THE WINE SENSE DIET

THE WINE SENSE DIET

BY ANNETTE SHAFER

LifeLine
Press

A REGNERY PUBLISHING COMPANY • WASHINGTON, DC

Library of Congress Cataloging-in-Publication Data

Shafer, Annette.
The wine sense diet / by Annette Shafer.
    p. cm.
Includes bibliographical references and index.
ISBN 0-89526-256-8
 1. Cookery, American—California style. 2. Menus. 3. Wine—Therapeutic use. I. Title.
TX715.2.C34 S48 2000
641.59794—dc21

99-057590

Published in the United States by
LifeLine Press
An Eagle Publishing Company
One Massachusetts Avenue, NW
Washington, DC 20001

Distributed to the trade by
National Book Network
4720-A Boston Way
Lanham, MD 20706

BOOK DESIGN BY MARJA WALKER
SET IN GARAMOND THREE AND NEWS GOTHIC

Printed on acid-free paper
Manufactured in the United States of America

10 9 8 7 6 5 4 3 2 1

Books are available in quantity for promotional or premium use. Write to Director of Special Sales, Regnery Publishing, Inc., One Massachusetts Avenue, NW, Washington, DC 20001, for information on discounts and terms or call (202) 216-0600.

The information in this book is not intended as a substitute for the medical advice of a physician. Before beginning any diet, consult with your doctor.

CONTENTS

To friends old and new who so graciously contributed to the adventure.

To Harry for his confidence in me.

To my grandparents for their early inspiration.

To my parents for their encouragement.

To Dodge for his enthusiasm, patience, and love.

FOREWORD
BY ROBERT MONDAVI

I LOVE TO EAT. I've always loved to eat. Some of my favorite childhood memories are of our family seated around the dining room table waiting with great anticipation for what Mama Rosa would bring from the kitchen. As Dad poured the wine—and he always let us have a taste if we wanted it—Mama would come in with a big bowl of steaming pasta or soup.

My parents, Rosa and Cesare, emigrated to the United States from Sassoferrato in the Marche region on the eastern coast of Italy. Where they came from, mealtime meant more than just a time to satisfy hunger; it was a time the family could share together. There was a special warmth and a spirit of conviviality that is natural to most Italian families. Eating and drinking were an important part of life. There were traditions being passed down to the next generation and a sense of generosity that was beyond words.

Mama even let me help in the kitchen sometimes. We made agnolotti, ravioli, linguini—all by hand. We worked together, side by side, kneading and shaping and talking all the while. Back in those days, I had no idea food and wine would become so important later in my life. Certainly from those experiences grew my great appreciation for food and wine—and an appreciation for a lifestyle I have adopted that keeps me healthy and active even though I'm now well into my eighties.

In those days, we always had a small garden outside the kitchen where Mama would harvest the most beautiful eggplants you've ever seen, and the reddest, juiciest tomatoes. She would snip herbs just before adding them to the dish that was being served that evening. I quickly learned the difference that the freshest, most high-

As Dad poured the wine—and he always let us have a taste if we wanted it—Mama would come in with a big bowl of steaming pasta or soup.

quality produce could make in a meal—an important lesson that would also apply later in life as quality winemaking became my central focus.

It is from my family that I also absorbed the enduring values of moderation in eating and drinking; of balance rather than excess; of the camaraderie that comes from gathering at the table with family and friends at mealtime, sharing food, sharing wine, sharing stories. This balance comes from incorporating time-honored traditions into my life—placing great value on family and community with food and wine as partners that contribute to overall well-being and happiness.

Those early, simple pleasures have given way to more sophisticated experiences as I encountered other cultures around the world. Yet each time I return to the Napa Valley I am reminded of the reasons why it is so dear to my heart. Our wines now stand with the finest in the world—that was my goal when I started out with my own Napa Valley winery in 1966. We have an abundance of the freshest ingredients and cuisine that rivals that of any other place on earth. The people are friendly and connected to the earth in a unique way: They exude a certain sophistication, but most are really farmers at heart.

I've lived and worked among the vineyards of the Napa Valley for sixty years now, yet every single day I remain awed by the beauty of this landscape and the power in the rhythms of nature stretched out before me.

While my appreciation for wine began back in those days when my father allowed all the children to taste at dinnertime, my interest continues to this day. Wine for me has been a profound mentor and teacher; the more I learn, the more I find I have to learn. This doesn't dissuade me but rather excites me to continue my pursuit of more knowledge.

My experience with wine while growing up made it a very normal, very necessary part of my daily life. As we find out more and more about wine's health benefits, my belief is stronger than ever that it should be a part of the mealtime ritual for those who can enjoy wine—excepting, of course, those who do not or should not drink for medical or religious reasons. I find, however, that sometimes the choices seem insurmountable; many people become frustrated by the apparent knowledge it takes to choose a good bottle of wine. You'll be glad to know that it's easier than you may think. As you will see in the pages to follow, the news is indeed good. There are so

I invite you to share my enthusiasm for food, wine, and a healthy way of life.

many good wines to choose from today that it's difficult to make a bad choice. We've made amazing progress in winemaking—and we're getting better all the time.

Because wine can seem enshrouded in mystery at times, many wine drinkers will stick to drinking one varietal they like. For instance, many people have heard a lot about Chardonnay, so that's what they drink. They might not feel confident enough to explore other white varietals such as Sauvignon Blanc—or Fumé Blanc as we call it—Viognier, and Pinot Grigio. Through the pages to follow, I hope you'll see that there are an infinite number of wine and food combinations, and the rewards of experimentation are tremendous. Those who know me know this favorite motto of mine: "Eat what you like, and like what you eat; drink what you like, and like what you drink." And it can be just that simple.

Wine is one of our most enjoyable foods (I like to refer to it as a food). It has been with us since civilization began. It's a part of our heritage, traditions, and the "gracious way of life." It has in it a touch of magic. The simple, pleasing sound of the pop of a cork is enough to announce the beginning of the happiest moment of daily life: the gathering of family and friends around the table at mealtime. To share the fruits of our labor. To share our heartaches and joys. To put aside our worries and fears for a while so that we can celebrate the bounty of nature and the greatest riches of being alive.

A book like this one is long overdue. And the fact that the Napa Valley can lead the way as an example makes me proud. The lessons that can be learned in the pages that follow are not complex—a heightened awareness and a good dose of common sense are all that's needed. "Wine sense" is simply common sense as it relates to wine, that extraordinary mealtime element, and as it's incorporated into a healthy lifestyle. Simple. That's it.

Food and wine bring everyone together around the table, joined happily in the daily celebration of two pleasures that are so universal that any barriers of personality, language, or culture disappear. I invite you to share my enthusiasm for food, wine, and a healthy way of life as you'll experience it through the eyes of those who live in our sumptuous valley. I encourage you and your family to incorporate these traditions into your own lives. I raise a glass: Here's to your health. Here's to enjoying the good life!

Robert Mondavi

NO DIETS HERE—THE WINE-HEALTH CONNECTION

YOU WON'T FIND A FAD DIET book on the shelf of any bookstore here. Or, if by chance you do, it's not a local best-seller. Town residents practically bathe in olive oil, and are always looking forward with great anticipation to their next loaf of warm, brick-oven-baked, crusty walnut bread or a wedge of aged Asiago cheese. Sharing a meal and a bottle of wine with friends and family is a favorite pastime. A special warmth and glorious energy emanates from the people here—a love of life, a *joie de vivre*, abounds.

A walk through the vineyards at sunset, a game of bocce with friends, a bike ride in the hills, or a jog through town—these are all welcomed events and a part of everyday life here. And the people are healthy. Really healthy.

The curious thing is that rather than thinking about how to cut calories, they are almost always talking about their next meal—even sometimes discussing dinner at lunch. There is a constant air of enthusiasm about food and wine and even more so about experiencing all that life has to offer. It's an attitude—a way of life.

It's easy to imagine these scenes originating in a tiny Italian hilltop village shielded from civilization's progress for perhaps centuries. Or even from a town along the coast of southern France where the much-heralded Mediterranean diet has been common practice for centuries. But it's not Italy or France. And it isn't really the *place* but rather the *lifestyle* that is prevalent. Could you capture this warmth and energy without leaving home or even without completely changing your daily routine? You'll be glad to know that you can and it's easier than you may think.

The place is California's Napa Valley. Here the healthy lifestyle is pervasive. It seems everyone radiates a positive, healthy outlook on life. What's their secret?

While their personal philosophies of healthy living may vary, some of the valley's most well-known personalities maintain an active lifestyle and passionately and reverently make the mealtime experience an important part of their daily routine. They emphasize the joy of the meal rather than depriving themselves of food, as many quick-fix diets recommend. They find utter enjoyment in the variety of food and wine that surrounds them, making moderation the only rule of the day. They have a first-hand understanding of the importance of wine in their lives.

DRINK WINE FOR GOOD LIFE AND HEALTH

Mealtime with wine is about pleasure, taste, and sharing with family and friends. And it's also about good health. It's all about lifestyle—a lifestyle that's full of joy and full of health.

Too many Americans, when it comes to diet and health, look for the "quick fix." We wait at the edge of our seats for news of the next diet regimen that promises to be a panacea—the antidote to all that troubles us: weight gain, clogged arteries, depression, lethargy, and on and on. We expect diets like the Cabbage Soup diet or the Zone diet to do it all for us. We'll deprive ourselves of food and rationalize. But then, we inevitably fall back into our old habits and the short-term benefits we initially saw, quickly disappear.

That's why it's important to adopt a natural, healthy lifestyle—like the Napa Valley lifestyle that incorporates wine in the diet—rather than some artificial regimen lifted out of a diet book. Unlike a quick-fix diet, a lifestyle with wine can have long-term benefits not only for a healthy heart but also for weight maintenance, longevity, improved quality of life, fending off harmful effects of aging, and much more.

We've all heard the formula to lose weight and be healthy: eat responsibly, exercise regularly. But the evidence is mounting for the health benefits provided by wine that make it an equally valuable component of a healthy lifestyle. With an emphasis on moderation, variety, and balance, you can participate actively in the celebration of wine and healthy living.

Years ago, when the CBS television show *60 Minutes* ran a story about red wine's role in preventing heart disease, the segment highlighted a study by French researcher

Drinking a moderate amount of wine, with meals and on a daily basis, gives wine its most significant contribution, physically and psychologically.

Serge Renaud that centered on what he called The French Paradox. Despite the seemingly excessive enjoyment of artery-clogging, heart-stopping, saturated-fat foods—including foie gras, butter, and cream sauces—the French still had a significantly lower incidence of heart disease than Americans. Renaud concluded that one of the most vital reasons was their alcohol consumption and noted that wine is France's most-consumed alcohol by far. He noticed that red wine, in particular, seemed to make even more of a difference. Since then, the news has gotten even better. Ongoing studies show that wine not only reduces risk of heart disease, it also might help:

- prolong your life and increase your quality of life in later years
- regulate weight
- improve your appearance and physical function as you age
- improve your psychological outlook and attitude
- improve cognitive reasoning
- ease the effects of stress and decrease tension and anxiety
- lower risk of the most common type of stroke
- decrease risk of peripheral artery disease
- decrease risk of high blood pressure (hypertension)
- reduce risk of atherosclerosis
- reduce risk of certain cancers
- lower risk for gallstones and kidney stones
- prevent food poisoning
- reduce risk for stomach ulcers
- reduce risk of blindness
- protect against Alzheimer's disease
- reduce risk of rheumatoid arthritis
- reduce risk of catching the common cold

Dr. R. Curtis Ellison, a physician at Boston University's School of Medicine, has found that amid all the studies detailing wine's healthy qualities, there is a message that has been overshadowed: It is the *pattern* of how wine is consumed that makes a difference in its benefit to overall health. Drinking a moderate amount of wine, with

"In Europe then we thought of wine as something as healthy and normal as food and also as a great giver of happiness and well being and delight. Drinking wine was not a snobbism nor a sign of sophistication nor a cult; it was as natural as eating and to me as necessary."

A MOVEABLE FEAST,
ERNEST HEMINGWAY, 1899–1961

meals and on a daily basis, gives wine its most significant contribution, physically and psychologically.

"It seems to me that what Ellison has found is what the Europeans have instinctually known for years and something we are just now beginning to pay attention to," says Dr. Eric Heiden. A physician specializing in orthopedic medicine, Dr. Heiden is also an Olympic record-holder—he represented the United States as a speed skater in 1980—and an avid wine drinker who lent me his medical expertise as I was researching the wine and health connection. "Some of the more recent studies appear to be attempting to specifically determine the benefits of red wine's antioxidant properties not only in their positive effect on the heart but also in a wide variety of other areas as well—such as cancer prevention, leukemia, alleviating some of the negative effects of menopause by helping to increase estrogen levels, and longevity."

The real key is to drink a little wine every day. It only takes a small amount of alcohol to help prevent heart disease, but it has to be introduced to the body on a regular basis. Some of wine's beneficial effects, particularly from the antioxidants, have been shown to be short-term, not cumulative—the positive effects last only a day or so. (But the positive effects from the alcohol are long-term.)

With the demands of working long hours, the endless school meetings and kids' sports practices, we're lucky sometimes if we even manage to put something—anything—on the table for dinner. Changing the routine will take a bit of effort—and for some a fair amount of juggling. But what a small change to make for such a big payoff! Unlike the deprivation dieters endure sucking on cabbage leaves for weeks on end, this change is pleasurable and even the smallest adjustment to your diet can make a difference right away.

WINE DRINKING PREVENTS HEART ATTACKS

Since heart disease and other cardiovascular diseases, like stroke and atherosclerosis, kill over half the people that die in the United States annually, the news about wine's benefit to the heart is of paramount importance. Even the United States Department of Agriculture (USDA), the federal agency responsible for publishing the Dietary Guidelines for Americans, has recently conceded that there is merit to these findings and has added wine consumption to its revised guidelines. The most recent version of the USDA's guidelines officially recognizes that "alcoholic beverages have been used to enhance the enjoyment of meals by many societies throughout human history." And since the news of alcohol's health benefits is heavily supported by current, conclusive research, the USDA conceded what scientists have been asserting for some time: "Current evidence suggests that moderate drinking is associated with a lower risk for coronary heart disease in some individuals." Moderate drinking as defined by the USDA is on the conservative side at two drinks a day for men and one drink a day for women, with one drink being equivalent to five ounces of wine.

In a 1995 follow-up to the French Paradox study, researcher Serge Renaud showed that moderate consumption of alcohol—three or four 4-ounce glasses of wine a day with meals—can actually reduce heart attacks by 50 percent.

There are at least three important ways wine has been shown to help prevent a heart attack. Wine can:

1. help prevent the development of atherosclerosis, a condition that affects most of us after a certain age
2. help prevent the formation of blood clots in the arteries
3. help dissolve blood clots that form within the arteries

Wine, like aspirin, is an anti-inflammatory. "Wine and aspirin both tend to make platelets less sticky so there is less of a chance that a blood clot will occur," says Dr. Eric Heiden. "That's why doctors will tell patients with a history of heart disease to take a daily dose of aspirin." He adds, "And I imagine some may now be advising their patients to include wine for similar reasons."

Results from a study in Denmark, sponsored by the Ministry of Health in Copenhagen, were also released in 1995. For the first time there was evidence that wine, over any other form of alcohol, was superior in delivering significant health benefits and providing substantial protection from many varied health risks. The control group consisted of people from ages thirty to seventy-nine. The population in Denmark is stable, and eating habits have not changed significantly over the years. Among their conclusions, the Danish researchers reported that:

THE ANTIOXIDANT ADVANTAGE

Resveratrol, catechin, quercetin, and epicatechin, responsible for red wine's primary antioxidant properties, are all found within the grape's skin. RESVERATROL is the flavonoid found to be one of the most effective antioxidants in wine. It prevents the oxidation of LDL (bad) cholesterol, thereby decreasing the likeliness of atherosclerosis. It has also been shown to inhibit "stickiness" of platelets, preventing blood clots and having other positive effects. The only downside is that it has been shown to dissipate in the bottle over time as the wine ages. The flavonoids CATECHIN and EPICATECHIN are known mainly for their antioxidant properties and are the most abundant antioxidants in wine. They have been shown to inhibit the "stickiness" of platelets as well. QUERCETIN is produced in some fruits and vegetables by ultraviolet light. The more sunlight, the greater its presence. It is found in green onions, shallots, red and yellow onions, leeks, garlic—and grapes. It is a powerful antioxidant and may act as an effective anti-cancer agent. It also counters the formation of blood clots by inhibiting the production of sticky platelets. And unlike resveratrol, it doesn't dissipate over time.

- heart disease had declined by 30 percent in Denmark, perhaps largely due to an increase in wine consumption among the Danes
- those who didn't drink wine had almost twice the risk of dying in any given year as those who drank wine daily
- drinking up to three to five glasses of wine a day for men, and up to two to four glasses of wine a day for women, lowered annual mortality rates in all cases
- drinking beer or spirits had no net beneficial effect on overall mortality

Other studies show similar results. Dr. David Goldberg, a physician and biochemist at the University of Toronto and a fifteen-year pioneer of research in this area, found significant evidence of wine's positive effect on the heart. As he reported in one study, "If every adult in North America drank two glasses of wine each day, cardiovascular disease, which accounts for just around 50 percent of deaths in this population, would be cut by 40 percent and more than $40 billion could be saved annually."

In a monumental move by the Bureau of Alcohol, Tobacco, and Firearms, the government agency that regulates the wine industry, vintners may soon be able to use one of two approved health labels on wine bottles:

1. "To learn the health effects of wine consumption, send for the federal government's Dietary Guidelines for Americans." Or,
2. "The proud people who made this wine encourage you to consult your family doctor about the health effects of wine consumption."

Industry spokesman John DeLuca, president of The Wine Institute, described the label approval as "defining a new chapter in the evolution of federal policy toward wine."

Most studies agree that to abstain from drinking wine—unless there is a preexisting problem with abuse, certain medical conditions, religious beliefs, or ethical prohibitions to drinking—is to neglect a major, and pleasurable, health benefit.

MODERATION IS THE KEY

Heavy drinking, however, can undo wine's beneficial effects. Heiden says, "More than moderate drinking can, among other things, seriously harm your health and actually

"When combined with meals rather than on an empty stomach, alcohol is much easier on your digestive system, allowing the components that create the positive health effect to enter your bloodstream more gently," says Boston University School of Medicine physician Dr. R. Curtis Ellison. **"Another benefit is that your blood alcohol level rises only about half as high, thereby also reducing wine's intoxicating effect substantially."** Research on the mealtime habits of many other cultures shows that the strong emphasis placed on drinking wine with meals tends to be a big factor in substantially limiting alcohol abuse. Researchers are also discovering that wine and food together promote favorable biochemical interactions reducing the risk of certain chronic diseases.

perpetuate hypertension and heart disease." A rise in triglycerides—the fatty compounds in blood whose elevated levels have been found to be a precursor to heart attack—an increase in blood pressure, and a greater incidence of irregularities of the heartbeat are among the harmful effects to the heart caused by heavy drinking.

Moderation means not only limiting the amount of alcohol you enjoy to two or so glasses a day, but incorporating wine-drinking into a moderated lifestyle, where work, play, and family all have their place. Including wine with your evening meal is an encouragement to celebrate life, to rejoice in the company of family members, to slow down enough to savor the wine and savor the meal. You're also more likely to think about the foods you prepare to complement the wine, to eat healthier, to enjoy the experience more, and to actually consume fewer calories.

The Wine Sense Diet is all about recapturing the wisdom of our ancestors who knew how to enjoy life—and lived it well.

THE PHYSIOLOGICAL EFFECTS OF DRINKING WINE

To make wine a part of your lifestyle, let's first briefly examine the properties in wine that bring out its beneficial effects.

In the simplest terms, drinking wine raises HDL (good) cholesterol, lowers LDL (bad) cholesterol, and helps to inhibit blood clotting inside the body, all of which make wine beneficial in preventing heart disease. But red wine has the added benefit of being high in antioxidants, which are major defenders of your body's health.

Antioxidants in Wine

Certain foods, particularly fruits and vegetables, contain antioxidants. (Mom was right when she told you to eat your broccoli and lima beans.)

Antioxidants are also produced naturally by the body. But as we age, our body produces fewer antioxidants, so we need to supply more. Until recently Vitamin E was thought to be the best antioxidant. But red wine contains other antioxidants that may be at least equally, if not more, effective.

Red Wine Has Added Health Benefits

Research has shown that grape skin—which is removed from the juice when making white wine—has antioxidants known as flavonoids. Flavonoids are also found in other sources, like red grape juice. But the fermentation process, which converts grape juice to wine, "frees" the flavonoids, making it easier for our bodies to absorb and use them.

Prefer white wine to red? Don't worry, you'll still receive significant health benefits.

WINE DRINKERS LIVE LONGER, HEALTHIER LIVES

While the most conclusive evidence points to wine's direct benefits for the heart, researchers are also finding that drinking wine has other health benefits and can add years to your life.

As early as 1980, researchers in the Honolulu Heart Study found that moderate drinkers live longer than those who don't drink or those who drink heavily.[1] A reduced mortality rate was also found as the result of the 1995 Harvard University Nurses' Health Study, which concluded that "the maximum mortality benefits were seen for women who drank a light-to-moderate amount of alcohol—between one and six drinks per week."[2] In 1996 the American Heart Association's Nutrition Committee reported, "The lowest mortality occurs in those who consume about two drinks per day."

These conclusions have been confirmed by studies from around the world. A large-scale study in mainland China found that those who drank a moderate amount of alcohol had a 19 percent reduction in overall mortality compared with lifelong nondrinkers.[3] In 1998 a French study concluded that among 34,000 middle-aged men, the group that consumed a generous two to five glasses of wine a day had a 24 to 31 percent reduction in overall death rate.

In a study reported in the *British Medical Journal* in 1994, those who had one or two drinks a day of wine, beer, or spirits had significantly lower rates for heart disease, as well as a lower rate of death from other types of cerebrovascular diseases, respiratory diseases, and cancers.[4]

A large-scale Kaiser Permanente Health Plan study on alcohol consumption and longevity in 1981, with more than 88,000 people monitored over ten years, showed that moderate drinkers (up to two drinks a day in this case) lived longer and were

WINE IN MODERATION EQUALS LOWER MORTALITY

Data from the Copenhagen City Heart Study, published in 1995, found that those who consumed wine daily were much less likely to die during the twelve-year study period than abstainers or consumers of other beverages with alcohol. Among more than 13,000 men and women aged thirty to seventy who were tracked from 1976 to 1988, wine consumers had half the risk of dying compared to those who never drank wine. The researchers reported, "Low to moderate intake of wine is associated with lower mortality from cardiovascular and cerebrovascular disease and other causes."[27]

about 27 percent less likely to die prematurely than either those who didn't drink at all or those who drank heavily.[5]

In 1990 an analysis of the medical records of 53,000 Kaiser Permanente Health Plan patients in California found that wine drinkers smoke less, are less likely to be overweight or to have a history of drinking problems, and are at a reduced risk for many health problems. Among the most significant healthy lifestyle factors are consuming a diet low in saturated fat, not smoking, getting moderate exercise, and enjoying alcoholic beverages in moderation.

In 1993 the National Health and Nutrition Examination Survey (NHANES), one of the largest studies of Americans' health and lifestyle habits, reported that moderate alcohol consumption could add an additional two-and-a-half years to the current expected life span.[6] Their results showed that "moderate drinking increases time until death from any cause by about 3 percent."[7]

DRINKING WINE HELPS REGULATE WEIGHT

We've all heard that alcohol adds "empty" calories to your diet. Many have avoided wine for this very reason. But in 1997 researchers at Colorado State University showed that two glasses of red wine with a meal *did not* promote weight gain because wine increases insulin sensitivity, which, in turn, helps regulate weight.

"Insulin is what allows your body to absorb carbohydrates, fuel for your body," says Dr. Eric Heiden. "If you're unable to absorb carbohydrates, your body is constantly looking for something else to absorb since it needs fuel. That's where the weight gain begins."

DRINK WINE AND LOOK YOUNGER LONGER

Something else many of us worry about is aging. Will we be less agile? Less attractive? Less able to remember important details? Not necessarily... if we drink wine. Wine can play a significant role in seeing that we maintain a high quality of life as we age.

For women, having an appropriate estrogen level is one key to maintaining a more youthful appearance. Various studies strongly suggest that alcohol may be involved in converting testosterone into estrogen in postmenopausal women. Since loss of estrogen—which keeps skin soft and supple—is a major cause of wrinkles in

INCREASE COGNITIVE JUICES
In one study of elderly male twins, the brother who consumed alcohol moderately scored consistently higher on a standard cognitive reasoning test than did his sibling, who didn't drink at all.[28]

older women, alcohol's potential ability to help keep levels up could theoretically slow the process.

Estrogen is also responsible for keeping bone density optimal, which means if wine helps with estrogen levels it could also reduce the risk of bone fractures and osteoporosis as women age.

IMPROVED PHYSICAL PERFORMANCE

Indeed, in studies among the elderly, moderate consumption of alcohol on a regular basis appears to aid in keeping bones stronger—which is very good news, as it can potentially reduce the risk for osteoporosis.[8]

One study of older women showed that moderate drinkers performed consistently better in tests of muscle strength, coordination, agility, and balance than nondrinkers or heavy drinkers.[9]

But does wine enhance physical performance? "There may be something to the fact that wine in moderation has a relaxing effect and seems to help relieve stress," says Dr. Heiden. "And if you're able to rest better then you should also be able to perform better—but that's a personal, not a clinical, observation," albeit an observation from an Olympic-level athlete who knows something about peak physical performance.

IMPROVED PSYCHOLOGICAL OUTLOOK AND ATTITUDE

If you have ever felt more relaxed after a glass of wine you'll be pleased to know that medical science now has evidence that wine offers mental, as well as physical, benefits. In fact moderate drinkers have been credited with increased cognitive reasoning abilities, a decreased risk of stress-related depression, less risk of tension, anxiety, and insecurity, and enhanced pleasant feelings and friendliness.

"A decrease in cognitive reasoning could possibly occur when the brain doesn't have enough blood flowing to it," explains Dr. Heiden. "And, as we age, our blood vessels get stiff. So, maybe by a combination of keeping the vessels more pliable and the blood platelets less sticky—two benefits we get from drinking wine—more blood can then continue to get to where it needs to go as we age."

Results from a study published in the *Lancet*, a British medical journal, in 1998 showed that adults—ages twenty-three to thirty-three—who drank moderately had a lower risk of poor physical health and psychological distress than peers who were either nondrinkers or heavy drinkers. The study suggests that people who have one to two drinks a day tend to have a more moderate and balanced lifestyle and seem better able to handle stress.[10]

WINE COMBATS DEPRESSION

What if all that was needed to overcome depression was not new drugs but one or two glasses of wine a day? Studies have shown that moderate drinkers are less likely to become depressed when under stress compared to nondrinkers or heavy drinkers.[11] The National Institute of Alcohol Abuse and Alcoholism has stated that "lower levels of alcohol consumption can reduce stress; promote conviviality and pleasant, care-free feelings; decrease tension, anxiety and self-consciousness."[12]

There is sometimes a tendency for depression to set in as we age. In the process, appetite seems to wane, so we don't get the nutrition we need and our bodily functions seem to slow. The good news is that moderate drinking among the elderly, as shown in a report published by the National Institute of Alcohol Abuse and Alcoholism in 1992, stimulates the appetite, promotes regular bowel functions, and can actually improve mood.[13]

OTHER CARDIOVASCULAR BENEFITS

Wine Lowers the Risk of the Most Common Type of Stroke

Numerous studies have linked habitual heavy drinking and binges resulting in alcohol intoxication to the increased risk of stroke, but drinking wine *in moderation* seems to lower the risk of the most common type of stroke. Dr. Heiden explains: "There are two kinds of strokes. An ischemic stroke is caused by a blockage in an artery supplying blood to the brain. The other, known as an aneurysm, is where the blood vessel bursts." He adds, "In the event of an ischemic stroke, patients are often given anti-inflammatories in hope that the platelets become less sticky and the blockage breaks up, allowing blood to flow freely once again. Wine has an anti-inflammatory effect."

Whether alcohol has a positive or negative affect on the occurrence of strokes has long been a controversial subject. A team of researchers from Columbia University in New York City has found that "a glass or two of wine, beer or spirits

WINE AND DIABETES PREVENTION

Wine may also reduce the risk of adult-onset diabetes for much of the same physiological reason that it helps to control weight. In one study moderate drinkers were less likely to develop adult-onset diabetes than nondrinkers.[29]

may reduce the risk of stroke caused by arterial disease.... Moderate alcohol consumption may have important health benefits in terms of reducing the risk of
ischemic stroke."[14] The researchers tracked 677 Manhattan residents over the age of
forty for a four-year period and found that moderate drinkers had a 49 percent lower
risk for stroke than nondrinkers.

According to the findings from an ongoing Physicians' Health Study, those who have
three or fewer drinks per day have a slightly lower risk of ischemic stroke than nondrinkers or those that have more than three drinks per day. The study concluded that small-
to-moderate consumption of alcohol reduces stroke risk by about 20 percent in men.[15]

Decreases Risk for Peripheral Artery Disease

A notable cause of death in the elderly is peripheral artery disease (PAD), or clogging
of the arteries in areas outside the heart—most commonly in the legs. In 1997
Harvard researchers concluded that daily drinkers were less likely to suffer from PAD
than nondrinkers or occasional drinkers. Again the Physicians' Health Study showed
that men who drank in moderation had a reduced risk for PAD of 32 percent compared to men who reported drinking less than one drink per week.[16]

"Peripheral Artery Disease is most often evidenced in poor circulation in the
hands and legs of the elderly," says Dr. Heiden. "So if the arteries can be kept more supple and the blood less sticky, then naturally circulation would be better to these areas."

Indeed, in a 1995 study from the University of Edinburgh, researchers found
that "moderate intake of wine has a statistically significant protective effect—reducing the debilitating effects of poor circulation."[17]

May Decrease Risk of Hypertension and Reduce Risk of Atherosclerosis

For decades, researchers have been looking at the relationship between alcohol consumption and hypertension. To date, most researchers have found no correlation
between moderate drinking, up to three drinks per day, and increased hypertension.
Any elevated risk seems to be linked only to heavy consumption. In fact, researchers
cite obesity as the most significant risk factor for hypertension.[18]

"Hypertension, or high blood pressure—the terms are interchangeable—is
often caused by obesity because you just have so much more volume to pump blood

through," Dr. Heiden told me. "Heavy alcohol consumption also causes high blood pressure both by elevating your cholesterol level and also by causing sclerosis of the liver, eventually shutting down liver function."

Atherosclerosis, or hardening of the arteries, is another health risk that might be reduced by drinking wine with meals.[19]

"In atherosclerosis, the muscles inside your arteries become hard and then, in turn, squeeze off the blood flow. So, if you are able to keep them smooth and supple, which moderate drinking of wine appears to help, the blood is allowed to flow freely," says Dr. Heiden.

MAY REDUCE CANCER RISK

Exciting preliminary results on wine's protective effects against some types of cancer are in the news. One such study, published by the National Cancer Institute in 1997, showed that while more research is needed to confirm the positive alcohol-related findings, "the indications are strong that wine drinkers are at a significantly reduced risk of at least four types of cancer, specifically cancers of the stomach and esophagus." Researchers speculated that the benefits from wine "may be the result of a protective ingredient such as the flavonoid resveratrol which isn't present in beer or liquor."[20]

The flavonoids in wine that act as antioxidants may be partially responsible for preventing cancer cells from forming. Resveratrol may inhibit the enzymes that can stimulate cancer cell growth and suppress immune response.[21]

The antioxidant quercetin, another flavonoid in red wine, has been found to inhibit the conversion of normal cells to cancer cells. This compound exists in a variety of plant foods, although it isn't activated until the final stages of digestion by enzymes in the lower colon. Quercetin in wine is activated during the fermentation of red grape juice to red wine, so it can, theoretically, go to work much earlier in the digestive process.

In explaining the significance of the latest studies concerning wine and cancer, Dr. Heiden commented, "If you can prevent the cell from transforming itself into a cancerous cell, which is why the antioxidants could play such a big role, then you've got it made."

The flavonoids in wine that act as antioxidants may be partially responsible for preventing cancer cells from forming.

A study conducted at the University of California at Davis showed that mice who were genetically prone to cancer had their life expectancy increased by 40 percent if they were fed red wine extracts. The researchers attribute the positive results to the antioxidizing properties of flavonoids in red wine.

Possible Reduced Risk of Lung Cancer

In a study released in 1999, researchers at Copenhagen University Hospital in Denmark found that wine was associated with a lower risk of lung cancer. The researchers theorized that the protective effect "may be related to the antioxidant properties of wine—which are more present in red wine."

Men who reported drinking one to thirteen glasses of wine per week had a 22 percent lower risk of lung cancer compared with drinkers of other types of alcohol. And those who consumed more than thirteen glasses of wine a week had a 56 percent lower risk than those drinking beer or spirits. Researchers were quick to add that even though wine may be moderately protective against lung cancer, it in no way suggests that wine drinking can compensate for the negative effects caused by smoking.[22]

May Reduce Risk for Bladder Cancer

The risk for the fourth leading type of cancer in men, bladder cancer, may be reduced with wine's help. Harvard School of Public Health researchers, funded by the National Institutes of Health and the American Cancer Society, found that men who drank the most fluid, over a ten-year period, had half the risk of the disease. They indicated that any extra fluid, whether it was water alone or in combination with wine or whiskey, helped to protect men from bladder cancer. Though stating that the most efficient way to provide the risk reduction is to drink six 8-ounce glasses of water a day, they also acknowledged that drinking ten glasses of a combination of other beverages, including coffee, tea, milk, beer, wine, or other alcoholic beverages, may provide a similar risk reduction.[23]

In commenting on this study, Michael Thun, who heads epidemiology research for the Atlanta-based American Cancer Society, acknowledges that alcohol can be a part of the mix, but warns, "Alcohol is definitely not the way to get your volume of fluid," because of the importance of *moderate* consumption.

Dr. Heiden agrees: "Alcohol is a diuretic. It has many healthful benefits, but it can cause you to become dehydrated." This diuretic action, in fact, is linked to the excessive drinker's hangover. Dr. Heiden explains: "Alcohol metabolizes into formaldehyde. If you're not hydrated, the formaldehyde becomes too concentrated, and that's what gives you the headache." So in general it pays to drink those six to eight glasses of water a day *plus* two or three glasses of wine.

LOWERS THE RISK FOR KIDNEY STONES

Drinking a glass of wine a day can reduce the risk of getting a kidney stone by 59 percent. Among a field of twenty-one beverages, wine was most strongly associated with a decreased risk for the formation of painful kidney stones. According to a study published by the *American Journal of Epidemiology*, both women and men show a reduced risk. The study's lead author, Gary Curhan, M.D., explains that "alcohol interferes with the secretion of the antidiuretic hormone that is responsible for telling the kidneys to concentrate the urine. Since the urine is then more diluted, you will tend to urinate more and that in turn will apparently help protect you against kidney stones." And given wine's alcohol content, it may do a better job than beer, which is lower in alcohol.[24]

MAY HELP PREVENT FOOD POISONING AND
REDUCE RISK FOR STOMACH ULCERS

Red and white wine may protect against bacterial diarrhea—welcome news for wayward travelers. Researchers at the Tripler Army Medical Center in Honolulu reported in 1995 that wine can kill off colonies of bacteria such as E. coli, salmonella, and shigella more effectively than bismuth salicylate, the active ingredient in Pepto-Bismol and other similar over-the-counter preparations. Your risk of becoming ill may be decreased dramatically since acid secretion in the stomach is stimulated by drinking alcohol in moderation—in particular wine or beer.[25]

By facilitating the spontaneous elimination of the bacterium known to cause ulcers, H. pylori, wine might help prevent ulcers from forming, according to a team of German researchers. The German researchers found that alcoholic beverages do indeed "have strong antimicrobial activity." The best results came from drinking about two glasses of wine a

MORE ADDED BENEFITS— FROM ARTHRITIS TO THE COMMON COLD
The risk for rheumatoid arthritis seems to be less among moderate drinkers. Positive results came from a 1994 study that showed that five to fourteen drinks per week decreased the risk of rheumatoid arthritis, in this case specifically for women.[30] Wine was the answer again, when a study published in 1993 showed the susceptibility to five strains of the common cold was higher among nondrinkers than moderate drinkers.[31]

day. The risk of infection declined 42 percent, compared to only 25 percent among those consuming similar quantities of alcohol from beer. Those who consumed a bottle of wine a week were about 70 percent less likely to have an active infection compared with non-drinkers. Heavy drinking, however, increased the risk of infection.[26]

MAY REDUCE RISK OF BLINDNESS

The leading cause of blindness in Americans over the age of sixty-five, Age-Related Macular Degeneration (AMD), is less likely to develop when wine is consumed in moderation, according to a National Health Nutrition and Examination Survey. Researchers theorize that wine's antioxidant properties might slow down the deterioration of the macula in the eye. The findings may prove to be of major significance because AMD is projected to become more prevalent as our population ages.

ALCOHOL AND ITS POTENTIAL BENEFIT TO WOMEN

While men have been the subjects of most of the studies conducted in the area of wine and health, there are more and more studies taking a look specifically at the effects of alcohol on women. Some highly publicized studies have attempted to link alcohol consumption to an increase in breast cancer among women. But Dr. R. Curtis Ellison at Boston University's School of Medicine notes, "The results of studies such as these are not yet conclusive. When comparing the mortality rate between breast cancer and heart disease—46,000 women die annually of breast cancer as compared to 500,000 women who die annually of cardiovascular disease—the most important effect at this stage is for us to recognize alcohol's proven ability to reduce heart disease."

GOOD HEALTH, GOOD FOOD, GOOD LIFE

Clearly, one or two glasses of wine a day with a meal, as part of a healthy lifestyle, can make a big difference in overall health. Now we'll show you with the Wine Sense Diet how you can maximize your enjoyment of life, while being fit, healthy, and happy.

JOIE DE VIVRE—THE NAPA VALLEY LIFESTYLE

AS THE FOG THAT HAS GENTLY BLANKETED the Valley begins to lift at dawn, I feel the cool morning mist on my face while I run through the quiet streets of the charming small town of St. Helena. The sun's first rays are just beginning to awaken the vines and light the western slopes. It's my time. It's a time I cherish. It's a sacred and necessary part of my day. It's the only time I have a moment to myself… to reflect, to plan, to appreciate those things that are most important in my life. I gain focus. I gain direction. I begin to feel more in control. And only then do I have the ability to truly savor yesterday's achievements and the invigorating challenges that lie ahead. I use this time to begin to reestablish that ever-elusive "balance" between the personal and the public. To embrace life. To live it rather than letting it "live" me.

Fortunately, the lifestyle in the Napa Valley encourages many moments such as these. For me, it's the quintessential place where a lifestyle of *joie de vivre*—or love of life—abounds. It seems those that exude the most joy here all have their comforting rituals that provide a steady anchor, as do I in my morning run. For others, it may be a short walk each morning, a shower to wind down after a hectic day, a yoga routine, some gardening time, or a trip to the gym. And, of course here in the Valley we share the ritual of popping a cork close to mealtime. An event in itself, it marks the transition from the daily demands of work to a time of sharing with friends and family, a time to slow down and appreciate the moment. This is the genesis of the Wine Sense Diet.

You may think, yes, that's all well and good for people who live in the beautiful and serene Napa Valley, but not all of us are so blessed by our environment. Therein lies the challenge as well as the potential for great rewards. Sometimes you'll have to work very hard to carve out that time. But it's worth it. Life doesn't just happen. It's a series of choices. Those choices are ours to make. Everyone, no matter where they live, can make the choice to find time to reflect, and time to share. I believe it is a necessary choice for a truly healthy, enjoyable life.

Recently I was in New York City. Now, to me, that's the ultimate place where everything happens at breakneck speed. It's exhausting just to try to keep pace! But, it occurred to me as I took a run around Central Park, for the first time in many years, that here is a place where I could find calm and quiet for a few stolen moments of the day. The city didn't slow down—I did. Everything in the universe felt right at that moment. I was able to clear my mind, gather my thoughts, and reenergize for the day ahead. I wasn't alone. There were couples walking and chatting, parents with baby strollers enjoying their quiet time, joggers, and rollerbladers... all getting a break from their day. That convinced me that it's possible anywhere.

SAVOR THE MOMENT

To be able to truly savor each moment, we need to find joy along the way. The key is to cherish the past but to let what's done be done, to respect the future, yet live for today. This is a way of life, a disposition that allows for a richer, more meaningful existence.

I know in my own life, it's all too easy for me to think about the presentation I gave yesterday or worry about the report that's due next week. But I work at keeping my focus on what's happening now. I remember a talk Michael Chiarello, chef/owner of Tra Vigne Restaurant in St. Helena and someone notorious for having several projects going on at once, gave to a group of young culinary students. When they asked how he managed to succeed when he had so many projects competing for his time, he said simply, "I focus carefully on the subject at hand. When I'm talking with someone, or working on a particular aspect of one project, I'm completely there. I'm not thinking about what I forgot to do yesterday or that another project is on deadline; my attention is 100 percent focused on the present." He adds, "You may be quite surprised how your effectiveness increases, and how your stress level decreases, by approaching each situation in this way."

Along with taking things one at a time, we need to take time out to find that quiet place where our sense of self resides to clarify our objectives. I've found that hav-

FIFTEEN STEPS TO JOIE DE VIVRE

1. Maintain a positive outlook
2. Savor each moment
3. Stay true to yourself
4. Take time for yourself
5. Develop comforting rituals to share with family and friends
6. Pursue your passions
7. Be gentle with yourself
8. Practice patience, generosity, and kindness
9. Honor yourself
10. Listen to your body
11. Include exercise in your daily routine
12. Challenge yourself
13. Celebrate success
14. Raise a glass of wine each day at mealtime to acknowledge your accomplishments and drink to your health
15. Nurture your sense of adventure

ing happiness and joy as an objective is a better guide to good health and fitness than the strict calorie counting and deprivation mentality of fad diets. It's all a matter of building healthy lifelong habits, based on a sense of *joie de vivre*.

LOOKING FOR THE OPPORTUNITY

Finding joy in life is an art. For me, it's a daily rediscovery. I live in the moment as much as I can, although that sometimes takes a lot of work! I take each situation as it comes—and each new person that I meet—with the expectation that I'll always learn a little something along the way. I face adversity as a challenge and celebrate successes.

A key ingredient for me is to honor myself in all that I do—whether it be a daily exercise routine, a well-thought-out meal plan, the commitments I choose to make, or the way I make decisions—always staying true to myself and my values. And, at the close of each day, I look forward to gathering at the dinner table with family, a good meal, and, always, a bottle of wine, to reflect and reminisce about what the day brought and inevitably develop an enthusiasm for what tomorrow has in store.

A REASONABLE APPROACH

It's important to me that everything I include in a healthy routine is eminently reasonable and can be accomplished. Our goals are best set incrementally—I didn't run a marathon the first day I put on my running shoes—and with a sense of balance and a hierarchy of priorities. All of us want to be healthy, but not all of us want to be bodybuilders, or to separate ourselves from our friends and family with four-hour workouts in the gym and hyper-strict diets. It's all a matter of deciding what we want, and assessing the time, the desire, and the ability we have to achieve it.

THE GLASS IS HALF FULL. THE DAY IS PARTLY SUNNY...

My "secret formula" for success is to keep a positive outlook, and to take care of myself through exercise and diet. Together, a positive outlook, exercise, and a natural, healthy diet makes it much easier for me to experience happiness—and to recognize the things that bring me joy.

A positive outlook, I've noticed, is a thread that weaves through many lives here in the Napa Valley. People here tend to schedule their priorities rather than prioritize their schedules. Everyone here is pursuing a passion—often a passion for producing fine wine. And their "pursuit of happiness" inevitably brings success.

It's all a delicate balance. "You can be a vegetarian and run six miles a day," says Caroline Myss and Dr. Norman Shealy in *The Creation of Health*, "but if you're in an unhappy relationship, dislike your job, have daily disagreements with those around you, you're losing energy. That can actually make you physically ill… truly unhealthy."

LIGHTEN UP

Keeping a positive outlook means working patiently to achieve your goals. It's important to be gentle with yourself, and to share that gentleness in kindness to others. Get rid of unrealistic expectations. Don't bemoan what you didn't achieve. Celebrate your accomplishments. Concentrate on moving ahead. In *The Creation of Health* Caroline Myss says, "For every regret we have over the past, or every resentful thought we attach to another person, we are losing energy. And most of us live in the past and in the future, attaching our emotions to what we regret and what we wish for."

Take delight in your daily life and use your seventh sense, intuition—your innate sense for bliss and enchantment. "If we follow it, it will direct us away from what hurts us and lead us directly to what brings us the greatest joy and health. Many have lost touch with this sense," says Paul Pearsell, a writer for *Natural Health* magazine.

A good way to enhance your quality of life and to improve your health is to spend time nurturing friendships. Arthur Stone, a psychiatry professor at the State University of New York at Stony Brook School of Medicine says, "Simple, enjoyable activities, such as having a few friends over for dinner, can immediately strengthen the immune system and even temporarily reduce blood pressure."

HONOR YOURSELF. RESPECT YOUR BODY.
YOU REALLY ARE WHAT YOU EAT!

Along with a healthy outlook, a healthy diet and adequate exercise readies me for the challenges each new day brings. I make a conscious effort to treat my body with

It's important to be gentle with yourself, and to share that gentleness in kindness to others. Get rid of unrealistic expectations.

respect, and to incorporate a wide variety of fresh fish, fruit, vegetables, and soy into my meals. Flavor and freshness are paramount.

My simple rules for eating are:

- **EAT ONLY WHEN YOU'RE HUNGRY.** That takes a lot of attention at first but then the body begins to regulate itself.
- **STOP EATING WHEN YOU'RE SATIATED, NOT OVERFULL.** There's quite a difference, and it takes some time to learn the distinction.
- **HAVE MEALS IN A PLEASANT, PEACEFUL PLACE.** Concentrate on the flavors and textures of what you're eating. Enjoy your surroundings, your conversation with family or friends. A glass of wine or two can serve as a reminder to slow down and enjoy. The fact that it's healthy, too, is quite a bonus!
- **DON'T EAT WHEN YOU'RE UPSET OR STRESSED.** Find another avenue through which to dispel anger or alleviate stress. Exercise works for me. Meditation might work for someone else. There are a number of creative, and very individual, approaches.

When I'm not training for a race, I watch my carbohydrates. I love my daily bread, but I do take care not to overindulge. I also make sure to include enough protein in my diet. Protein can come in many forms, even soy milk smoothies—a favorite!

It's important, while maintaining a diet low in saturated fat, not to exclude *all* fat. Fat is important because it gives us that sense of satiation that tells our bodies we're full. Without it, we tend to overeat, and consume more calories than we can burn off in normal exercise. Some fats are better than others. The best kinds of fats are monounsaturated fats like canola or olive oils.

While it's true that I generally eat very healthily, I make no apologies for the occasional greasy french fries and rich, thick chocolate shake, the thought of which is sometimes all that gets me through the last few miles of a marathon! The occasional indulgence is somehow good for your soul! Since I'm making admissions here, another is a love of ice cream. The real thing, not the low-fat, no sugar version. But what's amazing is that if I really pay attention to the flavors and textures, slowly savoring each spoonful, it doesn't take very much until I'm satisfied. That's very different from sitting in front of the television with a pint and a spoon. The key is to really pay attention. Live in the moment. Find delight in each and every bite.

HYDRATE, HYDRATE, HYDRATE

Drinking enough water is another element on which I place great emphasis. Our bodies need so much fluid to maintain all the natural functions. Running has helped me to better understand the significance of maintaining hydration. Even if you're not a runner and exercise only sporadically, drink more water each day. You'll be amazed at the difference something so simple can make. If you begin to feel fatigued, instead of grabbing a cup of coffee or a candy bar in the afternoon, think water first. To know how much is right for you, a good measure is to drink enough fluid to allow your urine to run almost clear. It's an easy habit to build. It's essential to the overall "balance."

EXERCISE... THERE'S SOMETHING FOR EVERYONE

And then there's exercise. Yes, it's necessary. The good news is that it can take many forms—running, walking, biking. Do whatever is right for you, do what you enjoy. Any routine that isn't fun and rewarding will seem like drudgery. And who enjoys misery?

Among its obvious benefits, exercise allows me to challenge myself. I've always wanted to be better—not better than the person "over there," just better than I was last week. And the standards are my own, not someone else's.

A GRAND REWARD

After all that exercise and the demands of a busy week, I treat myself to a massage. It's not only a treat, but has measurable therapeutic value as well. Interestingly enough, when I was little, I remember my grandmother always going for her weekly massage. So aside from sharing her love of cooking with me, she is also my inspiration to keep the massage tradition going. Although not an athlete, she found great value in those weekly trips. Among its other benefits, as we age, massage helps to stimulate circulation and keep muscles supple and pliable. Another who inspires me to continue to take massage time and who understands *joie de vivre* maybe better than anyone is wine expert Robert Mondavi who, as a part of his healthy routine, includes a daily massage. It is, as he puts it, "a glorious indulgence!" And at eighty-six, he's quite an inspiration!

EXPLORE

And, finally, remember that a sense of adventure keeps life exciting. Be curious about your surroundings, about people, about history—and, of course, about wine. Life is a sum of experiences. Go out and experience. And remember, a glass of wine with family and friends at mealtime is one of the best experiences we can have, a giant step toward ultimate happiness!

On the pages that follow, well-known Napa Valley locals share their personal philosophies of health, happiness, and good food.

As you'll see, they depend on fresh produce that's easy to prepare, an exercise regimen that fits in naturally with an active lifestyle, and a sense that the good things in life are meant to be shared and enjoyed with friends and family.

You'll find wine suggestions, recipes, and most of all, an invitation to be adventurous finding good wine, good food, and embracing the joy of living.

THE ANDRUSES OF PINE RIDGE WINERY

"We often open a bottle of wine while cooking."

NANCY AND GARY ANDRUS, both native Californians, have made it a point to enjoy life and all that surrounds them with their mantra: work hard and play harder! Nancy says, "We've both always been active and very much enjoy the outdoors. When we lived in Colorado, our life was skiing. Here in the beautiful Napa Valley we take long walks or runs among other activities when we're not on the road or harvesting grapes. Of course we both also love to eat and drink great wine, so balance is the key."

Even though they wholeheartedly agree that the Napa Valley encourages a healthy lifestyle, they know that it's possible to emulate that lifestyle anywhere in the country. Gary says, "Good wine and good food are available everywhere now. That's both good and bad for Nancy and me because moderating what we eat on the road is more and more challenging! With the business we're in, we're always on the road entertaining, so it's not always easy to be entirely reasonable with food and drink but we make every effort." The Andruses also have a winery in Oregon, so Gary's up there a lot, eating out. He says, "What I've found to help keep me in a healthy eating routine is to be truly conscious of portion size when dining in restaurants. I might decide to only eat half of everything on my plate even before the entrée comes. That helps." "Although," adds Nancy, "every once in a while our discipline slips a little and we just have to have a greasy burger and fries—sometimes there's just nothing better than that!" And, according to them both, the occasional dietary splurge is OK because their philosophy is to begin each day anew. "That's better than beating yourself up for eating things you shouldn't—you can begin again with renewed enthusiasm for eating healthily," says Nancy.

Wine is very much a part of their mealtime routine. Nancy says, "We often open a bottle of wine while cooking. A little of the pre-dinner wine is even likely to end up in whatever dish we're preparing." Neither of their parents really drank wine when they were young so they had to acquire their own appreciation for it. "It's something we're both passionate about," says Gary. "It's hard to remember that everyone doesn't have a similar comfort level with wine. It really doesn't have to be intimidating at all. I'd rather everyone think of it as a fun adventure. We really do drink anything and everything and love to try new wines." Adds Nancy, "And most important of all we have made it part of the mealtime routine at our home. It's meant to go with food and adds so much to the enjoyment of any dish."

Spring ~ Summer

Tri-Colored Tortellini Skewers with Parmesan Lemon Dip

Griddled Salmon with Mushroom and Cherry Sauce

Fresh Green Beans Sautéed with Pancetta

Lemon Risotto with Parmesan Cheese

Olive Oil Cake with Strawberries

Pine Ridge Napa Valley Chardonnay, Carneros District
Archery Summit Pinot Noir, Premier Cuvée (Oregon)

Fall ~ Winter

Winter Salad of Beets and Turnips

Honey Roasted Pork *or*
Sautéed Beef Steaks

Potato Zucchini Pancakes

Broccoli Sautéed with Garlic

Chocolate Mousse Torte

Pine Ridge Merlot, Crimson Creek
Beringer Howell Mountain,
  Bancroft Vineyard Cabernet Sauvignon

MAKES 10 SKEWERS

½ pound fresh or frozen tri-colored tortellini

⅛ teaspoon salt

1 tablespoon olive oil

6-inch bamboo skewers

Parmesan Lemon Dip (recipe follows)

TRI-COLORED TORTELLINI SKEWERS WITH PARMESAN LEMON DIP

The easiest way to prepare this recipe is to start with the roasted garlic, then make the Parmesan Lemon Dip, and then the tortellini.

Bring a large pot of salted water to a boil. Add tortellini and cook until tender, about 3 minutes. Drain and immediately pour the olive oil on the pasta, tossing gently. Place 3 warm tortellini on each skewer and serve immediately with Parmesan Lemon Dip.

MAKES 1 CUP

1 cup crème fraîche (see page 168)

¼ cup freshly grated Parmesan cheese

2 lemons, zest and juice

3 cloves roasted garlic, peeled (recipe follows)

PARMESAN LEMON DIP

Combine all the ingredients for the dip in a small mixing bowl. (Can be made up to 4 hours in advance.) Refrigerate until ready to serve.

Several heads of garlic (not elephant garlic)

olive oil

ROASTED GARLIC

Roasted garlic tends to be sweeter and milder than raw or sautéed garlic. You'll need only a small amount for the Parmesan Lemon Dip, but it's easy and practical to make more. With its mild flavor and buttery consistency, roasted garlic is also ideal to spread on any type of crusty French bread as an appetizer on its own.

Preheat oven to 350 degrees.

Cut garlic heads in half horizontally. Place skin side down on aluminum foil on top of a baking pan. Drizzle with a little olive oil. Fold the foil into a pouch. Roast for 45 minutes to 1 hour or until golden brown and soft.

GRIDDLED SALMON WITH MUSHROOM AND CHERRY SAUCE

In a large saucepan sauté mushrooms in 1 tablespoon butter until soft. Remove mushrooms and set aside. Add 1 tablespoon olive oil and leeks to pan and sauté leeks until soft but not brown. Add stock and wine and simmer until liquid is reduced by half. Add cherries, cook until tender, and stir in the mushrooms. Purée half the mixture then add back to the pan. Season with salt and white pepper. Keep warm until serving.

Lightly sprinkle some salt and white pepper on salmon. Dredge salmon filets in flour; shake off excess. Sauté salmon (presentation side down first) in remaining butter and olive oil in separate pan until the salmon has cooked two-thirds of the way, about 6 minutes. Turn and sauté until cooked through, about 2 minutes.

Serve salmon, presentation side up in a pool of warm mushroom and cherry sauce. Drizzle some sauce over the top and garnish with chives.

SERVES 6

2 cups mixed fresh wild mushrooms like shiitake, oyster, chanterelle (dried, reconstituted mushrooms can be substituted), sliced

3 tablespoons butter, divided

2 tablespoons olive oil

1 pound leeks, white part only, thinly sliced

1 pint fish stock or bottled clam juice

2 cups Chardonnay or other white wine

4 cups fresh cherries, pitted and quartered

salt and white pepper to taste

six 7-ounce salmon filets, skinned and boned

½ cup flour

4 tablespoons chopped chives

FRESH GREEN BEANS SAUTÉED WITH PANCETTA

Place beans in microwave-proof dish and add ¼ cup water. Place plastic wrap over the top, leaving a little gap for steam to escape. Microwave on high until tender, about 3 minutes. Drain.

Place pancetta in a medium pan and sauté over medium heat until crisp. Add beans and toss in pan. Add salt to taste and serve.

SERVES 6

¼ cup chopped pancetta

2 cups fresh green beans

salt to taste

LEMON RISOTTO WITH PARMESAN CHEESE

Melt a ½ tablespoon butter together with olive oil in a heavy saucepan over medium-low heat. Add onion and lemon zest and sauté for 3 to 5 minutes. Add rice and stir to coat with oil. Turn up heat to high and "toast," stirring, for 30 seconds. Immediately add wine and reduce heat to medium-low. Stir constantly until wine is absorbed. Add stock slowly—½ cup at a time—stirring constantly, and adding more only when the previous stock has been absorbed. When all the stock is absorbed and the rice is tender, stir in ¼ cup lemon juice. Stir in Parmesan and remaining butter. Cook briefly to blend and melt cheese. Season to taste with salt and pepper. Add remaining lemon juice to taste and serve immediately in warm bowls.

SERVES 8

1 tablespoon unsalted butter

2 tablespoons olive oil

½ cup minced onion

zest of 2 lemons

3 cups uncooked Arborio rice

1 cup white wine

9 cups chicken stock

¾ cup fresh lemon juice

1 cup freshly grated Parmesan cheese

salt and freshly ground pepper

OLIVE OIL CAKE WITH STRAWBERRIES

One may not associate olive oil with dessert, but this cake is sweet, scrumptious, and healthy for you. The olive oil gives the cake a moist texture and fruity taste.

Preheat oven to 375 degrees.

Separate the 5 eggs and beat the egg yolks with sugar in a large bowl for 3 to 5 minutes, or until very light in color. Mix in the orange and lemon zest. Set aside.

Combine flour and salt, and sift a little at a time into the sugar and egg mixture, beating continually until it is incorporated. Add the dessert wine and the olive oil in the same fashion.

In a separate bowl beat the 7 egg whites until they stand in stiff peaks, and then gently fold them into the mixture thoroughly.

Line the bottom of an 8-inch springform pan with parchment. Butter the lower ¼ of the sides. Pour the batter into the pan, making sure it is well distributed. Bake for 20 minutes. Lower the oven temperature to 325 degrees and turn cake (for even baking) if necessary and bake for an additional 25 minutes. Turn off the oven and leave the cake in the closed oven for 10 minutes more while the cake slightly collapses.

Remove from oven and allow the cake to cool for 10 minutes. Invert the cake onto a flat surface. Let it cool completely before serving. (Well sealed, this cake can be stored in the refrigerator for up to 4 days.)

Serve with strawberries or other fruit tossed in dessert wine along with vanilla ice cream or a drizzling of Crème Anglaise (recipe follows).

CRÈME ANGLAISE

Heat milk in heavy saucepan to just below boiling, stirring regularly to keep it from burning on the bottom. Remove from heat.

In a medium bowl, beat the egg yolks and sugar together until thick and light in color. Gradually beat in the milk. Pour the mixture back into the saucepan and cook, stirring constantly, over low heat (keep the milk from boiling or it will curdle) until the mixture coats the back of a wooden spoon, up to 15 minutes.

Add the vanilla extract. Remove from heat, and cool to room temperature by placing mixture in a mixing bowl set in ice water. Stir occasionally until cooled.

WINTER SALAD OF BEETS AND TURNIPS

Preheat oven to 375 degrees.

Remove greens and stems from beets and set aside. Place beets in an ovenproof bowl or baking dish, fill halfway with water, and cover tightly with a lid or aluminum foil. Bake until beets can be easily pierced with a knife, about 1½ hours. Remove from oven. When cool enough to handle, peel and julienne the beets.

Separate beet stems from greens. Bring a large pot of salted water to a boil, and blanch greens for 30 seconds. Transfer greens with a slotted spoon to a bowl of ice water. Drain and pat dry. Boil stems 1 minute in same water; transfer to ice water and, when cool, drain and dry them. Coarsely chop beet greens and stems.

In a large bowl, combine lemon juice, vinegar, mustard, and anchovy paste. Whisk in 1 cup of olive oil and stir in 2 tablespoons of Parmesan. Add beet greens and stems, and marinate 15 minutes.

Bring another large pot of salted water to a boil. Add turnips and boil until tender, about 10 minutes for very small turnips and up to 45 minutes for larger ones. Drain and dry. While still warm, peel and julienne turnips. (Very small turnips may be left whole or halved.)

Add beets, turnips, and remaining ¼ cup oil to beet greens, and let marinate 20 minutes. Add salt and pepper to taste.

Line a serving platter with lettuce leaves. Top with salad. Combine remaining Parmesan and parsley, and sprinkle over salad.

SERVES 6

5 medium beets with greens, washed
4 tablespoons fresh lemon juice
4 tablespoons red wine vinegar
2 tablespoons Dijon mustard
1 tablespoon anchovy paste
1¼ cups olive oil
6 tablespoons freshly grated Parmesan cheese
salt and freshly ground pepper
8 small turnips, washed
1 head green-leaf lettuce
1 head romaine lettuce
4 tablespoons minced parsley

6 cloves garlic, peeled

½ cup chopped fresh parsley, or ¼ cup dried

1 tablespoon chopped fresh thyme,
or 2 teaspoons dried

1 tablespoon olive oil

3 tablespoons honey

1 teaspoon salt

1 cup dry white wine

one 3- to 4-pound boneless pork loin, rolled and tied

salt and black pepper to taste

1 small onion, finely chopped

2 cloves garlic, peeled and smashed

1 cup tomato sauce (preferably homemade)

1 tablespoon unsalted butter

HONEY ROASTED PORK

In a food processor or blender, process the 6 cloves of garlic, parsley, thyme, olive oil, honey, salt, and 1 tablespoon of the wine into smooth paste.

With a sharp knife, make small slits in the meat and force generous quantities of the paste into the slits. Rub the remaining mixture all over the pork. Put the pork in a large roasting pan and pour in the remaining wine. Cover and marinate refrigerated for several hours or refrigerate overnight, turning the meat several times.

Preheat oven to 450 degrees.

Drain the marinade but reserve it for later. Sprinkle the top of the roast with salt and pepper and roast for 10 minutes. Reduce the oven temperature to 300 degrees and cook for approximately 1½ hours more or until a meat thermometer reads 160 to 170 degrees. Transfer the pork to a heated serving platter, remove the string, and keep the roast warm.

Pour off all but 2 tablespoons of drippings from the roasting pan. Add the onion and remaining garlic, and sauté gently for 2 to 3 minutes. Add the reserved marinade to the pan and stir over medium heat. Add the tomato sauce and cook until reduced to half. Remove from burner and swirl in butter. Adjust the taste with salt and pepper, if desired.

Carve the pork into thin slices and serve drizzled with the sauce.

SERVES 6 TO 8

3 pounds tender beef steaks like filet mignon, strip, or sirloin, ½ to ¾ inch thick

salt and freshly ground pepper to taste

4 tablespoons minced shallots

1½ cups red wine

3 tablespoons butter

SAUTÉED BEEF STEAKS

This dish relies on two simple, basic ingredients: good beef and good red wine.

Rub a piece of fat trimmed from steak in a heavy skillet (preferably cast iron) over medium-high heat. Cook steaks to desired doneness, turning once. *Test for doneness by gently pushing on steak with finger: A rare steak offers slight resistance, medium-rare springs back lightly, medium or beyond gets increasingly stiff and resistant.* Season with salt and pepper. Remove steaks to warm plates.

In same skillet, cook shallots in meat juices until translucent. (Add a little butter to the pan if it is too dry.) Add wine, bring to a simmer, and reduce by two thirds. Remove pan from heat, swirl in butter, adjust seasoning, and spoon sauce over the steaks.

POTATO ZUCCHINI PANCAKES

In large bowl, mix together the eggs, flour, salt, beer, and green onions. Set aside.

Coarsely grate the potatoes. Squeeze out any moisture, add the potatoes and zucchini to the batter, and blend well. Using wet hands, form 2 ½-inch loosely packed pancakes. Drop them into a non-stick skillet containing ¼-inch hot canola oil. Fry for 3 to 4 minutes on each side or until golden brown. Remove to a plate lined with paper towels. Repeat with the remaining batter. Keep the finished pancakes in a low-warm oven until ready to serve.

SERVES 6

2 large eggs, beaten

½ cup flour

½ teaspoon salt

¼ cup beer

¼ cup green onions, chopped, white part only

2 baking potatoes, peeled and kept in cold water until ready to use

1 cup grated zucchini (about 1 medium)

canola oil for frying

BROCCOLI SAUTÉED WITH GARLIC

Slice off and discard ends of fresh broccoli stalks. Peel the remaining stalks to make them more tender after cooking. Split stalks in half lengthwise, leaving florets attached. Place in microwave-proof dish and add ¼ cup water. Place plastic wrap over the top, leaving a little gap for steam to escape. Microwave on high until tender, about 3 minutes. Drain.

In a medium pan over medium heat, sauté garlic in olive oil 1 to 2 minutes or until it just releases its aroma. Add broccoli and sauté 2 to 3 minutes. Add salt to taste.

SERVES 6

2 bunches of fresh broccoli

4 cloves garlic, minced

⅓ cup olive oil

salt to taste

CHOCOLATE MOUSSE TORTE

Preheat oven to 350 degrees.

In a medium bowl, combine cookie crumbs and sugar. Pour in melted butter and stir to coat crumb mixture evenly. Press into an 8-inch springform pan and bake 10 minutes. Cool and refrigerate.

Prepare chocolate mousse and pour into prepared shell. Refrigerate at least 4 hours or overnight.

To serve, remove from pan, pipe spirals of Chantilly cream around the edge, and sprinkle cream with chocolate shavings.

SERVES 8

2 cups chocolate cookie crumbs (one 8½-ounce package chocolate wafers, crushed)

¼ cup coarse sugar

⅓ cup unsalted butter, melted

Chocolate Mousse (recipe follows)

Chantilly Cream (recipe follows)

chocolate shavings

CHOCOLATE MOUSSE

MAKES ABOUT 3 CUPS

1 ¼ cups whipping cream

6 ounces semisweet chocolate, melted and cooled

½ cup water

7 tablespoons sugar

4 egg yolks

In a medium bowl, whip cream until it holds soft peaks. Refrigerate.

Melt the chocolate in a double boiler over medium-low heat. Cool until tepid. In a separate saucepan, combine the water and sugar and bring to a boil. Boil 1 minute, making sure all the sugar is dissolved. Set aside.

Place egg yolks in a deep, 4- to 5-quart bowl of a double boiler. Whisk in the hot syrup a little at a time. Place over hot water and continue to whisk until the mixture holds stiff peaks, about 5 to 7 minutes. Remove from heat and beat with an electric mixer or by hand until it is cool. Stir in melted chocolate.

Fold in one eighth of the whipped cream. Gradually fold in remaining whipped cream. (If you fold in cream too quickly, it will cause chocolate to harden and form chocolate chips.)

At this point, the chocolate mousse can be served on its own or used to make the torte.

CHANTILLY CREAM

½ cup whipping cream, chilled

1 tablespoon sifted confectioners sugar

¼ teaspoon vanilla extract

NOTE: for best results chill mixing bowl and beaters (or whisk) before whipping cream.

In a medium bowl, whip cream until it begins to thicken slightly. Add sugar in a steady stream while you continue to beat the cream. Add the vanilla. Continue beating until cream holds stiff peaks. (Take care not to overbeat or cream will become grainy or turn to butter. Slightly underbeat the cream when piping from a pastry bag fitted with a star tip, because squeezing it though the tip whips it a bit more.)

THE BARRETTS OF LA SIRENA
AND CHATEAU MONTELENA WINERIES

"We take full advantage of the outdoors."

WITH WELL-KNOWN CLIENTS such as Screaming Eagle, Grace Family Vineyard, Paradigm, Oakford, Vineyard 29, Dalla Valle Vineyards, and others, it's amazing winemaker Heidi Peterson Barrett has any time for much of anything else. She even has her own label now, La Sirena. Although to some it may seem like insanity, those who know her and her equally busy husband Bo Barrett, who is a winemaker at Chateau Montelena, know that they successfully live life to its fullest.

They even manage to sit down around the dinner table each evening with their two children, Remi and Chelsea, for a meal and a chance to catch up on the day's events. Heidi says, "It's a comforting family ritual for us as we all come together at the end of the day. It's a chance to talk and reconnect." Bo adds, "One advantage we have is that we live so far up valley in Calistoga that there's no television reception. Although our children may not quite agree at the moment that it's a positive thing, it really gives us a chance to come together as a family."

Even with their busy lifestyles, finding time to exercise is never a challenge because they incorporate it into everyday activities. "We don't belong to a gym," says Heidi. "We don't have to since we're always walking the vineyards to check on the grapes or taking a hike with the kids. We're fortunate to live in such a beautiful area, and therefore we take full advantage of the outdoors."

Both Heidi and Bo grew up in households where wine was a normal part of the everyday mealtime routine, so they both feel it is important to help their children begin to appreciate wine at an early age. Heidi says, "Our kids usually have a taste of whatever we're drinking with the evening meal. They much prefer that to a watered-down version that some children in Europe routinely get at a young age. And," she continues, "the comments they make about taste and flavor constantly fascinate us. Their palates are so fresh and impressionable. They have a whole different perspective and it's one I continue to pay attention to. I have great memories of my Dad bringing wine home for me to taste when I was in the later years of high school. That's really when I started to get more interested in it." She adds, "And, here we are today immersed in such wonderful traditions and a healthy lifestyle—two big reasons why we love wine."

Spring ~ Summer

Grilled Salmon with Lemon

Artichokes

Mediterranean Salad

Chateau Montelena Chardonnay
or any good Chardonnay

Fall ~ Winter

Butternut Squash Soup

Smoked Turkey

Carrots with Sesame

Fresh Baked Walnut Bread

La Sirena Sangiovese
Shafer Firebreak (Sangiovese and Cabernet)
or a good spicy Zinfandel

GRILLED SALMON WITH LEMON

SERVES 8

olive oil

one 4- to 6-pound salmon filet, skinned, boned, and rinsed

1 teaspoon Sea Star* sea salt

2 teaspoons coarsely chopped fresh thyme

2 teaspoons coarsely chopped fresh tarragon

2 lemons, 1 thinly sliced and 1 cut into wedges

10 freshly picked lemon leaves, or other citrus leaves

*See "Sea Salt in Season" page 96

Rub a thin layer of olive oil on each side of the salmon. Coat the grilling rack with olive oil. Place the salmon in the rack and season one side at a time: sprinkle with Sea Star salt, then herbs, distribute the lemon slices evenly, and add the lemon leaves dark side down. Close the basket, flip it over, and repeat on other side.

Place on hot grill for 10 minutes per inch of thickness. Take care not to overcook. Remove salmon from rack to serving platter. Serve with lemon wedges.

MEDITERRANEAN SALAD

SERVES 8

2 Armenian cucumbers, sliced

4 tomatoes, sliced

4 ounces sliced feta cheese or fresh mozzarella

one 7-ounce jar Kalamata olives

¼ cup chopped fresh basil and/or mint

2 tablespoons olive oil

2 teaspoons lemon juice or balsamic vinegar

sea salt and pepper to taste

Arrange cucumbers, tomatoes, feta, and olives on individual salad plates. Add basil and drizzle with olive oil and lemon juice. Add Sea Star salt and pepper to taste. Chill ½ hour before serving.

BUTTERNUT SQUASH SOUP

SERVES 8

2 tablespoons butter

2½ to 3 pounds butternut squash, peeled, seeded, and cubed

1 yellow onion, peeled and coarsely chopped

2 stalks celery, coarsely chopped

2 carrots, coarsely chopped

5 cups chicken stock

¼ teaspoon Sea Star sea salt

½ cup light cream

½ cup nonfat yogurt

¼ teaspoon ground dry ginger, or ½ teaspoon crushed fresh ginger

2 tablespoons brown sugar

pinch ground black pepper

I like to serve this with a dollop of plain yogurt and a fragrant orange blossom on top.

Melt butter in a large stock pot over medium heat, add squash and chopped vegetables, and stir to coat with butter. Cook until onion is wilted but not browned, about 3 minutes. Add chicken stock and sea salt and bring to a boil. Cover and reduce heat to low, simmering until vegetables are tender, 25 to 30 minutes. Purée in a food processor or blender. Add the cream, yogurt, ginger, and brown sugar. Add additional sea salt & pepper to taste.

CHATEAU MONTELENA
ESTABLISHED 1882

Chardonnay
NAPA VALLEY
1997

PRODUCED & BOTTLED BY CHATEAU MONTELENA WINERY
CALISTOGA, CALIFORNIA · ALCOHOL 13.5% BY VOLUME

SMOKED TURKEY

Place water in a medium-size non-aluminum pot or plastic container. Stir in soy sauce, frozen apple juice, sesame oil, ginger, chili powder, and pepper flakes. Add ½ cup salt and stir to dissolve. Place egg in the marinade and, if needed, add more salt, stirring to dissolve, until the egg floats. Remove the egg (it's only a brine checker).

Wash poultry, pat dry, and place in pot. Marinate 12 to 24 hours or overnight in refrigerator. (You may need to weight it with a plate to make sure the poultry stays submerged.) Drain turkey, reserving the marinade.

Using a water smoker (follow the manufacturer's directions for the setup) with mesquite coals and grapevine hardwood soaked in water for 2 hours (or any smoker chunks and regular coals), smoke for 30 minutes (10 to 12 minutes per pound).

Preheat oven to 350 degrees.

Remove turkey from smoker to roasting pan. Brush with olive oil. Place a temperature probe or meat thermometer in the turkey, and roast in oven, basting occasionally with drippings until the probe indicates 160 to 165 degrees, about 30 minutes. Remove from oven and let rest 15 to 30 minutes. Carve and serve.

FOR GRAVY: Use up to ½ cup of the turkey drippings (any more will give it a very strong smokey, salty flavor) and chicken stock, fresh or canned, to make up the quantity of gravy you need.

SERVES 6

MARINADE:

2 quarts water

1 cup soy sauce

8 ounces frozen apple juice

1 tablespoon sesame oil

1 tablespoon freshly pulverized ginger, or 1 tablespoon dry powdered ginger

1 tablespoon Numex or Pasilla chili powder

1 teaspoon hot red pepper flakes

½ cup (or more) rock salt

1 uncooked egg in shell

1 bone-in turkey or chicken breast half, 3 to 3½ pounds

1 tablespoon olive oil

OPTIONS: You can use your barbecue instead of a smoker for the first half of cooking, using wood-like mesquite, or roast the turkey in the oven for the full time without using a smoker, covering it for half the cooking time and leaving it uncovered for the remainder. Also, a whole turkey (or chicken) can be used, increasing the recipe proportions according to the turkey's weight.

CARROTS WITH SESAME

Place carrots in a medium microwave-proof bowl and add stock. Cover loosely and microwave for 3 minutes on high. Drain. Heat a medium-size sauté pan over medium heat. Melt the butter, and when it begins to sizzle, add carrots, coating them with butter. Sprinkle with sesame seeds and serve.

SERVES 6

6 to 8 medium carrots, peeled and sliced diagonally into ⅛-inch pieces

¼ cup chicken or vegetable stock

1 tablespoon butter

1 tablespoon sesame seeds

OPTION: Steam carrots in a steamer for 5 to 7 minutes, just until tender, or simmer carrots in a covered sauté pan with stock, about 3 to 5 minutes.

THE CAKEBREADS OF CAKEBREAD CELLARS

"Wine is a part of the beauty and enjoyment of life."

"WINE IS A MAJOR CONTRIBUTOR to our good health and longevity," says Dolores Cakebread. "And a lighter, healthier style of cooking allows us the 'space' to enjoy a wide variety of food and wine daily." Jack Cakebread adds, "Exercise is also important in the balance. And a daily walk helps us not only make room for another day of culinary delights, but also allows us to relax, catch up, and enjoy our beautiful surroundings in a very special way." "Being outdoors is something we've enjoyed together for a long time. Even before we were married I helped Jack on his family's ranch as we would harvest almonds and peaches. And years later, when we lived in Oakland, we had our own garden as well as our morning walking ritual around Lake Merritt. Pull all of this together with friends and family," says Dolores, "and you have the perfect recipe for a healthy lifestyle!" With the Cakebreads, you'll find a staunch commitment to good healthy food and an atmosphere that not only encourages increased wine appreciation, but is also fun. Dolores says, "Wine is a part of the beauty and enjoyment of life. And of course you can drink any wine with whatever you want, but sometimes you can enhance both the food and the wine. That's an area we continually enjoy exploring." "And," says Jack, "we have a real commitment to American farm producers and chefs and to spread the word about the importance of good food and good wine to a healthy lifestyle." "As we do at the winery," says Dolores, "I also continually try to come up with meal combinations that are fresh, appealing, convenient, and healthy. It should be more simple for today's consumers, and we're working to make a difference there."

One of Dolores's greatest joys is gardening, because the fruits of her labor are readily evident with each new season. She even stocks a farmstand out in front of the winery when produce becomes abundant. "Since we knew food would be a very important part of what we do at the winery, we also wanted to plant a vegetable garden so the freshest produce would be at our fingertips," says Dolores.

"The wine business is an eating business. You just can't separate the two," says Jack. Dolores adds, "And we're dedicated to not only making quality wine but also to the education that helps more and more people learn how to truly enjoy and appreciate the meal before them each and every time."

Spring ~ Summer

Roast Beet and Spinach Salad with Candied Pecans and Goat Cheese

Sea Scallops with Warm Salad of Sweet Corn, Roasted Peppers, and Shiitakes with Chive Oil

Warm Polenta Cheesecake with Strawberries in Red Wine

Cakebread Cellars Sauvignon Blanc
Shafer Merlot

Fall ~ Winter

Roast Wild Mushroom Salad with Walnut Oil and Dry Jack Cheese

Rigatoni with Sausage and Red Wine

American Artisan Cheese Plate with Fresh Fruit and Whole Grain Toast

Cakebread Cellars Merlot
Ridge Zinfandel

3 bunches baby beets (preferably a mixture of red, gold, and chioggia beets), washed and tops removed

4 ounces baby spinach or arugula, washed and spun dry

1 tablespoon chopped fresh dill

½ cup Candied Pecans (recipe follows)

3 ounces crumbled goat cheese

VINAIGRETTE:

¼ cup sherry wine vinegar

1 large shallot, minced

salt and freshly ground pepper to taste

¾ to 1 cup olive oil

¼ cup honey

¼ cup sugar

¼ cup water

pinch of salt

1 pound pecan pieces

ROAST BEET AND SPINACH SALAD WITH CANDIED PECANS AND GOAT CHEESE

Preheat oven to 400 degrees.

Wrap beets in foil. Place in the oven and roast until easily pierced with a knife, about 1 hour. Remove from oven. Unwrap foil, wait until cool enough to handle, and peel and cut into thick slices. Set aside.

In a stainless steel bowl, place the sherry wine vinegar, shallot, and salt and pepper. Slowly whisk in olive oil.

In two separate bowls, place both spinach and beets with chopped dill. Pour vinaigrette (just enough to coat) over the spinach and the beets, and toss.

On chilled plates make a bed of spinach, top with beets, and sprinkle with Candied Pecans and goat cheese.

CANDIED PECANS

Preheat oven to 350 degrees.

Spray two sheet trays with non-stick spray. Place honey, sugar, water, and salt in large saucepan over high heat and boil to dissolve sugar. Add pecans and continue cooking until nuts are totally covered with syrup and bottom of pan is dry. Remove from heat, and pour out onto one of the sheet trays. Place in the oven and cook, stirring occasionally for 10 to 12 minutes until nuts are dark brown. Remove from oven and transfer nuts onto the other sheet tray. Place tray in freezer to cool them quickly. As soon as they are cool enough to handle, break them up to keep them from sticking together. Store in an airtight container in the freezer until ready to use.

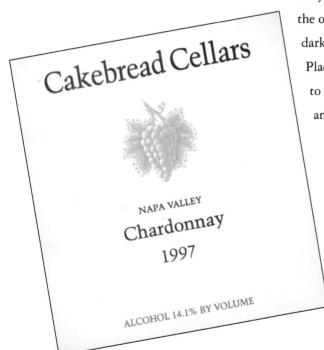

Cakebread Cellars

NAPA VALLEY

Chardonnay

1997

ALCOHOL 14.1% BY VOLUME

SEA SCALLOPS WITH WARM SALAD OF SWEET CORN, ROASTED PEPPERS, AND SHIITAKES WITH CHIVE OIL

Two hours before serving, purée chives and oil in blender on high speed until smooth. Reserve.

In a large pan, sauté shallots and garlic in butter over medium heat until soft, about 3 minutes. Add corn, mushrooms, and peppers. Turn to high heat and season with salt, pepper, and parsley. Sauté to heat through and soften mushrooms. Remove from heat and keep warm.

Brush scallops with 2 tablespoons olive oil and season with salt and pepper. Sear on both sides in a non-stick pan over high heat until brown.

Arrange a spoonful of corn salad in center of each plate. Top with three scallops. Arrange a small bundle of lettuce greens in the center to form a small bouquet. Drizzle with a little of the chive oil and serve.

SERVES 8

¼ cup chopped chives

1 cup canola oil

2 shallots, peeled and minced

2 cloves garlic, minced

2 tablespoons butter

4 ears white corn, shucked and kernels cut away

1½ cups sliced shiitake mushrooms

2 red peppers, roasted, peeled, and diced

salt and freshly ground pepper to taste

1 tablespoon chopped parsley

2 pounds sea scallops, cleaned

2 tablespoons olive oil

4 ounces baby spring salad greens

2 cups ricotta cheese

2 cups mascarpone cheese

1 cup sugar

1 teaspoon vanilla extract

1 tablespoon crushed fennel seed

¾ cup polenta

1 tablespoon butter

powdered sugar

2 pints fresh strawberries or raspberries, cleaned and sliced

¼ cup sugar

1 cup Cakebread Cellars Cabernet Sauvignon or other full-bodied red wine

WARM POLENTA CHEESECAKE WITH STRAWBERRIES IN RED WINE

Preheat oven to 300 degrees.

In a large mixing bowl, whisk together the ricotta, mascarpone, sugar, vanilla, and fennel until smooth. Add the polenta and stir to combine. Pour into a buttered springform pan. Bake for 1 hour and 20 minutes or until set. Place under broiler to lightly caramelize. Remove and allow to cool slightly.

Dust with powdered sugar and cut into serving portions. Serve over Strawberries in Red Wine (recipe follows).

STRAWBERRIES IN RED WINE

In a large bowl, toss strawberries with sugar. Adjust sugar to the sweetness of the berries. Cover with wine. Allow to steep for 1 hour. Transfer strawberries to serving bowl with a slotted spoon.

SERVES 4

1½ pounds assorted mushrooms, like shiitake, oyster, crimni, portabello, and chantrelles, cleaned, and trimmed (reserve stems), and cut into large pieces

3 cloves garlic, peeled, 2 minced and 1 smashed

3 tablespoons extra-virgin olive oil

1 tablespoon soy sauce

2 sprigs fresh thyme, or 1 teaspoon dry

salt and pepper

½ tablespoon walnut oil

6 ounces mixed lettuce leaves, cleaned

dry jack cheese (like Vella brand, or substitute fresh Parmesan cheese), shaved

2 tablespoons chopped chives

ROAST WILD MUSHROOM SALAD WITH WALNUT OIL AND DRY JACK CHEESE

Preheat oven to 400 degrees.

Toss mushrooms in a casserole dish with the 2 minced garlic cloves, olive oil, soy sauce, and half of the thyme. Season with salt and pepper. Cover with foil and place in oven for 20 minutes, or until mushrooms have softened and have released their liquid. Meanwhile, place mushroom stems and trimmings in a small sauce pan with remaining thyme and smashed garlic clove. Sauté over medium-low heat for 10 to 20 minutes. Strain, reserving liquid. Discard trimmings.

Remove casserole dish from the oven and drain the mushroom broth at the bottom of the casserole dish into the small saucepan. Turn the oven up to 450 degrees.

Return the casserole to the oven, and roast uncovered for another 20 minutes or until lightly browned. On the stovetop, bring the mushroom broth to a boil over high heat and reduce by half. Whisk in walnut oil.

To serve, form a bed of lettuce on a large platter or divide among four plates. Top with roasted mushrooms. Drizzle with the warm walnut oil and mushroom broth. Top with dry jack cheese shavings and chives.

RIGATONI WITH SAUSAGE AND RED WINE

Heat a wide-bottom skillet over high heat and sauté sausage with olive oil, breaking sausage up with back of a spoon. Sauté until sausage is cooked through and well browned. Drain off excess oil and return pan to medium heat. Add the onion, carrot, and celery, and cook to soften, about 10 minutes. Add the garlic, tomatoes, and red wine, deglazing the pan. Simmer for 20 minutes to reduce and thicken.

Cook pasta according to package directions. Drain and toss immediately with sauce, Parmesan, and parsley. Serve in warm bowls.

SERVES 4

4 links Italian sausage

2 tablespoons olive oil

½ onion, finely minced

1 carrot, finely minced

1 stalk celery, finely minced

3 cloves garlic, minced

14 ounces canned peeled tomatoes, seeded, and chopped

1½ cups red wine

1 pound rigatoni, penne, or fusili pasta

¼ cup freshly grated Parmesan

2 tablespoons coarsely chopped fresh flat-leaf parsley

AMERICAN ARTISAN CHEESE PLATE WITH FRESH FRUIT AND WHOLE GRAIN TOAST

Following the entrée, instead of a dessert, try a delicious alternative—a cheese plate using American cheeses.

Serve with grapes, pears, toasted nuts, and croutons or toasted whole grain bread.

Sonoma Dry Jack, California (cow)

Bellwether Toscono, California (sheep)

Great Hill Blue, Massachusetts (cow)

Bellwether San Andres, California (young sheep)

Matos St. George, California (cow)

HUGH CARPENTER OF CAMP NAPA CULINARY AND CULINARY PHOTOGRAPHER TERI SANDESON

TERI SANDESON, A FOOD STYLIST and photographer, and husband Hugh Carpenter, a cookbook author and owner of Camp Napa Culinary, have, admittedly, unbelievably hectic schedules. Despite their lack of time, they make every attempt to eat healthily by making easy-to-prepare and fast-to-cook dinners. Teri says, "Usually I'll create a salad while Hugh prepares the entrée and perhaps one dish to accompany it." "And as we work," says Hugh, "we have a glass of wine and either recap the day's events or use the time to brainstorm about the food we're creating. You never know, it might end up in the next book!"

As they prepare their evening meal they usually choose one wine—both to sip as the meal is being prepared and to have during dinner. "It's usually one we think will, for us, taste the best with whatever entrée we're having that evening," says Hugh. Then sitting in front of a cozy fire in the winter or outside on warm summer nights, the spirit of conversation is spurred by the food and enhanced by the wine."

When they first arrived in the Napa Valley in 1988, they constantly worried that they might make the wrong wine choice to serve at their dinner parties. Hugh says, "We were quickly put at ease though after attending several Napa Valley wine seminars during which, to our surprise, local winemakers radically disagreed about which wine to match with the food." "So," says Teri, "now we just serve whatever wine we enjoy the most. There has to be one wine expert, somewhere, that agrees with our choice!" They no longer worry about making a drastic mistake. "And," says Hugh, "we haven't had a complaint yet!"

"We just serve whatever wine we enjoy the most."

Spring ~ Summer

Papaya Salad

Halibut in Lemon Ginger Marinade

Pan Fried Potatoes with Pepper and Garlic

Fresh Berries with Raspberry Cabernet Sauce

Chappellet Old Vine Cuvee
Pine Ridge Chenin Blanc

Fall ~ Winter

Baby Greens with Blue Cheese Pecan Dressing

Sichaunese Chicken with Eggplant

Steamed Rice

Lemon Ice Cream

Cakebread Sauvignon Blanc
Trefethen Merlot

SERVES 4

DRESSING:

1 clove garlic, very finely minced

2 tablespoons chopped fresh cilantro

2 tablespoons chopped fresh mint leaves

2 tablespoons lime juice

¼ cup orange juice

2 tablespoons low-sodium soy sauce

2 tablespoons light brown sugar

¼ cup light olive oil

2 firm papayas, peeled, seeded, and cubed

4 cups baby lettuce greens or mixed torn lettuce greens, rinsed and patted dry

PAPAYA SALAD

In a medium bowl, combine all dressing ingredients. Adjust seasonings to taste.

Place papaya and greens in a large bowl. Add dressing. Toss and serve immediately.

SERVES 4

MARINADE:

1 tablespoon finely minced lemon zest

⅓ cup freshly squeezed lemon juice

¼ cup white wine

3 tablespoons canola oil

2 tablespoons low-sodium soy sauce

1 tablespoon oyster sauce

¼ teaspoon Asian chile sauce, or ½ teaspoon red pepper flakes

¼ cup minced green onions

1 tablespoon very finely minced ginger

2 pounds fresh halibut steaks, 1 inch thick

HALIBUT IN LEMON GINGER MARINADE

In a small bowl, combine all marinade ingredients. (Can be made and refrigerated up to 8 hours in advance.)

Pour the marinade over the halibut, and turn the halibut to coat evenly. Marinate between 10 and 30 minutes.

TO GRILL: Preheat grill to medium heat (350 degrees). Place the halibut in the center of the grill, cover, and grill, brushing with remaining marinade periodically until the halibut begins to flake when prodded with a knife and fork, about 4 minutes each side.

TO BROIL: Place the halibut on a broiler pan 4 inches from the broiler heat, and broil, brushing once with marinade, until halibut begins to flake when prodded with a fork, about 4 minutes on each side. If the halibut begins to brown too much, remove from the broiler and continue to bake in a 500 degree oven.

Transfer halibut to a heated serving platter or four heated dinner plates and serve immediately.

PAN FRIED POTATOES WITH PEPPER AND GARLIC

Place a 12-inch cast iron skillet over medium-high heat. Add oil and garlic. When garlic begins to sizzle, add potatoes, green onions, and peppercorns. Cover, reduce heat to low, and cook until the potatoes become dark brown, crunchy on the exterior, and tender in the center, about 15 minutes. (During cooking, stir potatoes every 5 minutes and add a splash of water or white wine to prevent scorching.) Season with salt and serve immediately.

SERVES 4

8 cloves garlic, finely minced

¼ cup extra-virgin olive oil

2 pounds small red potatoes (about 20), scrubbed, halved (soak, covered in cold water, if prepared more than 30 minutes in advance of cooking)

3 whole green onions, diagonally-sliced into ½-inch pieces

1 tablespoon mixed peppercorns, toasted in hot skillet and crushed or coarsely ground

water or white wine

salt

FRESH BERRIES WITH RASPBERRY CABERNET SAUCE

Place berries in a large bowl. Pour Raspberry Cabernet Sauce over berries and marinate 10 to 30 minutes. Spoon fruit into 4 small bowls and spoon a little marinade over the top.

SERVES 4

1 cup fresh blueberries, rinsed

1 cup fresh strawberries, rinsed, sliced or quartered

1 cup fresh raspberries, rinsed

1 cup fresh blackberries, rinsed

2 cups Raspberry Cabernet Sauce (recipe follows)

OPTION: Top with a dollop of crème fraîche (see page 168)

RASPBERRY CABERNET SAUCE

Place all ingredients in a medium sauté pan and boil over high heat until reduced to two cups. Cool slightly and transfer to a blender. Pulse until completely puréed. Pour through a sieve and refrigerate until ready to use. (Can be stored for several months for future use.)

12 ounces frozen raspberries

1 cup sugar

1 bottle (750ml) red wine

2 grinds black pepper

BABY GREENS WITH BLUE CHEESE PECAN DRESSING

In a small bowl, combine dressing ingredients. Adjust seasonings to taste.

In a large bowl, combine greens and pepper. Pour dressing over the greens, add pecans, and toss evenly. Serve immediately.

DRESSING:

¼ cup crumbled blue cheese

6 tablespoons extra-virgin olive oil

3 tablespoons balsamic vinegar

2 tablespoons low sodium soy sauce

¼ teaspoon fresh finely ground black pepper

¼ teaspoon salt, or to taste

4 cups baby lettuce greens or torn mixed lettuce greens, washed and dried

1 red bell pepper, stemmed, seeded, and chopped

½ cup toasted and finely chopped pecans

SERVES 4

1 pound boned and skinned chicken breast meat, sliced into 1-inch pieces

1 tablespoon each oyster sauce, hoisin sauce, low-sodium soy sauce, dark sesame oil, and rice wine

3 tablespoons cooking oil

1 tablespoon water

1 yellow onion, cut into ½-inch cubes

4 small Japanese eggplants, trimmed, and cut into ¼-inch-wide slices

1 tablespoon cornstarch

SAUCE:

⅓ cup chicken broth

3 tablespoons Chinese rice wine or dry sherry

2 tablespoons oyster sauce

1 tablespoon hoisin sauce

1 tablespoon red wine vinegar

1 tablespoon dark sesame oil

1 teaspoon sugar

1 teaspoon Asian chili sauce

¼ cup chopped fresh cilantro sprigs

SICHUANESE CHICKEN WITH EGGPLANT

In a medium bowl, combine the chicken with the oyster, hoisin, and soy sauces, sesame oil, and rice wine. Mix well and refrigerate.

In a small bowl, combine the sauce ingredients and refrigerate. (Can be made up to 8 hours in advance.)

Heat 1 tablespoon of oil in a wok over high heat. Add the chicken and stir until it loses its pink color. Transfer the chicken to a plate. Add the remaining oil to the wok and stir in the onions and eggplant. Toss until the vegetables begin to sizzle, then add the sauce. Cover, stirring occasionally until the eggplant softens, about 4 minutes. Return the chicken to the wok and combine the cornstarch with an equal amount of cold water. Add a little at a time so that the sauce thickens slightly. Transfer to a heated platter, or dinner plates. Serve immediately.

LEMON ICE CREAM

In a large bowl, beat the cream and sugar until well mixed. Stir in the lemon juice and mix well. Place the mixture in an ice cream maker and freeze according to the manufacturer's directions.

Place 1 large scoop or 3 small scoops of ice cream in the center of each bowl. Garnish with a sprig of mint or a twist of candied lemon peel. Serve immediately.

SERVES 12

4 cups heavy (whipping) cream or half-and-half

2 cups sugar

1 cup freshly squeezed lemon juice

mint sprigs or candied lemon

CATHERINE CARPY OF FREEMARK ABBEY WINERY

"Any wine you like is the perfect cooking wine."

Working at Freemark Abbey under the tutelage of her father, Chuck Carpy, who has a long Napa Valley lineage, Catherine Carpy knew she would one day have very big shoes to fill. Catherine says, "They are indeed, and even bigger than I had imagined, but wine is in my blood so I enjoy the challenge. I love the business!"

Having a full-time job, an equally busy husband, and two young children, Catherine admittedly struggles to find the time even to just return phone calls, and barely has time left to think about dinner, much less really "cook." Catherine says, "I do still make every attempt at healthy preparations and foods—so we really eat very simply. If I'm ever motivated to get more elaborate, I have to rely on a professional's recipe. But I do have some favorites that I can call my own—born out of a necessity to be speedy and kid-friendly—and are relatively simple to make." At this stage of the game what is really important is that dishes can be eaten at any temperature. "They have to be great hot from the oven all the way to room temperature, not only because of our schedules, but also toddler temperament! I know anyone who's a parent will understand that," she says.

She adds, "One thing I can wholeheartedly recommend, and is something I make a part of our mealtime ritual, is a glass of wine for the cook (that's me) while preparing dinner. It helps me wind down from my day and begin to enjoy the evening with family." Catherine's "cooking wine" as she calls it, is typically a refreshing white wine, usually the Freemark Abbey Riesling. "Though," she's quick to add, "of course any wine you like is the perfect 'cooking wine.'"

As for balance, she says, "I'm not sure I can expect balance at this point of my life. It's more like controlled chaos. But I'm loving every minute of it!"

Spring ~ Summer

Garden Pasta Toss

Sweet White Corn on the Cob

Cantaloupe with Riesling Sorbet

Freemark Abbey Riesling
Markham Merlot

Fall ~ Winter

Cheesy Vegetable Lasagna

Garlic Bread

Green Salad with Mandarin Oranges

Freemark Abbey Merlot
Rombauer Chardonnay

DRESSING:

¼ cup red wine vinegar

¼ cup olive oil

2 cloves garlic, lightly smashed

salt and pepper

4 medium vine-ripened tomatoes

¼ cup chopped fresh sweet basil leaves

¾ cup fresh cubed mozzarella cheese
(½-inch pieces)

vermicelli for 4, cooked per package directions

OPTIONAL:

2 medium grilled zucchini, sliced

2 medium grilled yellow squash, sliced

1 small grilled eggplant, sliced

1 to 2 ears sweet, white corn kernels,
lightly steamed or grilled

GARDEN PASTA TOSS

I like to make the dressing for this dish in a wine bottle and make a larger batch to have on hand for other meals. When the summer days are sweltering, this dish is best served at room temperature. The ingredients and quantities may vary with preference, or what's available in the garden. And, have fun experimenting with different tomato varieties. If you prefer balsamic vinegar to red wine vinegar, use less than the given amount of olive oil.

In a small bowl or empty wine bottle, combine vinegar, oil, garlic, and salt and pepper to taste. Place tomatoes, basil, mozzarella, and any optional vegetables in a medium bowl, and pour the mixture over it. Place cooked pasta in a large serving bowl, add vegetables, and toss.

SERVES 4 TO 6

YIELDS 5 CUPS

SORBET:

3 cups water

1½ cups sugar

1¼ cups Freemark Abbey Riesling

1 tablespoon lemon juice

1 medium-large vine-ripened cantaloupe,
diced into 1-inch pieces

CANTALOUPE WITH RIESLING SORBET

Combine the water and sugar in a medium saucepan and heat to a simmer. Cover, and simmer 5 minutes. Remove from heat. Stir in the wine, and set aside to cool to room temperature. Refrigerate, loosely covered, until chilled, at least 2 hours.

Freeze in an ice cream maker according to manufacturer's directions.

Arrange cantaloupe in bowls. Place a scoop of sorbet on top and serve immediately.

FREEMARK ABBEY

1998
NAPA VALLEY

JOHANNISBERG RIESLING

RESIDUAL SUGAR 1.4% BY WT   ALCOHOL 12.8% BY VOLUME

CHEESY VEGETABLE LASAGNA

This recipe has evolved over the years, and can vary depending on what's on hand: sliced olives, kidney beans, a few sliced carrots, green peppers, or whatever your preference is—it's your chance to be creative!

Bring a large pot of water to boil over high heat. Lay dry lasagna noodles in a 9 x 13-inch pan in three layers to measure the amount. Add to the pot and boil until tender. Remove, rinse quickly under cold water, and drizzle with a little olive oil.

Meanwhile, in a medium sauté pan heat olive oil over medium-high heat. Add zucchini and yellow squash, and sauté until heated through, about 1 to 2 minutes. Add onion and garlic; continue to sauté 1 to 2 minutes more. Remove from heat, add oregano and basil, and set aside.

Preheat oven to 375 degrees.

Layer prepared ingredients in the 9 x 13-inch pan in the following order: ¼ of the sauce, ⅓ of noodles, ½ zucchini mixture, ½ hard boiled eggs, ½ tomatoes, ⅓ of each cheese. Repeat. Finish with the final ⅓ noodles, ¼ sauce, and ⅓ cheese over the top.

Cover with foil. (Take care to not let foil touch cheese during baking.) Bake in oven until bubbling, about 45 minutes. Broil uncovered for a few minutes until top browns. Remove from oven and let stand 15 to 20 minutes before serving.

SERVES 6 TO 8

1 package dried lasagna noodles

1 to 2 tablespoons olive oil

2 small zucchini, diced

1 medium yellow squash, diced

1 small yellow onion, coarsely chopped

2 cloves garlic, minced

2 tablespoons fresh chopped oregano

¼ cup fresh chopped basil leaves

1 large jar tomato sauce

4 hard boiled eggs, thinly sliced or coarsely chopped

one 15-ounce can diced tomatoes, drained (or the equivalent of fresh tomatoes in season)

8 ounces mozzarella cheese, sliced ⅛-inch thick

8 ounces white cheddar, coarsely grated

OPTION: The onion can be kept raw for a little added crunch. Also, one pound cooked, lean ground beef or turkey may be added to the tomato sauce.

GARLIC BREAD

In a small saucepan over medium-low heat, melt butter and stir in garlic. Slice bread horizontally but not all the way through. Place on enough foil to wrap entire loaf. Using basting brush, brush garlic butter on both slices. Wrap in foil and bake (with lasagna) for the last 20 minutes.

SERVES 8

¼ cup butter

2 cloves garlic, minced

one long loaf sourdough (French) bread

GREEN SALAD WITH MANDARIN ORANGES

Place lettuce pieces in large bowl. Add oranges and hearts of palm. In a small bowl, whisk together remaining ingredients and drizzle enough over salad to coat the lettuce leaves. Toss and serve.

SERVES 4

1 small head butter lettuce, washed, spun dry, and torn into bite-size pieces

1 small can mandarin oranges, or ½ cup fresh orange sections, pith removed

3 spears canned hearts of palm, coarsely chopped

¼ cup olive or canola oil

2 tablespoons red wine vinegar

1 tablespoon each chopped fresh oregano and basil

1 teaspoon chopped fresh thyme

½ teaspoon minced fresh garlic

MICHAEL CHIARELLO OF TRA VIGNE RISTORANTE

"Our cooking was always centered around the most wonderful produce available."

SINCE CHILDHOOD, MICHAEL CHIARELLO has, in his words, "always lived a healthful life encompassing a very balanced way of living." Michael says, "Our cooking was always centered around the most wonderful produce available in any given month, which was more a European tradition than American at the time. I learned very early that both freshness and availability of good ingredients were crucial to the success of any recipe. For example, if wild mustard greens were in season we would cook large batches with a little garlic and olive oil. They would be eaten hot that night accompanied with a little fennel roasted pork tenderloin." And dinner options for the next night would spring up from the previous night's meal. Michael explains, "The next evening, we'd mix a little vinegar with the garlic and olive oil and marinate the mustard greens. We would then coarsely chop them and place them atop a thick slice of toasted Italian bread and finally sprinkle on a little freshly grated pecorino cheese." In his childhood days, the protein portion of the meal played a less significant role than in a typical American household.

What was also not so typical was the family's winemaking. Michael says, "In the fall, we would make a couple of barrels of red wine. Like most Italians in our neighborhood, we made a field blend of what was left from the second crop. The kids would pick the grapes, and Mom and Dad would make the wine. We made just enough to enjoy every night with our supper." And, as is traditional in Italian households, Michael and the other children would always get a little wine with added water, he says, "kind of like wine with training wheels." He adds, "By the winter when we were ready with the new wine, the previous year's wine would just have been consumed and we were ready for another cycle." Now at his restaurant Tra Vigne in St. Helena, Michael says, "as these cycles of eating and drinking have been the backbone of my family's style of living, so they are incorporated into our style of cooking here. Everyone should take a little time this year to start some annual traditions of their own—they will be passed on for generations to come."

Spring ~ Summer

Shaved Artichoke and Asparagus Salad

Pastina Risotto with English Peas, Prosciutto, and Carrot Broth

Strawberries "Pazzo" with Vanilla Bean Cornmeal Loaf Cake

Patz & Hall Hyde Vineyard Pinot Noir
Mason Sauvignon Blanc
Etude Pinot Blanc

Fall ~ Winter

Salad of Romaine with Red Onions, Asiago, and Lemon Vinaigrette

Fusilli Michelangelo

"Semi-Freddo" Tra Vigne style

Cafaro Merlot
Luna Sangiovese

SHAVED ARTICHOKE AND ASPARAGUS SALAD

This salad, capitalizing on the sweetness of the fresh and tender artichokes of spring, can also become a main course served with a piece of sautéed or grilled fish, such as halibut.

Bring a large pot of salted water to a boil.

Cut off and discard the top third of the artichokes. Snap off the dark, outer leaves until only the pale, yellow-green leaves remain. Cut off all but 1 inch of the stem. With a paring knife, trim artichokes and their stems of all remaining dark green parts. Cut in half lengthwise through the hearts and remove fuzzy chokes with a spoon. Slice halves lengthwise very thinly and put in a bowl of water with 2 tablespoons of the lemon juice.

When the salted water boils, add asparagus and blanch until slightly undercooked, about 2 to 3 minutes. Immediately drain and plunge into a bowl of ice water. Drain again. Mix ¼ cup of olive oil with rosemary. Brush oil mixture on asparagus spears and grill until just tender, turning occasionally to ensure even cooking, about 2 to 3 minutes. Set aside.

Drain artichokes well and put in a bowl with the remaining lemon juice, olive oil, rosemary, and parsley. Season with salt and pepper. Toss well. Moisten asparagus with some of the dressing.

To serve, mound a portion of artichoke salad on each of 6 plates and top each with 3 asparagus spears. With a vegetable peeler, shave strips of Parmesan or pecorino over the top.

PASTINA RISOTTO WITH ENGLISH PEAS, PROSCIUTTO, AND CARROT BROTH

Pastina, a small pasta shaped like Arborio rice, is a year-round favorite at Tra Vigne. We're always thinking of new dishes to create around it. We had fun with the carrot juice in this recipe because, along with the refreshingly sweet character it adds to the dish, it also creates a little drama with its vibrant color.

Heat stock to simmering in a medium saucepan.

Heat olive oil in a large saucepan over medium-high heat. Add garlic and cook until light brown. Add onion and a pinch of salt. Lower heat to medium and cook until onion is soft but not brown, about 3 minutes. Add pastina, stir well, and add 1 cup stock. Cook, regulating heat so stock maintains a slow simmer. Stir occasionally so pastina does not stick to bottom of pan. Season with salt and pepper.

As stock is absorbed, add more by cupfuls, until pasta is about ¾ done, about 10 minutes. Add peas, remaining stock, and cook until peas are tender and pasta is al dente, about 3 minutes. Remove from heat and stir in butter, oregano, thyme, Parmesan, and 3 tablespoons prosciutto bits.

Warm carrot juice in a small pan over medium heat. Do not allow to get too hot, or solids will precipitate.

To serve, spoon pastina into the center of 4 warmed dinner plates. Pour about 2 tablespoons (1 ounce) carrot juice over each serving. Garnish with a light sprinkle of prosciutto bits.

SERVES 4

4 cups fresh chicken stock, or low-sodium canned chicken broth

2 tablespoons extra-virgin olive oil

1 tablespoon minced garlic

¾ cup finely chopped onion

salt and freshly ground pepper to taste

¾ pound dried pastina pasta (or orzo, riso, or stellini)

1½ cups shelled English peas

1 tablespoon unsalted butter

1½ teaspoons fresh finely chopped oregano

1½ teaspoons fresh finely chopped thyme

¾ cup freshly grated Parmesan cheese

¼ cup cooked, crisp prosciutto or bacon, finely minced

½ cup fresh carrot juice

STRAWBERRIES "PAZZO" WITH VANILLA BEAN CORNMEAL LOAF CAKE

SERVES 6

2 cups fresh strawberries, washed, stemmed, quartered

6 tablespoons balsamic vinegar

½ cup superfine sugar

pinch salt and pepper

CAKE:

½ pound unsalted, sweet butter

1 teaspoon finely minced lemon zest

½ vanilla bean, scraped

1⅔ cups sugar

1 teaspoon vanilla extract

5 eggs

1¾ cups cake flour

⅓ cup cornmeal or polenta

½ teaspoon salt

From my rich Italian heritage comes a dessert most have a hard time believing will taste good until they try it. You'll be amazed!

In a small bowl, combine vinegar, sugar, salt, and pepper. Toss in strawberries. Marinate for a short time, 10 to 15 minutes.

Preheat oven to 325 degrees.

Grease and lightly flour a 9 x 5-inch loaf pan. Place butter and lemon zest in bowl of mixer. Scrape in seeds from vanilla bean and beat until smooth. Gradually beat in sugar until light.

Add vanilla extract to the eggs. Then, one at a time, add eggs to butter mixture, beating well after each addition.

In another bowl, combine flour, cornmeal, and salt. Sift this mixture over the batter in 3 additions, mixing to blend after each.

Spoon into prepared loaf pan and bake for 1 hour and 15 minutes or until a toothpick comes out clean. (You may need to cover the cake during the last minutes of baking so that the top doesn't burn.)

Cool in the pan for 10 minutes before turning out onto a rack.

Place a slice of cake on a dessert plate and spoon strawberries with some extra marinade over top.

SALAD OF ROMAINE WITH RED ONIONS, ASIAGO, AND LEMON VINAIGRETTE

SERVES 4

1 medium head romaine lettuce

½ medium red onion, cut into very thin slices

2 ounces whole, aged Asiago, thinly shaved with a vegetable peeler

VINAIGRETTE:

¼ cup freshly squeezed lemon juice

¼ teaspoon grated lemon zest

1 tablespoon Dijon mustard

½ teaspoon coarsely ground sea salt

½ teaspoon freshly ground pepper

¾ cup fruity, extra-virgin olive oil

Wash and dry lettuce. Break into bite-size pieces, and place into a medium-size serving bowl. Add the onion and shaved cheese.

In a separate bowl, whisk together vinaigrette ingredients (or combine in a 12- to 16-ounce jar and shake vigorously).

Drizzle enough vinaigrette onto salad to barely coat the leaves. Toss and serve immediately.

FUSILLI MICHELANGELO

What started as my rendition of pasta for a staff meal at a restaurant in Florida is now one of the most requested dishes at Tra Vigne. And its name, Michelangelo, is a bit nostalgic for me since it's a nickname my mother called me when I was young—I was always, even then, inventing new combinations in the kitchen.

Mix tomatoes in a small bowl with the boiling water, sugar, vinegar, and marjoram. Cover. Let tomatoes rehydrate until soft, about 10 minutes. Drain well, squeezing out excess liquid, if necessary. Slice tomatoes into fine strips. Set aside.

Bring a large pot of water to a boil, add salt, and cook pasta until al dente, about 10 minutes. Drain, reserving about ½ cup of the pasta cooking water.

While pasta is cooking, heat olive oil in a large sauté pan over medium-high heat. Add mushrooms and do not stir until they begin to brown, about 1 minute. Stir. Continue to sauté until browned, about 5 minutes. Season with salt and pepper. Add garlic and cook quickly until light brown. Add basil leaves and rehydrated tomatoes and cook quickly, removing pan from heat as necessary, so tomatoes do not burn.

Add tomato sauce to mushrooms in sauté pan and bring to a simmer. Add pasta as soon as it is done and toss well with ½ cup cheese and enough of the reserved pasta cooking water to moisten well. Add 2 cups arugula and toss until it's barely wilted.

Spoon into a warmed serving bowl or onto a platter and scatter remaining arugula on top. Sprinkle with nuts and dust with the remaining cheese. Serve immediately with chili flakes and the small bowl of reserved, mashed jalapenos (see Quick Tomato Sauce page 62).

SERVES 4

⅓ cup dried tomatoes (not packed in oil)

3 tablespoons boiling water

1½ teaspoons sugar

1 tablespoon plus 2 teaspoons balsamic vinegar

1 teaspoon finely chopped fresh marjoram (or ½ teaspoon dried)

salt and freshly ground pepper to taste

¾ pound dried fusilli pasta

¼ cup extra-virgin olive oil

4 cups ¾-inch diced mushrooms (preferably a mixture of several kinds)

1½ tablespoons minced garlic

½ cup loosely packed basil leaves

2 cups Quick Tomato Sauce (recipe follows)

¾ cup freshly grated Parmesan cheese

4 cups arugula

2 tablespoons toasted pine nuts

chili flakes (optional)

MAKES ABOUT 3½ CUPS OF SAUCE

one 28-ounce can plum (Roma) tomatoes

3 tablespoons extra-virgin olive oil

1 jalapeño chili

½ cup finely chopped onion

1 tablespoon minced fresh garlic

1 bay leaf

salt and freshly ground pepper

¼ cup chopped sun-dried tomatoes, packed in oil, drained

1 tablespoon finely chopped fresh oregano

NOTE: As a variation for summer tomato sauce, substitute 2 pounds of vine-ripened tomatoes for canned tomatoes. Peel tomatoes, cut in half crosswise, and squeeze out juice and seeds over a strainer, suspended over a bowl. Chop tomatoes. Follow recipe, omitting sundried tomatoes. Makes about 2¼ cups of sauce.

QUICK TOMATO SAUCE

A little trick I learned from my mother was to add a small, whole, hot chili to the sauce. It adds a little spiciness and at the same time absorbs some of the sauce as it cooks. It makes a great condiment when mashed with a little of the sauce and passed, so diners can add as much or as little as they desire to their individual portion.

Drain juice from canned tomatoes into a bowl. Extract as much of the juice as possible. Then, preferably using your hand, squeeze tomatoes to a pulp. In separate containers, reserve juice and pulp.

In a heavy saucepan, heat olive oil over medium-high heat. Tilt pan to collect oil in a little pool against side and drop jalapeño into oil, cook until lightly browned, about 2 minutes. Remove jalapeño and reserve.

Add onion to pan and cook until onions have softened, about 2 minutes. Add garlic and cook quickly until light gold. Add tomato juice and bring to a boil. Simmer rapidly several minutes. Add tomatoes, then rinse remaining pulp out of can by filling halfway with water and add that to pan. Add bay leaf, jalapeño, and salt and pepper to taste. Return to boil.

Add sun-dried tomatoes and stir. Lower heat to medium and simmer, stirring occasionally to prevent scorching. Add oregano after 15 minutes and continue cooking until mixture thickens and tomatoes have turned an orange-red, about 30 minutes. Discard bay leaf. Peel, seed, and mash jalapeño with a spoonful of sauce and pass at the table.

"SEMI-FREDDO" TRA VIGNE STYLE

Traditionally in Italy, semi-freddo refers to a half frozen dessert. Here we have a version that was developed at Tra Vigne for our sister restaurant, Tomatina, where we wanted to serve a fun, quick dessert for adults with a play on the Italian theme. Our semi-freddo is simply a scoop of your favorite gelato, a shot of espresso, and a dollop of unsweetened whipped cream on top. Serve with your favorite biscotti. It's that simple! If you want to try your hand at making your own gelato, here is Tra Vigne pastry chef Gerry Moss's recipe:

BASE: In a large stainless steel bowl, mix together sugar and flour. Add 2 egg yolks and 1 egg, mixing thoroughly. Scrape the seeds from the vanilla bean and add to the mixture reserving the pod. Slowly whisk in milk. Add vanilla pod. Place bowl over a saucepan of boiling water, making a double boiler. Whisk until thick. Strain. Cool.

GELATO: Whisk milk and cream into the base mixture. Place in ice cream freezer and freeze according to manufacturer's instructions.

1 quart cooled base (see below)
1 cup whole milk
1 cup heavy cream

BASE:

1 cup superfine sugar
1 tablespoon plus 1 teaspoon flour
2 egg yolks
1 egg
1 vanilla bean
2½ cups milk

VARIATIONS: Cinnamon—Steep a cinnamon stick or two in the warm base mixture while it's thickening. Chocolate—Add enough unsweetened cocoa to the base mixture until it's the color of a rich chocolate milk.

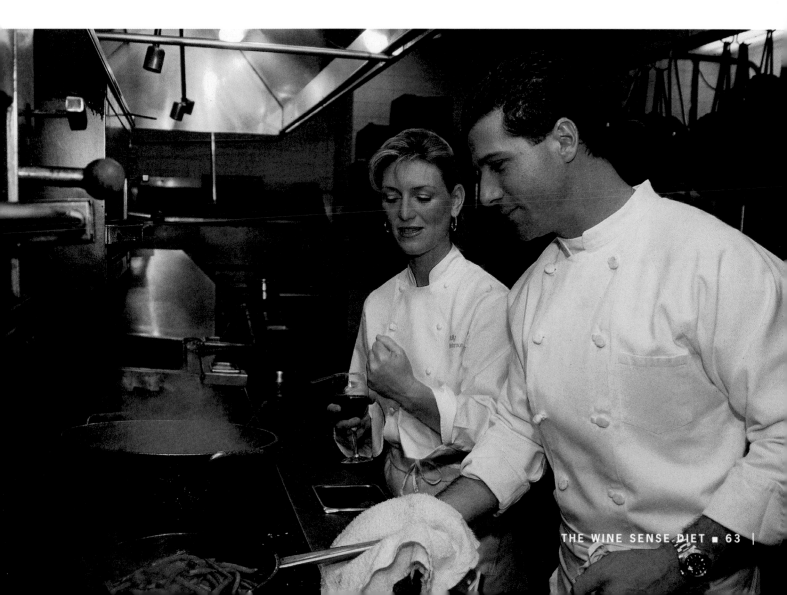

"It's a chef's paradise!"

GREG COLE HAS TURNED A PASSION for cooking into a prospering business. Chef at his own Napa Valley restaurant, Celadon, since 1996, Greg feels he finally has a venue from which to coax the true personality out of the bountiful, seasonal ingredients that surround him. "Within practically arms reach we have beautiful fresh produce to work with many months of the year, unbelievable wine, and an audience who has a natural interest in healthy living and well-prepared food. It's a chef's paradise!"

Cole began his training at the Culinary Institute of America right out of high school. Greg says, "I always knew I wanted to cook. After school, and after a stint cooking in Tahoe, I landed in the Napa Valley in 1985 and realized right away this was an ideal place for me to try out my culinary wings." The restaurant has curbed the outdoor activity he really enjoys, but he says, "Now I'm doing what I love most, and my weekly walk with my two-year-old, Sophia, is about as outdoors as it gets at the moment!"

Sophia can often be found at Celadon in the early evenings with mom, Beth, in tow. She is already adept at asking for dishes she enjoys and isn't shy about asking other diners to share their fried wonton skins! Cole says, "It's important to me that Sophia understands early what I do when I go to work. I want to share my joy for what I do." And as for her introduction to another of the couple's passions, wine, Greg says, "Even though neither Beth nor I really grew up drinking much wine, we now make it a point to include it as a normal part of our mealtime. It's so crucial that Sophia grows up seeing it has an important part to play as it's enjoyed with food."

Greg's and Beth's long work days make family mealtime rituals all the more important. "While it's not easy, especially with the career I've chosen (Beth is a full-time nurse) we always make it a point to start out the day together with breakfast, even if I've had a late night at the restaurant. And on my nights off, we stay home and cook together. Family is so important to us."

And as if one restaurant isn't enough, says Greg, "I've always wanted to try my hand at a traditional American steakhouse, and I know that this area would support one." So, look for his newest endeavor, which opened New Year's Day, 2000.

Spring ~ Summer

Sweet Corn and Potato Soup

Shrimp Green Curry

Stir-Fried Wild Rice

Celadon's Popular Peach Cake

Voss Sauvignon Blanc
Lazy Creek Gewürtztraminer

Fall ~ Winter

Algerian-Inspired Lamb Shanks with Cardamom and Orange

Almond and Golden Raisin Couscous

Bittersweet Chocolate Terrine with Sun-Dried Cherries

Duckhorn Napa Valley Merlot
Rombauer Cabernet Franc

1 tablespoon butter

1 yellow onion, peeled and diced

4 Yukon Gold potatoes, diced

2 ears sweet corn, kernels cut off cob

1 teaspoon chopped fresh thyme,
or ½ teaspoon dried

1 teaspoon minced fresh garlic

1 teaspoon salt

⅛ teaspoon black pepper

one 14.5-ounce can low sodium chicken broth,
or fresh chicken stock

½ cup half-and-half

½ cup whole milk

SWEET CORN AND POTATO SOUP

Heat butter in a small saucepan over medium heat. Add onion, potatoes, corn, thyme, garlic, salt, and pepper and cook for 4 minutes stirring consistently. Add chicken broth, cover, and simmer for 20 more minutes. Add half-and-half and milk. Continue heating the soup until just before it boils. Serve.

SERVES 4

1 teaspoon canola oil

2 pounds shrimp, peeled and cleaned

salt and freshly ground black pepper to taste

CURRY:

1 teaspoon canola oil

2 tablespoons green curry paste

1 small onion, diced

1 red bell pepper, cored and diced

1 yellow bell pepper, cored and diced

2 tablespoons minced ginger

1 tablespoon minced garlic

zest of 1 lemon

zest and juice of 1 lime

2 cans unsweetened coconut milk

2 tablespoons fish sauce (found in asian markets and supermarkets) or low sodium soy sauce

¾ cup torn basil leaves

½ cup cilantro leaves

SHRIMP GREEN CURRY

In a large sauté pan, heat 1 teaspoon oil over medium-high heat. Add the shrimp, salt, and pepper and sauté until the shrimp turn pink. Remove from sauté pan and hold in a warm place.

In the same large sauté pan, heat 1 teaspoon oil. Add the green curry paste and sauté for 1 minute. Add the onions and diced pepper and cook for two minutes. Add the ginger, garlic, lemon and lime zest, and cook for 3 minutes more. Add the coconut milk, fish sauce, and lime juice and bring to a simmer. Add ½ cup basil and ¼ cup cilantro. Add shrimp and heat through.

Serve garnished with remainder of green herbs and alongside Stir-Fried Wild Rice (see page 67).

STIR-FRIED WILD RICE

Bring water and salt to a boil in a medium-size saucepan. Add rice. Return to a boil, reduce heat to a simmer, and cook until soft, about 50 minutes. Remove from heat and drain in colander. Set aside.

Heat canola and sesame oils in a large sauté pan over medium-high heat. Add garlic and sauté until it releases its aroma, about 1 minute. Stir in rice. Add chicken stock and soy sauce. Stir fry until rice is hot. Serve with Shrimp Green Curry (see page 66).

SERVES 4

6 cups water

pinch salt

1 cup uncooked wild rice

1 tablespoon canola oil

1 tablespoon sesame oil

1 teaspoon minced garlic

½ cup chicken stock, or low sodium canned chicken broth

¼ cup low sodium soy sauce

CELADON'S POPULAR PEACH CAKE

Preheat oven to 350 degrees. Lightly grease and flour a 10-inch round cake pan.

In a small bowl, mix together sugar, cinnamon, and pecans. Set aside.

In a large mixing bowl, cream together butter, oil, and sugar. Beat in egg. Slowly beat in buttermilk and vanilla.

In a separate bowl, sift flour, salt, and baking soda together twice. Add to wet ingredients and mix until just combined. Stir in peaches.

Pour into pan and sprinkle on topping. Bake for 40 minutes, or until a toothpick inserted in the center comes out clean.

TOPPING:

¼ cup sugar

1 teaspoon cinnamon

½ cup coarsely chopped pecans or walnuts

CAKE:

¼ cup butter

¼ cup canola oil

¾ cup sugar

1 egg

1 cup buttermilk

1 teaspoon vanilla extract

2 cups all-purpose flour

½ teaspoon salt

½ teaspoon baking soda

2 cups fresh peaches, peeled and diced

ALGERIAN-INSPIRED LAMB SHANKS WITH CARDAMOM AND ORANGE

SERVES 4

4 lamb shanks, external fat trimmed

pinch salt and black pepper

¼ cup olive oil

1 pound onions, coarsely diced

¼ cup peeled garlic cloves

1 tablespoon finely chopped fresh ginger

2 cardamom seeds, skin removed

pinch saffron (optional)

1 teaspoon chili flakes

2 teaspoons fennel seed

½ cinnamon stick

2 teaspoons curry powder

1 tablespoon salt

1 teaspoon ground cloves

1 teaspoon caraway seed

½ cup blanched, slivered almonds

½ cup golden raisins

two 10-ounce cans diced Roma tomatoes

1 bottle white wine

1 orange, grated zest and juice

1 pound carrots, peeled, coarsely diced

½ pound fennel, coarsely diced

Season lamb shanks with salt and black pepper. Heat 2 tablespoons olive oil in a dutch oven. Add the shanks and brown on all sides, about 5 minutes. Remove and keep warm.

Preheat oven to 350 degrees.

Add 2 tablespoons olive oil, onions, and garlic cloves to dutch oven and sauté until onions soften, about 3 minutes.

In a small bowl, combine ginger, cardamom seeds, saffron, chili flakes, fennel seeds, cinnamon stick, curry powder, salt, cloves, caraway seeds, almonds, and raisins. Add to vegetable mixture, and continue sautéing for 5 minutes. Add tomatoes, orange zest, juice, and wine. Bring to a simmer.

Add the lamb shanks, place in the oven, and braise until the meat is very tender, approximately 1 to 1½ hours. Add carrots and diced fennel. Cover and bake until vegetables are tender, about 15 minutes more.

Serve with Almond and Golden Raisin Couscous (recipe follows).

ALMOND AND GOLDEN RAISIN COUSCOUS

SERVES 8

1 quart water

1 tablespoon salt

¼ teaspoon black pepper

¼ cup olive oil

2 cups couscous

2 tablespoons butter

¼ cup coarsely chopped, blanched almonds

¼ cup golden raisins

2 tablespoons chopped Italian parsley

2 cups chicken stock

pinch salt and black pepper

In a large pot, combine water, salt, black pepper, and olive oil and bring to a boil. Place couscous in a large bowl and pour mixture over couscous. Cover with plastic wrap, and let sit until couscous has absorbed all the liquid, about 10 minutes.

Heat butter in a large sauté pan. Add almonds, and cook until golden brown. Stir in raisins, parsley, and salt and pepper. Add chicken stock and couscous, and cook until heated through, about 5 minutes.

Arrange on four serving platters. Evenly divide braised lamb shanks, sauce, and vegetables over couscous.

BITTERSWEET CHOCOLATE TERRINE WITH SUN-DRIED CHERRIES

Line a small loaf pan with wax paper.

Melt chocolate in a double boiler over low heat. Stir in butter until melted. Gently whisk in cream and red wine. When mixture is smooth, remove from double boiler.

Sift in ¼ cup powdered sugar, and mix until incorporated. Add 1 cup cherries, mix well. Pour into loaf pan and refrigerate overnight.

To unmold, submerge the loaf pan in hot water about ¾ the way up the sides of the pan. Loosen the terrine at the top edge with a knife. Invert terrine onto cutting board. Slice using a thin bladed, sharp knife, dipping it in hot water prior to each slice. Serve garnished with a sprinkling of powdered sugar and a few sun-dried cherries.

SERVES 8

8 ounces bittersweet chocolate, finely chopped

1 tablespoon unsalted, sweet butter

½ cup heavy cream

¼ cup red wine

1 cup plus 1 tablespoon powdered sugar

1 cup plus ¼ cup sun-dried cherries

JAMIE DAVIES OF SCHRAMSBERG VINEYARDS

"LIKE MANY," SAYS JAMIE, "my husband Jack and I were drawn to the Napa Valley by a desire for a life more tied to the land. Our own livelihood and that of our neighbors is provided by the valley's abundance of fertile soils and its moderate climate." Jamie often visits her garden to see what will be on the menu that evening. She says, "It's only natural that we eat seasonal produce fresh from our own gardens, seek out foodstuffs crafted by the hands of friends, and serve local wines." This link to the earth is what she calls "the basis of our wine country diet."

And since Schramsberg is a producer of sparkling wine, it's no surprise that Jamie is a proponent of popping the cork often—not just for special celebrations. "Sparkling wine is a natural companion to this lifestyle," she says. You'll see Jamie encouraging others to try sparkling wine not only as an aperitif, but throughout a meal. Jamie says, "It adds a lift, a graceful sizzle to any occasion. It's light and fresh on the palate and can awaken many menus, from seafood and cream sauces to spicy Asian dishes to desserts." She adds, "I bet you'll find it's an excellent choice with just about everything."

"Sparkling wine is a natural companion to this lifestyle."

Spring ~ Summer

Jamie's Fruit Salad *or*
Nectarine and Avocado Salad

Smoked Salmon Hero Sandwiches

Grapefruit, Raspberries, and Kiwis in Champagne

Butter Cookies

Schramsberg Brut Rose
Schramsberg Blanc de Noirs
or any sparkling wine you enjoy

Fall ~ Winter

Watercress Salad

Champagne Chicken *or*
Sea Bass in Parchment with Leeks and Ginger

Steamed Green Beans

Wild Rice with Dried Cranberries

Calistoga Apple Torte

Schramsberg Blanc de Blancs
Schramsberg J. Schram
sparkling wine

SERVES SIX ½-CUP PORTIONS

DRESSING:

1½ tablespoons raspberry vinegar

1 teaspoon sugar

¼ teaspoon salt

3 tablespoons low-fat or non-fat sour cream

1 tablespoon finely chopped fresh mint

pinch dry mustard

pinch ground nutmeg

1 tablespoon canola oil

2 medium ripe pears, cored and
diced into ½-inch pieces

2 cups seedless red grapes, halved

1 large rib of celery, peeled, finely diced

6 red lettuce leaves

JAMIE'S FRUIT SALAD

In a small bowl, whisk the vinegar, sugar, and salt until blended. Whisk in the sour cream, mint, mustard, and nutmeg. Whisk in the oil. Add pears, grapes, and celery and toss until well coated.

Place lettuce leaf on individual salad plate and top with fruit salad.

SERVES 4

¼ pound watercress

¼ pound arugula

2 firm, ripe avocados, peeled and sliced

2 firm, ripe nectarines, sliced

½ red onion, thinly sliced

DRESSING:

½ cup olive oil

2 tablespoons raspberry vinegar

½ teaspoon Chinese five spice seasoning

NECTARINE AND AVOCADO SALAD

Wash, dry, and coarsely chop watercress and arugula. Place a bed of greens on each plate. Arrange sliced avocado, nectarines, and onions over greens.

In a small bowl, whisk together olive oil, vinegar, and Chinese five spice seasoning. Drizzle dressing on salad just before serving.

SERVES 4

1 large loaf sourdough french bread,
or 2 to 3 small baguettes

8 ounces cream cheese, softened

4 ounces smoked salmon, thinly sliced

½ cucumber, thinly sliced

½ red onion, thinly sliced

½ cup sliced black olives

1 bunch watercress

freshly ground black pepper

SMOKED SALMON HERO SANDWICHES

Warm the bread and slice lengthwise. Spread each half with cream cheese. Layer salmon, cucumber, onions, olives, and watercress as desired. Grind black pepper over top. Close and slice diagonally.

GRAPEFRUIT, RASPBERRIES, AND KIWIS IN CHAMPAGNE

Remove skin from grapefruit with a knife, leaving segments exposed. Remove each segment without the pith over a serving bowl to catch juice. Press half of the raspberries through a sieve over the grapefruit. Add the remaining whole berries to the bowl. Sprinkle with sugar. Pour in sparkling wine or champagne just before serving. Arrange kiwi slices over top and garnish with mint.

SERVES 4

3 grapefruits

1 basket fresh raspberries, or 1 package frozen

1 tablespoon sugar

1 cup Schramsberg Napa Valley sparkling wine (or champagne)

mint, for garnish

3 kiwis, peeled and sliced

BUTTER COOKIES

In a large bowl, cream butter and sugar. Add vanilla and egg and beat until light and fluffy. Stir in flour. Using a small ice cream scoop, drop on cookie sheet 2 inches apart to allow for spreading. Press a pecan half into each cookie.

Bake for 10 minutes or until edges are golden. Remove to cooling rack.

MAKES 16 TO 20 COOKIES

1 cup butter, softened at room temperature

1 cup sugar

1 teaspoon vanilla extract

1 egg

2 cups cake flour

4 ounces whole pecans

WATERCRESS SALAD

Bring large pot of water to boil. Immerse bean sprouts in boiling water for 30 seconds, remove, rinse under cold running water, and drain. Immerse the snow peas in boiling water for 1 minute, drain, rinse under cold running water, and drain again.

Cut snow peas diagonally into 1-inch pieces. Place watercress, bean sprouts, snow peas, and green onions in a serving bowl. In a small bowl mix together olive oil, vinegar, sesame oil, salt, and pepper. Drizzle dressing over vegetables to moisten lightly. Mix gently.

SERVES 6

½ pound mung bean sprouts

½ pound snow peas

2 bunches watercress, stems removed

4 green onions, chopped (including some green tops)

⅓ cup olive oil

2 tablespoons rice wine vinegar

1 teaspoon oriental-style sesame oil

salt and freshly ground black pepper to taste

one 3- to 4-pound chicken, cut into 8 pieces

¼ cup flour for dredging

3 tablespoons canola oil

1 tablespoon unsalted butter

2 tablespoons minced shallots

2 cups champagne or sparkling wine

1 tablespoon brown sugar

1 lemon, rind grated and juiced

¼ cup toasted pine nuts

¼ cup coarsely chopped fresh parsley

CHAMPAGNE CHICKEN

Coat chicken pieces with flour, set aside.

Heat 2 tablespoons oil and butter in a heavy skillet over medium heat. Add chicken and cook until it's lightly brown, 5 to 10 minutes. Remove chicken and keep warm. Add remaining oil and shallots to pan and sauté 2 to 3 minutes. Add champagne, brown sugar, grated zest, and lemon juice. Cover and simmer until chicken is tender, about 45 minutes. Remove chicken to warm serving platter. Keep warm.

Reduce remaining sauce over high heat. Pour over chicken, sprinkle with pine nuts, and garnish with parsley.

SERVES 6

1 tablespoon butter

1 tablespoon olive oil

3 to 4 medium leeks, washed, white and some green parts julienned

six 4-ounce sea bass fillets (about 1-inch thick)

1 clove garlic, finely minced

3 slices fresh ginger root, thinly julienned

½ cup Blanc de Noirs sparkling wine

2 carrots, julienned

1 red bell pepper, julienned

3 green onion tops, thinly sliced

salt and pepper to taste

SEA BASS IN PARCHMENT WITH LEEKS AND GINGER

Preheat oven to 400 degrees.

Heat butter and olive oil in a medium sauté pan over medium-high heat. When sizzling, add leeks and sauté until just translucent, about 2 to 3 minutes. Add garlic, ginger root, and sauté 1 minute. Add sparkling wine and simmer until almost all liquid evaporates, about 3 minutes. Remove from heat and set aside to cool.

Cut cooking parchment into six 16 x 24-inch pieces. Fold each piece in half crosswise and cut out to form heart shape. Open hearts flat and place one-sixth of the leek mixture on one half of each heart, leaving a 1-inch border. Top with one-sixth of the carrots, bell pepper, and onion tops. Place a fish fillet on top each portion of vegetables. Season lightly with salt and pepper.

Fold parchment over fish, forming a half moon shape and make small pleats around open side to seal edges together. Place packets on baking sheet and bake for 5 to 8 minutes or until packets puff and start to brown. Serve at once; let guests open packets at the table.

CALISTOGA APPLE TORTE

Preheat oven to 350 degrees.

In a large mixing bowl, beat eggs and brown sugar until smooth and light. Stir in flour, baking powder, salt, and vanilla extract. Add nuts and apples to batter, and pour into a greased 9-inch pie pan.

Bake for 30 minutes or until golden brown. In a small bowl, whip the whipping cream with confectioners' sugar and cinnamon.

Cut torte into wedges and serve warm with the whipped cream.

SERVES 8

2 eggs

1 cup firmly packed brown sugar

¼ cup all-purpose flour

2½ teaspoons baking powder

pinch salt

2 teaspoons vanilla extract

1 cup coarsely chopped walnuts, pecans, or almonds, toasted

1½ cups peeled, cored, and coarsely chopped apples

½ pint whipping cream

1 tablespoon confectioners' sugar

¼ teaspoon ground cinnamon

THE DUCKHORNS OF DUCKHORN WINERY

"We fell in love with the land, the people, and were forced to get back to the basics."

ALTHOUGH THEY'RE AVID wine drinkers now, both Margaret and Dan Duckhorn had very different experiences with wine as they were growing up. Margaret lived in Europe in her late teens, and, as she says, "It was there that I was first introduced to wine. It was always on the table at mealtime without question. That's when I also began to really develop an interest in cooking as well."

It was the opposite for Dan: "I really didn't think much about wine, nor drank it regularly with meals until I got involved in managing a company that had a vineyard and grapevine grafting business in the Napa Valley in the 1970s." "It was that job," Margaret says, "that actually brought us to the Napa Valley from Piedmont, CA. I always thought we'd eventually move back. But, as you can see, we fell in love with the land, the people, and were literally forced to get back to the basics."

"In those early days," Dan says, "the Napa Valley was even more rural than you see today." Margaret adds, "Sharing mealtimes with our friends was our primary source of entertainment. I'm so thankful for that experience, because that ritual has stayed with us and still allows us to remember our appreciation for those basics in life. We've built some great friendships through hospitality over the years." An important part of the socializing then was also exploring wine, learning how to taste and assess wine. "It was great for conversation," recalls Margaret, "since we learned more and more each time we tasted. It's really all about practice and experience." They both wholeheartedly believe that everyone has the "equipment" to learn how to experience wine, and, as Margaret says, "you just have to pay attention and focus each time you taste."

All their children were raised in the Napa Valley. "We encouraged our children to taste a little wine very early," says Dan. "Their senses are so impressionable at a young age. It's good to have that early experience. None of our kids have ever abused wine, because they know how to enjoy it in the right context, in moderation, along with food."

Margaret says, "For the grandkids, I make learning about wine a fun ritual. When they come to visit us, I have special little shot glasses shaped like wine glasses for them to taste the wine." Dan adds, "They get a real kick out of it and already understand that it's not only our livelihood but something that belongs on the table each night as we sit down to share a meal and a special family time."

Spring ~ Summer

Sliced Tomatoes with Lemon Vinaigrette

Simple Sea Bass with Basmati Rice or Dilled Couscous

Crusty French Bread

Duckhorn Sauvignon Blanc
Shafer Red Shoulder Ranch Chardonnay

Fall ~ Winter

Green Salad with Honey Mustard Vinaigrette

Turkey Chili

Crusty French Bread

Paraduxx Red Wine
Saintsbury Pinot Noir

or

King Eider Chicken

Steamed Brown Rice

Easy Broccoli

Spottswoode Sauvignon Blanc
Duckhorn Merlot

SLICED TOMATOES WITH LEMON VINAIGRETTE

In a small bowl, whisk together all vinaigrette ingredients.

Arrange tomatoes on a large platter. Drizzle with vinaigrette.

SERVES 4

VINAIGRETTE:

¼ cup lemon juice

½ cup olive oil

¼ teaspoon minced fresh garlic

¼ teaspoon freshly grated lemon zest

1 tablespoon minced red onion

1 tablespoon minced fresh chives

½ teaspoon coarsely ground sea salt

¼ teaspoon freshly ground pepper

4 tomatoes (preferably colorful heirloom tomatoes), sliced

SIMPLE SEA BASS WITH BASMATI RICE OR DILLED COUSCOUS

Heat the olive oil in a large sauté pan over medium-high heat. Add leeks, sauté for 2 to 3 minutes, then place sea bass in pan and sear until slightly brown on each side. Add Sauvignon Blanc and reduce heat. Cover and poach until fish is firm. Remove fish from juices, continue simmering juices until reduced to one to two tablespoons. Spoon over fish.

Serve over basmati rice steamed in vegetable broth or Dilled Couscous (recipe follows).

Serve with your favorite green vegetable or green salad, and crusty french bread.

SERVES 4

2 tablespoons lemon flavored olive oil (or 2 tablespoons olive oil and 1 teaspoon fresh lemon zest)

1 leek, thoroughly rinsed and finely chopped

1½ pounds sea bass filet

½ cup Sauvignon Blanc

DILLED COUSCOUS

In a medium saucepan, sauté chopped shallot in olive oil over medium heat. Cook until translucent, then add couscous. Stir to combine, and add water and salt. Cover and cook for the time recommended on the couscous package or until the couscous is soft.

Remove from heat. Add lemon zest and dill. Fold in with a fork, fluffing the couscous. Serve immediately.

SERVES 4

1 medium shallot, peeled and finely chopped

2 teaspoons olive oil

1½ cups couscous

¼ teaspoon coarsely ground sea salt

2 cups water

1 teaspoon finely grated lemon zest

¼ cup chopped fresh dill

GREEN SALAD WITH HONEY MUSTARD VINAIGRETTE

In a small bowl, whisk together all vinaigrette ingredients. Drizzle on lettuce and toss just before serving.

SERVES 4

VINAIGRETTE:

½ cup extra-virgin olive oil

2 tablespoons red wine vinegar

1 tablespoon fresh lemon juice

1 teaspoon Dijon mustard

1 tablespoon honey

¼ teaspoon minced fresh garlic

1 medium head red leaf lettuce, leaves rinsed and spun dry

TURKEY CHILI

Place beans in medium saucepan with the vegetable broth. Cover and cook over low heat until tender, about 30 to 40 minutes. Drain. (Eliminate this step if using canned beans.)

In a large pot over medium heat, sauté the onion in olive oil until translucent, about 3 minutes. Add the garlic and stir for about 1 minute taking care not to burn it. Add turkey and continue sautéing until cooked through and nicely browned, about 10 minutes. Stir in cumin, chili powder, and oregano.

Add beans, tomatoes, and Zinfandel to turkey mixture. Simmer slowly until liquid is reduced, about 20 to 30 minutes.

Serve with a green salad and crusty French bread.

SERVES 4

1 cup dried kidney beans, soaked overnight, or canned beans, drained

2 cups canned low sodium vegetable broth

2 large onions, 1 chopped and 1 quartered

1 tablespoon olive oil

2 cloves garlic, minced

1 pound coarsely ground fresh turkey

2 teaspoons cumin

2 tablespoons chili powder

1 tablespoon chopped fresh oregano

1 can chopped tomatoes with their juice

½ cup Zinfandel

DUCKHORN VINEYARDS

1998
NAPA VALLEY
SAUVIGNON BLANC

Produced and bottled by Duckhorn Vineyards
1000 Lodi Lane, St. Helena, CA 94574 BWCA 4857
ALCOHOL 13.9% BY VOLUME

SERVES 4

4 to 6 boneless, skinless chicken breasts or thighs

2 tablespoons olive oil

2 to 3 garlic cloves, peeled and sliced

1 medium shallot, peeled and minced

1 cup sliced fresh mushrooms

¼ cup King Eider dry vermouth or other dry vermouth

½ teaspoon berry balsamic vinegar

1 teaspoon freshly minced lemon zest

KING EIDER CHICKEN

Cooks' tip: Sip a little of the King Eider over ice as an aperitif as you prepare the chicken.

In a large pot, brown both sides of chicken over medium-high heat in 1 tablespoon olive oil. Remove and set aside. Add garlic and shallot to the pan and quickly sauté in remaining olive oil. Add mushrooms and cook until the mushroom liquid is evaporated. Remove. Place chicken back in pan, reduce heat to medium-low, and add vermouth, vinegar, and lemon zest. Cover. Gently poach for 15 minutes. Add sliced mushroom mixture back to pan and more vermouth as needed to keep pan from becoming too dry. Cook for another 10 minutes. Check chicken for doneness; meat should be firm and white, and juices should run clear.

Serve over steamed brown basmati rice cooked in vegetable broth.

SERVES 4

3 cups broccoli florets

¼ cup vegetable broth

1 tablespoon freshly grated Parmesan cheese

salt and pepper to taste

EASY BROCCOLI

Place broccoli florets in a microwavable bowl. Add vegetable broth. Cover with plastic wrap, leaving a small gap for steam to escape. Microwave on high for 2 minutes. Let stand for 1 minute. Drain. Sprinkle with cheese. Add salt and pepper to taste.

DAWNINE DYER OF DOMAINE CHANDON
AND CONSULTING WINEMAKER BILL DYER

DAWNINE DYER, who works at Domaine Chandon, and Bill Dyer, formerly with Sterling Vineyards and now consulting on several winemaking projects, know how important it is, despite their busy lifestyles, "to come together each day to renew our spirits."

They live on a mountain that overlooks the Napa Valley. Dawnine says, "The view in itself is worth getting up for each morning! Our favorite morning ritual is to greet the day as we walk to the hilltop together and then back to the house, taking in the vista before we go our separate ways." For added exercise, they both go out in the vineyards, often walking row after row and observing the vines' progress during each stage throughout the year. "And," says Dawnine, "when I have the time, I like to stop by the community pool on the way home from work to get in a quick swim. It's great in helping me wind down from the hectic workday pace."

"In the evening," says Dawnine, "we'll gather in the kitchen to prepare a meal as we discuss the day, upcoming calendar obligations, and revel in the process of creating something usually very simple yet very soulful and satisfying." Quite often they'll sip on whatever wine was left from the night before and make crostini from yesterday's bread as they cook. Dawnine says, "It's a great way to deal with my daily bread habit!"

"We look for fresh, locally available ingredients whenever we can. In summer, pastas are our mainstay, especially when time is short. In winter, we naturally tend to want heartier meals, and we're inside earlier with more time for preparation."

Dawnine shares a quick tip she's learned through the years: "Many of the dishes we prepare daily serve as a base when we're entertaining. We'll just dress them up a bit and they easily become a first course. That leaves less to chance when hungry guests are arriving!"

"To come together each day to renew our spirits."

Spring ~ Summer

Crostini with Tomatoes, Olive Oil, and Basil

Linguini with Summer Squash Blossoms and Fava Beans *or*
Papardelle with Fresh Morels and Young, Tender Carrots

Sourdough Baguette

Green Salad with Champagne Vinaigrette

Cheese Plate with Apricots and Figs

*Domaine Chandon Blanc de Blancs
a crisp Sauvignon Blanc or Viognier*

Fall ~ Winter

Crostini with Fig and Olive Tapenade

Fresh Olives

Mussels in Sparkling Wine

Crusty Olive Country Bread

Salad with Winter Greens

or

Celery Root and Potato Gratin

Spinach or Romaine Salad

Seeded Wheat Bread

Cabacou with Warm Lavender Honey and Walnuts

*Domaine Chandon Blanc de Noirs
Pinot Noir*

2 medium tomatoes, or 4 Roma tomatoes, peeled (optional), seeds removed, diced, and well-drained

2 tablespoons olive oil

2 teaspoons balsamic vinegar

2 garlic cloves, peeled (1½ minced, reserve one half)

1 tablespoon thinly sliced (ribbons) basil leaves

coarsely ground sea salt and freshly ground pepper to taste

4 slices crusty Italian bread, or any day-old bread

CROSTINI WITH TOMATOES, OLIVE OIL, AND BASIL

In a medium bowl, combine the tomatoes, 1 tablespoon olive oil, balsamic vinegar, minced garlic, basil, and salt and pepper. Place bread on a grill or under a broiler. Grill or broil until golden on each side, about 2 to 3 minutes. Remove from heat and rub the surface with the half garlic clove. Brush lightly with remaining olive oil. Top with tomato mixture. Cut each slice of bread into thirds. Serve immediately.

12 to 16 small squash blossoms

4 green onions, including some of the green, thinly sliced

3 tablespoons olive oil

1 pound shelled fava beans, skinned•

2 garlic cloves, minced

salt and freshly ground pepper to taste

1½ cups crème fraîche (see page 168) or non-fat sour cream

2 tablespoons thinly sliced (ribbons) fresh basil

1 package fresh or dried linguini (enough for 4 servings)

2 tablespoons chopped fresh chives

•**NOTE:** If your schedule doesn't allow for the time-intensive process of preparing the fava beans, fresh, steamed green peas or young, tender, quick-blanched green beans can be substituted.

LINGUINI WITH SUMMER SQUASH BLOSSOMS AND FAVA BEANS

Skinning the fava beans for this recipe is a time-consuming process, but some enjoy the spring ritual. For this fava bean pasta I prefer white wine: a Sauvignon Blanc or a delicate Viognier.

Bring a large pot of water to boil over high heat.

Meanwhile, in a medium pan, sauté squash blossoms and green onions in 1 tablespoon olive oil over medium-high heat until lightly browned. Remove from pan and set aside. In the same pan, gently sauté fava beans in 1 tablespoon olive oil until just tender, about 2 to 3 minutes. Add garlic and sauté for 1 minute more, taking care not to let it burn. Season with salt and pepper. Stir in crème fraîche and basil, and simmer on low heat for 2 to 3 minutes.

Place pasta in the boiling water and cook until al dente. Drain. Add 1 tablespoon olive oil to pasta and toss to prevent it from sticking together. Place in warm serving bowl. Add fava bean mixture and toss gently. Sprinkle with chopped chives and serve.

PAPARDELLE WITH FRESH MORELS AND YOUNG, TENDER CARROTS

For me, nothing goes with the fresh morels like a flavorful Pinot Noir.

Bring a large pot of water to boil over high heat.

Meanwhile, in a medium pan, sauté the mushrooms and shallots in butter over medium heat until mushroom juices are reduced, about 3 to 5 minutes. Reduce heat to medium-low and add the carrots, thyme, chervil, and parsley, and cook for 1 to 2 minutes. Season with salt and pepper.

Place pasta in boiling water, and cook until al dente.

Meanwhile, add the chicken stock to the mushroom mixture and simmer until liquid is reduced by half. Then, add half-and-half and reduce until the sauce has the consistency you prefer. Stir in lemon juice. Remove from heat, cover.

Drain pasta. Place in warm serving bowl. Spoon 1 to 2 tablespoons sauce over pasta to keep it from sticking together. Mix gently. Then, add remaining sauce. Toss gently. Serve.

SERVES 4

½ pound fresh morels, chanterelles, or other wild spring mushrooms, wiped clean or gently rinsed, thinly sliced•

3 shallots, peeled and diced

1 tablespoon unsalted butter

10 small, first-of-the-season carrots, julienned

3 sprigs chopped fresh thyme (or 1 teaspoon dried)

3 sprigs chopped fresh chervil (or 1 teaspoon dried)

1 tablespoon chopped fresh parsley

salt and freshly ground pepper to taste

1 cup chicken stock, or canned low-sodium chicken broth

½ cup half-and-half or heavy cream

1 tablespoon freshly squeezed lemon juice

1 package fresh or dried papardelle pasta (enough for 4 servings)

•**NOTE:** If fresh mushrooms aren't available, dried, reconstituted mushrooms can be used—although the flavor will not be quite as delicate.

SERVES 4
VINAIGRETTE:

1 tablespoon Dijon mustard

1 teaspoon minced shallots

pinch salt

¼ cup champagne vinegar

½ to ¾ cup olive oil

market mix of baby greens

nasturtiums

GREEN SALAD WITH CHAMPAGNE VINAIGRETTE

Nasturtiums mixed in this salad add appetizing color!

Whisk vinaigrette ingredients together in a small bowl and drizzle over baby greens and nasturtiums. Toss and serve.

SERVES 4

1 cup coarsely chopped pitted Kalamata olives

½ cup chopped Mission figs

3 tablespoons olive oil

1 tablespoon fresh lemon juice

1 teaspoon Dijon mustard

1 tablespoon brandy

freshly ground pepper to taste

1 tablespoon capers

4 slices crusty Italian bread, or any other day-old bread

1 garlic clove, halved

CROSTINI WITH FIG AND OLIVE TAPENADE

Place olives, figs, 2 tablespoons olive oil, lemon juice, Dijon mustard, brandy, and pepper in a food processor. Purée until combined. Add capers and incorporate with quick pulses.

Place bread on a grill or under the broiler. Grill or broil until golden on each side, about 2 to 3 minutes. Remove from heat and rub the bread with the garlic clove halves, and brush lightly with remaining 1 tablespoon olive oil. Top bread slices with tapenade, then cut each into thirds. Serve immediately.

SERVES 4

3 shallots, peeled and diced

2 garlic cloves, chopped

1½ tablespoons unsalted butter

2 tablespoons chopped fresh thyme

2 bay leaves

1 tablespoon black peppercorns

3 cups Brut sparkling wine or champagne

2 lemons

4½ pounds black mussels

1 cup chopped Italian flat-leaf parsley

½ cup (small can) diced tomatoes

MUSSELS IN SPARKLING WINE

Adapted from a recipe by Domaine Chandon's chef Robert Curry, this is a favorite of ours when the evenings begin to cool as fall approaches. When I cook with sparkling wine or champagne, I usually like to drink it with the meal, too. If I had to choose an alternate wine for the mussels, I would probably choose a delicate Pinot Noir.

In a large pot, sweat the shallots and garlic in ½ tablespoon butter. Stir in thyme, bay leaves, peppercorns, and sparkling wine. Add the juice from half a lemon, then cut the lemon into two or four pieces and add to the pot. Add the mussels. Cover and steam just until mussels open, about 2 minutes. Place mussels in a warm serving bowl. Cover to keep warm.

From the remaining liquid, strain out bay leaves, peppercorns, and lemon rind. In a large pan, bring the liquid to a simmer and reduce by half. Whisk in 1 tablespoon butter. Add parsley and tomatoes. Adjust the flavor with additional lemon juice if needed. Pour mixture over the mussels and serve with purchased crusty olive country bread.

SALAD WITH WINTER GREENS

In a small bowl, whisk together dressing ingredients. Drizzle dressing over greens just to coat. Toss and serve.

SERVES 4

DRESSING:

2 tablespoons verjus·

2 tablespoons balsamic vinegar

½ cup olive oil

1 tablespoon grainy, mild mustard

1 shallot, peeled and chopped

salt and pepper to taste

8 cups bite-size mixed winter greens like frisse, radicchio, and endive (any winter greens may be added or substituted), washed

·**NOTE:** unfermented juice of unripe grapes often used in France—sometimes in the place of vinegar

CELERY ROOT AND POTATO GRATIN

I like a Cabernet Sauvignon or an earthy Rhône wine with this dish.

Preheat oven to 375 degrees.

Rub a 2-quart gratin dish with a garlic halve and then truffle oil.

Place the celery root parings and the other garlic halve in a 3-quart saucepan with the vegetable broth. Set a steamer over the top and bring to a boil. Quarter the celery root, then slice into ¼-inch pieces. Steam in vegetable broth for 5 minutes and remove to a large bowl. Steam potatoes for 5 minutes or until tender and add to the celery root. Strain the cooking liquid, reserving 1½ cups, and mix in a small bowl with the cream and mustard. Pour over the vegetables and toss well. Season with salt and pepper.

Transfer the vegetables to the gratin dish, smooth them out, and sprinkle cheese over top. Bake until bubbling and browned on top, about 30 minutes.

SERVES 4

1 clove garlic, halved

1 teaspoon truffle oil

1 celery root (about 1 pound), scrubbed and peeled (reserve parings)

2 cups vegetable broth

1 pound potatoes, preferably Yellow Finn or Yukon Gold, peeled and sliced thin

½ cup cream, or half-and-half

2 teaspoons Dijon mustard

salt and freshly ground pepper to taste

1 cup freshly grated Gruyere cheese

SERVES 4

Cabacou (goat cheese marinated in oil with herbs)

6 tablespoons lavender honey, or a flavorful star thistle honey

grilled or toasted bread

candied walnuts (recipe follows)

1 cup walnut halves

3 tablespoons honey

¼ cup sugar

¼ cup water

pinch salt

pinch cayenne pepper

CABACOU WITH WARM LAVENDER HONEY AND WALNUTS

Phillipe Jeanty, of Bistro Jeanty in Yountville and formerly longtime chef at Domaine Chandon, brought this idea back from a vacation in Provençe several years ago. It's become a staple for us, the flavors are so clean and simple. The cayenne on the walnuts is really great, and they can be prepared well in advance. Robert Curry, presently chef at Domaine Chandon, helped me pull this recipe together. I get my Cabacou from Laura Chenel, a local cheese purveyor in the Valley—it's the best!

For an individual serving, place a few slices of Cabacou on a small plate, drizzle with about 1 tablespoon honey, and garnish with walnuts. Serve with bread.

CANDIED WALNUTS

Preheat oven to 350 degrees.

Spray two sheet trays with non-stick spray. Place honey, sugar, water, salt, and cayenne in small saucepan over high heat and simmer until sugar is dissolved. Add walnuts and continue cooking until nuts are totally covered and bottom of pan is dry. Remove from heat and spread out onto one of the sheet trays. Place in the oven and cook for 10 to 12 minutes, stirring occasionally, until nuts turn dark brown. Remove from oven and turn out onto other sheet tray. Cool. As soon as they are cool enough to handle, break them up.

PAULA KORNELL OF CARMENET VINEYARDS

"Cooking and sharing good wine and food with friends is the absolute ultimate."

REFERRING TO HER HERITAGE, Paula Kornell, formerly with Robert Mondavi and now general manager of Carmenet Vineyards (just over the Napa Valley border in Sonoma county), says, "I guess you could say I'm half spaghetti and half sauerkraut!" Paula is a Napa Valley native whose mother, while also born in the Valley, has Swiss-Italian roots and whose father, a native of Germany, came from a family of Sekt-makers. "That's German sparkling wine," Paula explains. She considers herself extremely lucky to have been surrounded by great wine and food since she was very young. Paula says, "The lifestyle is an easy one to adopt, and of course I've been fortunate to be able to add a little flair of my own!" And those who know Paula would agree that for her, anything less wouldn't make much sense!

Paula says, "Carrying on European traditions, wine was always a part of mealtime. It would have seemed strange not to see a bottle of wine on the table each evening." And that is particularly true since she grew up around wine, sparkling wine, from her father's winery, Hans Kornell. "What others saved for a special occasion, I had the privilege of indulging in every day! Now, though, more and more people are finally getting the point that sparkling wine can easily be a part of their daily routine, especially with all the good health news about wine."

A healthy lifestyle is about much more though than just food and wine. "To me it's not always a strict regime," she says. "It's really almost more about being able to share good food and good wine with friends. And of course getting out for a little exercise with friends is also much more enjoyable than going alone!" Because of the nature of her work, Paula is on the road a lot. She's not always able to stick to one exercise routine or even a regular mealtime, but she doesn't believe that's really necessary or truly realistic, at least for her. "Being on the road a lot, I try to be outside as much as I possibly can—and even visiting the hotel gym when there is one. As for my meals, I try not to beat myself up if I'm stuck on a plane eating just out of sheer boredom. I know those who travel can empathize!"

"My personal philosophy of food," she says, "is to find the ingredients as fresh as possible and keep preparations simple. I usually cook without a lot of sauces and fuss but always with at least one glass of wine in my hand!" She says, "Cooking and sharing good wine and food with friends is the absolute ultimate—the body and soul of my life."

Spring ~ Summer

Avocado and Lime Soup

Salmon Steaks Wrapped in Sorrel

Watermelon and Feta Salad

Corn on the Cob

White Peaches with Riesling and Fresh Rosemary

Alexander Vineyards Gewürtztraminer
Archery Summit Pinot Noir, Arcus Estate

Fall ~ Winter

Moroccan Artichokes

Rabbit and Olive Stew

Soft Polenta with Asiago

Baked Bosc Pears in Cream

Robert Mondavi Fumé Blanc, Reserve
Carmenet Moon Mountain Cabernet

AVOCADO AND LIME SOUP

SERVES 6

4 cups chicken broth
4 large ripe avocados
¼ cup lime juice
1 teaspoon crushed garlic
2 cups skim milk
dash of sea salt and black pepper
6 thin lime slices

Purée chicken broth, avocados, lime juice, garlic, and skim milk in a blender. Season with salt and pepper. Cover and refrigerate until cold.

Divide soup among 6 bowls. Top each with lime slice.

SALMON STEAKS WRAPPED IN SORREL

SERVES 6

½ pound fresh sorrel
6 salmon steaks 1 to 1½ inch thick
unsalted butter
salt and pepper to taste

Place a large pinch of sorrel on a piece of aluminum foil. Set salmon steak on sorrel and top with a pat of butter. Season with salt and pepper, and top with another pinch of sorrel. Wrap salmon in foil so that juices do not escape.

Place over medium heat on grill, for approximately 15 to 20 minutes, or bake in the oven at 350 degrees for 15 to 20 minutes, taking care not to overcook. Serve.

WATERMELON AND FETA SALAD

SERVES 6 TO 8

1 small seedless watermelon cut in small cubes
¼ pound crumbled fresh feta cheese
½ cup balsamic vinegar
black pepper
¼ cup sliced fresh mint (ribbons)
6 fresh mint sprigs

Mix all ingredients except mint sprigs in a large serving bowl. Let stand for 1 to 2 hours to allow flavors to blend. Garnish with fresh mint sprigs and serve.

WHITE PEACHES WITH RIESLING AND FRESH ROSEMARY

SERVES 8

8 fresh white peaches, peeled and sliced
½ cup Riesling
4 tablespoons finely chopped fresh rosemary

Mix all ingredients in a large serving bowl. Allow peaches to steep by refrigerating at least 3 hours before serving.

MOROCCAN ARTICHOKES

Place artichokes in a large pan over medium heat. Add orange juice, lemon juice, and pepper flakes. Top each artichoke with an orange and onion slice. Cover and simmer until the bottom of the artichoke is tender, about 40 to 45 minutes.

Cut artichokes in half and remove fuzzy part with spoon. Arrange artichokes on plate with onion and orange slice. Add pinch of salt.

SERVES 6

6 medium artichokes, stemmed, tops trimmed, and outer thistles removed

½ cup orange juice

½ cup lemon juice

¾ cup olive oil

4 teaspoons red pepper flakes

6 orange slices

6 yellow onion slices

salt

RABBIT AND OLIVE STEW

Preheat oven to 350 degrees.

Heat olive oil in a large oven-proof pan over medium-high heat. Add rabbit and brown on all sides. Add diced onion, garlic, and fennel, and cook until onions are translucent, about 3 minutes. Add wine and tomato paste and boil until wine is reduced by half. Add the stock, olives, and tomatoes.

Cover and bake for 2 hours. Remove from oven, let rabbit cool slightly, then pull meat off the bones. Fold in parsley. Season with salt and pepper to taste. Serve over Soft Polenta with Asiago (recipe follows).

SERVES 6

3 tablespoons olive oil

1 rabbit, cut into pieces (your local butcher will do this upon request)

1 yellow onion, diced

2 tablespoons minced fresh garlic

¼ cup chopped fresh fennel

1 cup white wine

2 tablespoons tomato paste

½ cup chicken stock

1 cup green or Spanish olives, pitted and sliced

1 cup diced fresh tomatoes

½ cup chopped fresh parsley

salt and pepper to taste

SOFT POLENTA WITH ASIAGO

Polenta is traditionally made by whisking dry cornmeal into boiling water. This method helps to keep the consistency smooth, preventing lumps.

Heat olive oil in a large saucepan over medium heat. Add the onion and stir until translucent, about 3 minutes. Sir in 2½ cups water and all of the chicken broth. Add bay leaf and bring to a boil.

In a small bowl, whisk together the cornmeal and the remaining 1 cup of water.

Once the other mixture has come to a rolling boil, remove the bay leaf and gradually whisk in the cornmeal, reduce the heat to low and cook, stirring constantly, until the cornmeal is very thick, about 20 to 25 minutes. Remove from heat and stir in the cheese. Taste the polenta before adding additional salt.

BAKED BOSC PEARS IN CREAM

Preheat oven to 350 degrees.

Grease baking dish lightly with butter and sprinkle with half the sugar. Arrange pears cut side down in pan, dot with butter, and top with remaining sugar. Bake until soft, about 20 to 30 minutes. Transfer juices to small saucepan and whisk in cream. Reduce by half over low heat stirring often.

To serve, place berry purée on one half of plate and sour cream on the other half. Place pear on top of the sauces. More sauce can be spooned over the top of the pear.

SEA SALT IN SEASON

Salt is one of the building blocks of good food—it's natural, clean, pure, and, in the right quantities, healthy.

WHAT SEEMS TO BE a new culinary phenomenon is not really new at all… it's salt—and it's back in fashion. But not just any salt: It has to be pure sea salt, the kind that's been hand-harvested in many cultures for centuries.

"Salt has always been among the world's most important commodities. One of the four elemental components of taste—along with sweet, sour, and bitter—salt sharpens and pulls together other tastes," says Berry Fussell in *Bon Appétit* magazine. Throughout human history, salt has been a powerful commodity, traveling along its own "route," being honored in its own museum in Oshima, Japan, and having its curative powers documented in carvings and shrines. In medieval England, guests sat above or below the salt, because proximity to the host—who always sat next to the salt—was indicative of rank. Although the salt trade has been documented in ancient Phoenicia and China, the first industrial salt production occurred in Italy. Soldiers guarding shipments were paid in salt, and if they didn't perform properly, they were deemed "not worth their salt." Napoleon knew the importance of salt because his men didn't have enough in their diets; the result of their poor health was the loss of several battles. Thomas Jefferson called salt "a necessity of life."

Now those in the food and wine industry are seeing a salt renaissance through sea salt. *Wine Spectator* magazine has recently commented on sea salt: "As chefs get more elemental, simplicity reigns. Every ingredient is therefore crucial—and salt is such an integral part of cooking." Some chefs say sea salt makes food taste more like itself. Some say it is pure magic and, unlike precious jewels or metals, it is necessary to sustain life.

Holly Peterson Mondavi is not only a wine and food lover like her sister, winemaker Heidi Peterson Barrett, she is also a sea salt lover. As a seasoned chef, Holly experienced cooking in great kitchens around the world and found the most essential element to be the sun-dried grey sea salt from the coast of Brittany. When she couldn't find a consistent reliable source in the United States, she started her own company, Sea Star. Holly says sea salt is "the most delicate flavor in the world, and it doesn't cover or conflict. It pulls out more of the flavors of whatever is in a dish. And, coincidentally, it actually has a lower sodium content, and higher flavor content, than processed and commercial salt. Not only is it essential physiologically," says Holly, "it also gives life and character to the food we eat. Salt is one of the building blocks of good food—it's natural, clean, pure, and, in the right quantities, healthy." Following is Holly's Sea Star recipe for Gravlox.

GRAVLOX

In an herb grinder or food processor, grind together the peppercorns, coriander grains, and juniper berries. In a medium bowl, combine this mixture with sea salt and sugar. Add dill and lemon zest and toss.

Layer this mixture with the salmon in a glass or other non-reactive dish that's slightly larger than the salmon. (Place the salmon on top of one layer of the salt mixture and then cover with remaining mixture.)

Cover with plastic wrap and let cure in refrigerator for 2 days, turning the salmon once each day.

Remove from the refrigerator and scrape off half of the mixture. Drain. Pour the milk over the salmon, cover, and refrigerate one more day.

When ready to serve, remove salmon from the milk, drain, and pat dry. Slice very thin.

1 tablespoon black peppercorns

2 tablespoons coriander grains

1 tablespoon juniper berries

½ cup crushed Sea Star sea salt

¾ cup superfine sugar

1 bunch fresh dill, lightly chopped

2 lemons, zest only

1 side of fresh salmon, skinned and filleted

½ gallon milk (organic if available)

OPTION: Serve on toasted brioche with crème fraîche and arugula tossed in a citrus vinaigrette.

JOHN AND DIANE LIVINGSTON found themselves in the Napa Valley twenty-five years ago. Diane says, "It wasn't the wine we were interested in at that time. We were really looking more for a place to raise our six children, then ages five to twelve. It wasn't until we'd moved that we became enamored with wine and the lifestyle it perpetuates."

Diane spent her childhood in Philadelphia and John spent his in Boston. Neither was raised with wine in the house. But when they moved to the Valley, they bought a piece of property with a small vineyard on it. And out of curiosity, they began making wine, which eventually led to the development of Livingston Moffett Vineyards.

"Both John and I maintain an active lifestyle, which is easy to do here," says Diane, "because you're somehow just more aware of being active and it easily becomes a part of what you do." As often as they can, they play tennis or golf. You'll usually catch John running early in the morning, likely training for the next Napa Valley marathon. "We love the outdoors and both find a way to do some kind of exercise daily," says John.

"We also really try to maintain a healthy low-fat diet," says Diane. "And, of course, now we drink wine every evening with our meal. We really do." The message is that with a little attention, wine becomes, as Diane says, "a natural part of your mealtime experience so easily"—part of a healthy Napa Valley lifestyle that can be enjoyed anywhere.

"Of course, now we drink wine every evening with our meal."

Spring ~ Summer

Oriental Chicken Salad

Spiced Strawberries and Cabernet with Chocolate Shortbread Stars

Livingston Wines, Stanley's Selection Cabernet
Cakebread Chardonnay

Fall ~ Winter

Marinated Grilled Pork Loin

Roasted Winter Root Vegetable Purée

Salad of Watercress, Apples, Toasted Walnuts, and Feta Cheese

Mini Baked Alaska "Snowballs"

Moffett Vineyard Cabernet
Harrison Zebra Zinfandel

ORIENTAL CHICKEN SALAD

SERVES 8

1 pound dry linguini noodles or noodles of your choice

¾ cup low-sodium soy sauce

¼ cup peanut oil

2 whole chicken breasts, skinned, poached, cut into bite-size pieces

1 red bell pepper, coarsely chopped

one 8-ounce can bamboo shoots, drained

one 6-ounce jar miniature corn on the cob, drained and thickly sliced; reserving 2 for garnish (½ cup blanched fresh corn kernels can be substituted)

½ cup chopped fresh cilantro

2 cups light mayonnaise, or 1 cup light mayonnaise and 1 cup nonfat yogurt

1 tablespoon Dijon mustard

1 teaspoon Szechuan chili oil

½ pound fresh snow peas, blanched and julienned

1 teaspoon toasted sesame seeds

Boil noodles in 4 quarts boiling water until al dente. Drain and place in serving bowl.

In a separate bowl, whisk together ½ cup soy sauce and peanut oil, pour over noodles and toss. Cool to room temperature. Add chicken, pepper, shoots, corn, and cilantro.

In a small bowl, combine mayonnaise with Dijon mustard, remaining soy sauce and Szechuan chili oil to taste. Mix with noodles and refrigerate until ready to use. (Can be made the day before and refrigerated overnight.)

Add snow peas when ready to serve. Garnish with sesame seeds and reserved corn.

SPICED STRAWBERRIES AND CABERNET WITH CHOCOLATE SHORTBREAD STARS

SERVES 8

1½ cups Cabernet Sauvignon (Livingston "Stanley's Selection," if available)

½ cup water

¼ cup ground cinnamon

⅛ teaspoon ground cloves

6 peppercorns

¼ cup extra fine granulated sugar

pinch allspice

2 pints fresh strawberries, rinsed, drained, and hulled

mint leaves

Place wine, water, cinnamon, cloves, peppercorns, sugar, and allspice in a medium saucepan and bring to a boil. Reduce heat and simmer 30 minutes. Chill until ready to use.

Slice strawberries into a medium serving bowl. Ladle just enough Cabernet sauce over top to cover. Spoon a little sauce into individual serving bowls, add strawberries, and garnish with mint leaves. Serve with Chocolate Shortbread Stars (recipe follows).

CHOCOLATE SHORTBREAD STARS

MAKES 24 TO 36

½ pound butter, very cold

1 teaspoon vanilla extract

pinch salt

1 cup powdered sugar

2 cups flour

½ cup Dutch process powdered chocolate

Preheat oven to 300 degrees.

Combine all ingredients in food processor until dough forms a ball. On a floured wooden board, roll dough to ½ inch thickness, working quickly so that dough doesn't warm up and become sticky. Cut out with star cookie cutter and place on cookie sheet. Prick each cookie a few times with a fork.

Bake just until done; avoiding any browning, about 10 minutes. (The cookies will keep for a week or more in an airtight container.)

MARINATED GRILLED PORK LOIN

In a large pot, combine garlic, ginger, sherry, peppercorns, sesame oil, brown sugar, soy sauce, and Cabernet Sauvignon. Reduce heat and simmer 1 hour. (May be refrigerated for several weeks for later use.)

With marinade at a simmer, add pork loin and poach for 10 minutes. Remove from marinade, drain slightly, and grill or broil 8 minutes each side, adding half the rosemary sprigs to the coals or bottom of the pan (if broiling, rosemary sprigs may need to be removed from pan to prevent burning).

Slice ½ inch thick and place on platter surrounded by remaining fresh rosemary.

SERVES 8

MARINADE:

2 garlic cloves, minced

¼ cup freshly grated ginger root

½ cup sherry

¼ cup peppercorns

¼ cup sesame oil

½ cup brown sugar

4 cups low-sodium soy sauce

1 bottle (750ml) Cabernet Sauvignon (Livingston Stanley's Selection, if available)

one 4-pound boneless, whole pork loin

10 sprigs fresh rosemary

ROASTED WINTER ROOT VEGETABLE PURÉE

Preheat oven to 400 degrees.

In a large roasting pan that has been rubbed with olive oil, toss potatoes, parsnips, carrots, onions, and garlic. Cover with aluminum foil and bake 1 hour.

Place roasted vegetables in food processor and blend until smooth. Add milk, butter and salt. With quick pulses, combine until incorporated. Serve immediately or chill covered, overnight.

Bake covered until heated through, about 35 minutes. (If chilled overnight, let stand at room temperature 30 minutes before baking.)

Garnish with chives.

SERVES 8

2 tablespoons olive oil

4 large baking potatoes, peeled and quartered

1 pound parsnips, peeled and cut into chunks

1 pound carrots, peeled and sliced 1 inch thick

2 medium onions, peeled and quartered

4 garlic cloves, peeled

½ cup lowfat milk

¼ cup unsalted butter

1 teaspoons salt

1 tablespoon chopped fresh chives

SALAD OF WATERCRESS, APPLES, TOASTED WALNUTS, AND FETA CHEESE

Combine watercress, apples, walnuts, and feta in a medium-size serving bowl.

In a separate bowl, whisk together vinegar, oil, sugar, and salt. Drizzle enough over salad just to moisten. Toss and serve.

SERVES 8

2 bunches watercress, rinsed and dried (about 2 cups)

4 McIntosh apples, washed, cored, and diced into bite-size pieces

½ cup coarsely chopped walnuts, lightly toasted

1 cup crumbled feta cheese

¼ cup red wine vinegar

⅓ to ½ cup canola oil

1 teaspoon sugar

salt to taste

SERVES 12

MERINGUE:

4 egg whites

⅛ teaspoon cream of tartar

¾ cup superfine sugar

¼ cup sifted powdered sugar

¾ cup finely chopped almonds

twelve 3-inch circles parchment paper

TOPPING:

6 egg whites

⅛ teaspoon cream of tartar

1¼ cups superfine sugar

½ gallon peppermint ice cream, or your favorite

MINI BAKED ALASKA "SNOWBALLS"

Preheat oven to 200 degrees.

In a medium bowl, beat 4 egg whites until foamy. Slowly add ⅛ teaspoon cream of tartar and superfine sugar, beating until stiff peaks form.

In a separate bowl, mix together powdered sugar and almonds, and gently fold into beaten egg whites.

Place parchment paper on cookie sheet and make 12 meringues using a pastry bag with no tip, piping in one continuous circle beginning in the middle of the circle and moving outward. Bake for 2 hours. Let cool and store in an air-tight container until ready to use. (These may be made up to one month in advance.)

In a small bowl, beat the 6 egg whites until foamy. Slowly add cream of tartar and superfine sugar and continue beating until stiff peaks form.

Place one scoop (snowball shape) of ice cream on a meringue cookie. Cover with topping. Broil quickly until just before topping begins to brown. Remove from oven and serve immediately.

KAREN MACNEIL OF THE CULINARY INSTITUTE OF AMERICA AT GREYSTONE AND DENNIS FIFE OF FIFE VINEYARDS

"BALANCE IS A CONCEPT we talk about all the time in the wine business," says Karen MacNeil, journalist and wine curriculum instructor at the Culinary Institute of America at Greystone. "Balance, in fact, is one of the hallmarks of a great wine. And it's not very easy to achieve. My husband, Dennis, and I think living a healthy life is also all about balance. But because we love wine, food, and restaurants, we spend just about every waking second working at some aspect of one of the three. Frankly, that doesn't make for a very balanced existence. We can only say that work doesn't seem like work when you're passionate about it—which is a balance of sorts, isn't it?"

Both she and Dennis enjoy most evenings preparing dinner together while always tasting several new wine selections. Karen admits, "Dinner sometimes runs really late. There's so much good wine to try!" They call it "research." The wines they try may be a comparitive set of wines to a varietal Dennis currently produces, or they may be wines from a distinct area of the world forming the basis of a lecture Karen will deliver the next day.

With all the wining and dining, how do they stay so fit and trim? "Oh yes," says Karen, "there is one other admission in order here: we exercise like mad!" And that certainly helps balance the scale.

"Work doesn't seem like work when you're passionate about it."

Spring ~ Summer

Eat-With-Your-Fingers Spicy Grilled Shrimp

Tomato, Beet, and Endive Salad with Feta and Orange-Apricot Vinaigrette

Summer Corn Pudding

Spicy Chicken with Preserved Lemons

Nectarine-Blackberry Cobbler

Fife Vineyards "Redhead Vineyard" Zinfandel

Fife Vineyards L'Attitude 39 (a Rhône style blend)

Joseph Phelps Vin Du Mistral Grenache Rosé

Fall ~ Winter

Rosemary-Balsamic Honey and Goat Cheese Crostini

Spicy Lamb Stew

Buttery Mashed Potatoes

Pears Poached in Red Wine

Fife Vineyards Max Cuvee (a Rhône style blend)

Fife Vineyards "Redhead Vineyard" Petite Syrah

Edmunds St. John Syrah

SERVES 4

1 pound fresh or frozen jumbo or very
large shrimp, shell on

1 cup Kosher salt

MARINADE:

½ cup olive oil

1 teaspoon paprika

1 teaspoon turmeric

1 teaspoon ground cumin

1 teaspoon cracked black pepper

½ teaspoon salt

1 tablespoon minced garlic

1 tablespoon tandoori paste*

1 teaspoon tamarind paste (optional)*

*NOTE: Tandoori paste is available in better supermarkets and most specialty shops. Patak's is a very good
brand. Tamarind paste is available in Asian grocery
stores.

EAT-WITH-YOUR-FINGERS SPICY GRILLED SHRIMP

*I usually brine the shrimp first to make them more plump and juicy. This is very easy to do, and
the results are remarkable. The shrimp also stay very moist because they are grilled in their shells.*

TO BRINE THE SHRIMP: Pour 1 cup of boiling water into a large bowl. Add the
salt and stir until it is dissolved. Stir in 1½ quarts of cold water. Add the fresh or
frozen shrimp (do not peel). Place bowl in the refrigerator for 1 to 1½ hours. Drain
shrimp and rinse with cold running water. Spread on paper towels and pat dry.

Mix all marinade ingredients together in a medium bowl. Add shrimp, tossing
to coat. Cover bowl with plastic wrap and refrigerate for at least 1 hour.

Lightly brush a clean grill with vegetable oil. Heat to medium-high. Place shrimp
on the grill. Using tongs, turn each shrimp when the side exposed to the heat turns a
bright red and takes on grill marks, about 3 to 5 minutes. Cook briefly on second side.
Shrimp is completely done when the shell begins to split open down the back.

Heap shrimp on a platter and serve family style, with plenty of napkins.

SERVES 4 TO 6

3 medium chiogga beets, washed, tops trimmed

4 heads Belgian endive

1 tablespoon olive oil

2 medium vine-ripened red tomatoes

2 medium vine-ripened yellow tomatoes

½ cup packed basil, cut into thin ribbons

⅓ pound Greek feta (California goat cheese
can be substituted), crumbled

salt and freshly ground pepper

VINAIGRETTE:

¼ cup extra virgin olive oil

¼ cup orange juice

1 tablespoon apricot preserves

2 teaspoons plain yogurt

1 teaspoon red wine vinegar

1 teaspoon Dijon mustard

½ teaspoon dried basil

¼ teaspoon cumin

½ teaspoon salt

freshly ground pepper to taste

pinch of sugar

TOMATO, BEET, AND ENDIVE SALAD WITH FETA
AND ORANGE-APRICOT VINAIGRETTE

*This salad is simple to make, a riot of flavor, and a bold splash of color. I like to use chiogga
beets because they are very sweet and, when cut, have vibrantly-colored red and white stripes.
However, red or yellow beets can be substituted.*

Place beets in a covered saucepan filled with water. Bring water to a boil, reduce
heat slightly, and cook 40 minutes to 1 hour until beets are cooked through. (If the
water gets low, add more to the pot.) Set aside to cool. When cool, hold beets under
cold running water and rub off their skins. Slice into ¼-inch slices. Set aside. (Can be
done one day ahead.)

Brush the endive with olive oil and grill briefly until endive is just beginning
to turn golden brown. Set aside. Slice tomatoes into ¼-inch slices. Set aside.

In a small bowl, combine the basil and feta.

Cut each endive in half and place the halves on a large circular platter. The tips
of the endive should extend over the edge of the platter. Arrange the tomatoes with
beets, alternating colors, in a large circle over the endive. Sprinkle the basil-feta mixture over all. Lightly salt and pepper.

Combine the vinaigrette ingredients in a jar and shake vigorously. Adjust seasonings. Drizzle enough vinaigrette over the salad just to moisten.

SUMMER CORN PUDDING

Fresh corn makes this the quintessential summer side dish.

Preheat oven to 325 degrees.

Husk corn. Remove kernels by holding each ear perpendicular to a plate, and cut the kernels from the cob using a sharp knife. Then, to extract the most corn flavor, use the tines of a fork to scrape the cob, releasing the bit of sweet flavorful liquid known as the corn "milk." Scrape this milk onto the plate along with the kernels.

Place corn and corn milk in a large bowl. Mix in cheddar, basil, flour, nutmeg, salt, and pepper.

In a separate bowl, whisk together the eggs, half-and-half, and brown sugar. Stir this liquid mixture into the corn. Fold in the cherry tomatoes.

With the teaspoon of butter, grease a 1½-quart baking dish. Gently scoop the corn pudding mixture into the dish.

Melt the two tablespoons of butter and mix with the pine nuts. Spoon the buttered nuts over the corn pudding. Set the baking dish in a roasting pan. Pour enough boiling water into the roasting pan so that the water reaches about one quarter of the way up the outsides of the baking dish.

Bake 60 to 70 minutes, until pudding sets and top turns golden.

SERVES 6

3 cups fresh corn (4 to 6 ears)

⅓ cup grated sharp white cheddar cheese

½ cup chopped basil

1 tablespoon flour

¼ teaspoon nutmeg

½ teaspoon salt

1 teaspoon cracked black pepper

2 large eggs

1 cup half-and-half

1 tablespoon brown sugar

15 to 20 cherry tomatoes

2 tablespoons plus 1 teaspoon butter

1 tablespoon pine nuts

¼ cup low-sodium soy sauce

¼ cup sweet Marsala

1 tablespoon minced garlic

2 teaspoons ground cumin

1 teaspoon paprika

8 tablespoons olive oil

8 chicken thighs, bone in but skin removed

1 large onion, chopped

½ cup all-purpose flour

2 teaspoons cinnamon

1 teaspoon cayenne

1 teaspoon salt

2 preserved lemons (recipe follows)

SPICY CHICKEN WITH PRESERVED LEMONS

Making preserved lemons is extremely easy and their flavor is wonderfully exotic and refreshing. Because preserved lemons keep for months, you can make a jar and use it over the course of several seasons. If you don't have preserved lemons, regular fresh lemons can be substituted. I use free range chickens because I think they taste better. Also, I like the way dark meat works in this recipe, but one could certainly use small chicken breasts on the bone (skin removed).

In a large dish, combine the soy sauce, Marsala, garlic, cumin, paprika, and 4 tablespoons of the olive oil. Add the chicken, toss to coat, and marinate for several hours or overnight in the refrigerator.

Preheat oven to 350 degrees.

Heat 2 tablespoons of the remaining olive oil in a large skillet. Add the onion and sauté over medium-low heat until onion just begins to brown, about 15 minutes. Set aside.

Drain the chicken, reserving the marinade. Combine the flour, cinnamon, cayenne, and salt in a plastic bag. Add the chicken and shake bag to coat chicken evenly.

Heat the remaining 2 tablespoons of olive oil in a large oven-proof covered skillet, casserole dish, or Dutch oven (large enough to hold the chicken in one layer). Add the chicken and brown gently on both sides. Scatter the onions over the chicken. Drizzle with the reserved marinade.

Using the palm of your hand, roll the preserved lemons back and forth a few times on the kitchen counter. This will help extract the juices from the flesh. Place the lemons on a plate (to catch the juices) and gently slice them into ⅛-inch-thick slices. Top the chicken with the preserved lemon slices and pour the lemon juices over.

Bake, covered, 45 minutes. Remove cover and bake 10 to 15 minutes more until chicken is nicely browned.

6 lemons

2 tablespoons salt

large (4 liter) glass mason jar with a metal clamp and rubber seal*

*NOTE: Large mason jars with a clamp and rubber seal are available at kitchenware stores and lifestyle stores such as Cost Plus, Pier One, and Crate & Barrel.

PRESERVED LEMONS

It's almost impossible to describe the sweet, tangy, exotic flavor of preserved lemons. But once you try them, you'll never be without a jar around the house.

Wash jar with hot, soapy water, rinse well, and dry.

Clean lemons well by scrubbing them under running water with a vegetable brush. Pierce each lemon all over (about 10 times) with a fork. Be sure the fork pierces through the peel to the flesh.

Place salt in the jar, cover with about a cup of boiling water and stir to dissolve salt. Add lemons. Fill jar completely with tepid water, close securely with the clamp, then shake jar several times. For the next week, shake jar once a day (to keep salt distributed). After that, simply let the jar sit on a counter. Lemons will be ready in 6 weeks and will keep for 8 months or more.

To use, simply remove lemons as you need them, leaving the remaining lemons in the same jar. Do not wash lemons before using them.

NECTARINE-BLACKBERRY COBBLER

Preheat oven to 375 degrees and set rack in center of oven.

Combine sugar, cornstarch, and vanilla in a large, heavy saucepan. Add nectarines and blackberries and stir gently to mix. Over medium-low heat, bring fruit just to a simmer. Turn heat as low as possible, and cook about 5 minutes, occasionally stirring fruit. Transfer to a deep, 10-inch tart dish that has been lightly greased with the 1 teaspoon butter. Set aside.

Cut the 6 tablespoons of butter into small cubes. Place in the freezer for 20 minutes until butter hardens.

In a food processor, briefly pulse butter, flour, salt, sugars, and baking powder, until mixture resembles coarse cornmeal. Do not over process. Transfer mixture to a bowl and gently stir in half-and-half, until mixture is moistened.

Lightly dust your hands with flour and knead dough a few times. Roll out dough ¾ inch thick. Using a round biscuit cutter about 1½ to 2 inches in diameter, cut dough into rounds. Arrange the biscuits on top of the fruit. Place tart dish on a cookie sheet to catch any spills as the fruit bubbles up. Bake about 35 minutes or until the biscuits are just beginning to turn golden and the fruit bubbles around them. Cool slightly on a wire rack.

Serve warm with vanilla ice cream.

SERVES 8

FILLING:

½ cup sugar

2 teaspoons cornstarch

1 teaspoon vanilla

3 cups unpeeled ripe nectarines, diced into ½-inch cubes

2 cups fresh or frozen blackberries

1 teaspoon unsalted butter

TOPPING:

6 tablespoons unsalted butter

1½ cups all-purpose flour

½ teaspoon salt

1 tablespoon sugar

2 teaspoons brown sugar

2¼ teaspoons baking powder

¾ cup half-and-half

flour for dusting

vanilla ice cream, optional

½ cup honey

⅓ cup water

1 sprig fresh rosemary (4 inches)

3 tablespoons balsamic vinegar

6 ounces fresh goat cheese

12 slices firm walnut bread, each slice 2 inches thick, toasted

ROSEMARY-BALSAMIC HONEY AND GOAT CHEESE CROSTINI

This simple appetizer provides a warm, friendly start to a cozy evening. Experiment with strong-flavored, interesting honeys such as pistachio or chestnut.

In a small saucepan, combine honey and water. Bring to a boil over high heat. Add rosemary sprig and simmer gently, uncovered, until reduced to ½ cup, 8 to 12 minutes.

Remove and discard rosemary. Stir in vinegar and cool.

Spread goat cheese thickly on toast. Drizzle with honey syrup and serve.

SERVES 4

2 tablespoons olive oil

½ cup diced onion (about ½ of an onion)

1 teaspoon red curry powder

1 teaspoon ground cumin

1½ pounds boneless lamb shoulder, cut into 1½-inch cubes

one 15-ounce can beef stock

1 cup red wine or ½ cup port

2 to 3 parsnips, chopped into bite-size pieces (about 1 cup)

2 to 3 medium to large carrots, chopped into bite-size pieces (about 1 cup)

½ cup whole pitted black olives

zest of half a lemon (save the other half to use in the poaching liquid for dessert)

salt and freshly ground pepper

SPICY LAMB STEW

This is a spicy California version of my Irish grandmother's lamb stew. Serve it over very buttery mashed potatoes for a hearty one-bowl meal. You can add a side of greens—such as chard—sautéed in olive oil with a little garlic and finished with a squeeze of lemon. A simple spinach or watercress salad with red wine vinaigrette is also nice.

Heat a large dutch oven or deep sauté pan over medium-high heat and add olive oil.

Add chopped onions and sauté until translucent, 1 to 2 minutes. Add curry and cumin, stir, and sauté 1 to 2 minutes more to release the flavors and aromas from the spices.

Brown the lamb in two batches. Return all meat to the pan.

Add beef stock, wine or port, parsnips, and carrots. Bring to a boil and simmer, covered, on low heat (or transfer to a preheated 350 degree oven) for 1 hour.

Add olives and lemon zest. Taste and season with salt and freshly ground pepper. Cook (or bake) uncovered until lamb is fully tender, about 15 to 20 minutes more. Serve over very buttery mashed potatoes.

PEARS POACHED IN RED WINE

Beautiful to serve and easy to prepare, pears poached in red wine are a favorite dessert in fall and winter. I like Bosc pears, which have pretty long necks and retain their shape well. I use either red wine or port to flavor the poaching liquid. When using port, you can reduce the sugar a bit or use up to a cup of water.

In a covered saucepan large enough to hold the pears in a single layer, place the pear peels, sugar, wine, cinnamon, and zest. Bring to a boil. Reduce heat and simmer 5 to 10 minutes. Remove pear peels and discard.

With a slotted spoon, gently add the pears to the poaching liquid. If necessary, add more wine or water to completely cover the pears. A small plate, set over the pears, will help keep them submerged. Leave the cover ajar and simmer gently 15 to 20 minutes or until a skewer poked into a pear center meets little resistance.

Using the slotted spoon, remove the pears from their liquid and stand upright in a serving dish deep enough for the reduced liquid to be poured over. Remove zest and cinnamon stick (or strain liquid) and continue simmering to reduce the liquid to a syrupy consistency.

Pour syrup over the pears. Serve room temperature or chilled from the refrigerator. These pears are delicious served simply with their syrup, or serve them with a scoop of vanilla ice cream or a light, lemony cookie.

SERVES 4 TO 8

4 firm pears, washed, peeled (reserve peels), stems intact

¾ cup sugar

3 cups good red wine or port

1 cinnamon stick (2 inch)

Large strips of orange or lemon zest (use zest from the other half of the stew lemon)

KAREN MITCHELL OF THE MODEL BAKERY

"Our philosophy is that you shouldn't deprive yourself of good food—just moderate."

"SURVIVAL IS SIMPLE," says Karen Mitchell, "all I need is my daily bread! That's part ritual and part comfort food for me." For the owner of St. Helena's Model Bakery, the availability of yummy hearth-baked breads is not a problem. "We're baking bread in the same brick ovens Italian masons built decades ago," says Karen. Her passion for bread is truly the Napa Valley's good fortune!

In the food business for twenty-five years, and a caterer for many of them, the philosophy she's developed is a simple one and is shared by her husband, John: "Our philosophy is that you shouldn't deprive yourself of good food. Just moderate—but it's ok to really treat yourself every once in awhile." As you may have guessed, bread isn't all that she bakes... there are those deadly chocolate "rad" cookies and those gooey sticky buns.

Exercise... did anyone say exercise? With all that bread and all those sweets, both she and John do still manage to stay fit. Karen says, "We belong to a local gym for those days when we need a little extra motivation and structure to exercise. If we didn't, all those carbs might catch up with us! But we also take advantage of many outdoor activities that are right at our fingertips particularly when we take a break at our Lake Tahoe cabin." John adds, "When I get a break from work and can get Karen away from the bakery, we head up to the lake to fly fish and mountain bike. There are wonderful streams and trails everywhere." "And we walk a lot," says Karen. "Whether it's Tahoe or Napa Vally, the area is great for that."

"As for meals at home," says Karen, "we stay happy and healthy with a relaxed style of cooking." In the summer their meals are centered around the abundance of Karen's organic vegetable garden. "After a long day at the bakery, it's a pleasure to come home and 'shop' for dinner in my own garden. I take a big colander out and pick what's ready. In the fall we are lucky to find fresh wild mushrooms in our local farmer's markets or from our friends who forage."

Karen and John even have a small Syrah vineyard on their property. John says, "We're fortunate to have our own small vineyard with the wine made by the Livingstons. We have a glass or two with each evening's meal. We drink while preparing dinner—it helps us unwind, slow down from the busy day full with activity." There's the key: to slow down enough to enjoy good food, good wine, and each other.

Spring ~ Summer

Fresh Tomato Salad with Basil

Grilled Salmon with Cucumber Raita

Grilled Eggplant with Fresh Ricotta

Summer Peaches Baked with Almond Macaroons

Robert Mondavi Fumé Blanc
Swanson Rosato
Bandol

Fall ~ Winter

Risotto with Fall Mushrooms

New York Strip Steak with Roquefort Butter *or*

Butterflied Leg of Lamb with Black Olive Tapenade

Roasted, Stuffed Red Peppers

Caramel Pears

Joseph Phelps Vin du Mistral (a Rhône blend with Syrah)
Syrah

GRILLED SALMON WITH CUCUMBER RAITA

Lightly salt cucumbers, toss, and place in a colander for ½ hour to release juices and drain.

In a medium bowl, combine cucumbers, yogurt, pepper, lemon juice, garlic, and herbs. Chill until ready to serve.

Preheat grill to medium heat.

Rub olive oil and coarsely ground pepper over salmon. Cover the top of the fish with dill. Sprinkle some dill sprigs over coals just before placing salmon on grill. Cover grill and cook through without turning, approximately 20 to 30 minutes. Salmon should be firm to the touch and pink (not opaque).

Serve with the Cucumber Raita.

GRILLED EGGPLANT WITH FRESH RICOTTA

Preheat grill to medium heat.

Brush eggplants with olive oil and grill until golden and soft, or broil 4 inches from the heat, about 3 to 4 minutes a side. Remove from heat. Season with salt and pepper. Spread each slice with fresh ricotta cheese. Roll loosely from bottom to top and arrange on serving platter. Drizzle lightly with balsamic vinegar, and sprinkle with basil.

SUMMER PEACHES BAKED WITH ALMOND MACAROONS

Preheat oven to 375 degrees.

Arrange peach halves cut side up in a greased baking dish large enough for peaches to fit in a single layer. Fill each peach half with macaroons, dot with butter, and add a dash of wine.

Bake until golden brown, approximately 20 to 30 minutes. Spoon pan juices over each peach after baking. Serve with fresh cream or ice cream.

RISOTTO WITH FALL MUSHROOMS

Fall mushrooms, like porcini and chanterelles, are wonderful treasures and deserve the careful preparation of a good risotto. This is soul food for me. I even love the leftovers for breakfast!

Heat chicken stock in a medium saucepan, cover, and keep warm.

In a separate medium saucepan over medium heat, sauté mushrooms in 1 tablespoon olive oil until most of the liquid has evaporated, about 3 to 5 minutes. Add garlic and sauté quickly until the garlic releases its aroma, about 1 minute. Remove from pan and set aside.

In the same pan, sauté onions in the remaining olive oil until golden, add rice, and stir until rice has a chalky appearance. Add wine, and stir until all the liquid is absorbed. Add ½ cup of chicken stock at a time, stirring until it is incorporated before adding more. Continue adding the chicken stock until all is absorbed except the last ½ cup, approximately 20 minutes. Check the rice for doneness—it should be plump, yet firm, and the mixture should appear creamy.

Add mushrooms and then the remaining broth. Stir until the broth is absorbed. Remove from heat. Add parsley and ½ cup grated cheese. Add salt and pepper to taste.

Serve in warm bowls and pass the remaining grated cheese.

SERVES 4 AS A SIDE DISH OR 2 AS AN ENTRÉE

½ pound fresh porcini, chanterelles, or other fall mushrooms, cleaned and thinly sliced

1 medium onion, peeled and diced small

2 tablespoons olive oil

1 clove garlic, minced

1½ cups arborio (short grained) rice

½ cup white wine

4 to 5 cups fresh chicken broth, or canned low-sodium chicken broth

½ cup chopped (flat-leaf) Italian parsley

1 cup freshly grated Parmesan or Romano cheese

salt and freshly ground pepper to taste

NEW YORK STRIP STEAK WITH ROQUEFORT BUTTER

Preheat grill or broiler.

Rub steak with olive oil and pepper. Place on grill or on broiler pan under boiler and sear on one side and turn. Grill or broil to desired doneness. Slice into thin strips and serve with Roquefort Butter (recipe follows).

SERVES 4

1½ to 2 pounds New York strip, cut 2 to 3 inches thick

2 tablespoons olive oil

coarsely ground pepper to taste

ROQUEFORT BUTTER

Mix well in a medium bowl and set aside until ready to serve.

¼ pound Roquefort cheese or aged blue cheese

3 tablespoons unsalted, sweet butter

coarsely ground pepper to taste

1 tablespoon red wine

MARINADE:

2 cups Syrah or other red wine

2 teaspoons freshly ground black pepper

3 cloves fresh garlic, peeled and crushed

3 tablespoons minced fresh rosemary

2 tablespoons olive oil

4- to 5-pound leg of lamb, boned and trimmed to 2 to 2½ inch thickness

1 cup Kalamata or Nicoise olives, pitted

1½ cloves garlic, finely minced

3 tablespoons olive oil

3 to 4 anchovy filets, rinsed

2 tablespoons fresh lemon juice

freshly ground pepper to taste

1 tablespoon brandy or Cognac

2 tablespoons capers, drained

COOK'S HINT: Use any leftover tapenade to top bruschetta as an appetizer for tomorrow's dinner.

BUTTERFLIED LEG OF LAMB WITH BLACK OLIVE TAPENADE

In a medium bowl, whisk together Syrah, pepper, garlic, rosemary, and olive oil.

Place lamb in a non-reactive dish and cover with marinade. Refrigerate overnight or at least 1 hour before cooking.

Preheat grill to medium heat or preheat broiler. Grill flat, approximately 15 to 20 minutes a side: skin/fat side down for 15 to 20 minutes, turn and finish grilling for another 15 to 20 minutes until medium rare or desired doneness (45 to 60 minutes total). Or broil starting with skin side up in broiler pan 5 inches from heat until well seared—about 12 to 15 minutes per side (24 to 30 minutes total). Let stand covered with foil for 5 to 10 minutes before carving, to allow juices to reabsorb.

Slice ½ inch thick and serve with Black Olive Tapenade (recipe follows).

BLACK OLIVE TAPENADE

Purée olives, garlic, olive oil, anchovy filets, lemon juice, pepper, and brandy in food processor or blender until smooth. Add capers and pulse to incorporate. Adjust seasoning. Serve with lamb.

ROASTED, STUFFED RED PEPPERS

In the fall, large meaty red bell peppers are plentiful in the Valley. We often grill them with steaks or chops and slice them into thick pieces, drizzled with fruity olive oil and sprinkled with herbs and garlic. If you have the time, stuffed, roasted peppers are a hearty accompaniment to your main course.

Preheat oven to 375 degrees.

In a medium-size saucepan over medium heat, sauté onion in 1 tablespoon olive oil until translucent, about 3 to 5 minutes. Add garlic and cook until it releases its aroma, 1 to 2 minutes. Remove from heat and add herbs, breadcrumbs, olives, and Parmesan cheese.

Arrange peppers, cut side up, in a greased gratin dish large enough to fit the peppers in a single layer. Fill each pepper half with some of the bread crumb mixture. Drizzle with remaining 1 tablespoon olive oil. Bake for 30 minutes or until lightly browned.

Can be served hot from the oven or at room temperature.

SERVES 4

1 small onion, peeled and diced
2 tablespoons olive oil
2 cloves garlic, peeled and minced
2 tablespoons chopped fresh parsley
2 tablespoons chopped fresh basil or oregano
2 cups breadcrumbs (or cooked rice)
½ cup sliced black olives, Kalamata or Nicoise
½ cup freshly grated Parmesan cheese
4 large red bell peppers, halved, cored, and seeded

CARAMEL PEARS

This is an excellent and simple dessert for a busy lifestyle. When we have time to linger over dessert, we love to drink a dessert wine such as Far Niente Dolce or Joseph Phelps Eisrebe.

Preheat oven to 350 degrees.

Arrange pear halves in greased baking dish. Sprinkle lemon juice on each half, followed by a dot of butter and ½ teaspoon of sugar. Bake until golden, approximately 20 to 30 minutes spooning juices over pears while baking. Remove from oven.

Pour juices into a small saucepan and heat slowly on low heat. When the mixture starts to caramelize and turn brown (take care not to let it burn) add cream and stir well. Keep cooking until the sauce is thick and caramel colored. Pour over baked pear halves. Sprinkle with almonds, and serve.

SERVES 8

4 firm Bartlett pears, peeled, cored, and halved
1 tablespoon fresh lemon juice
2 tablespoons unsalted, sweet butter
4 teaspoons sugar
1 cup heavy cream or half-and-half
¼ cup sliced almonds, lightly toasted

ROBERT MONDAVI AND MARGRIT BIEVER MONDAVI OF ROBERT MONDAVI WINERY

"The more we learn and experience together, the more we are reminded that simple pleasures really are the best."

"THE LIFESTYLE WE ENJOY isn't only about food and wine, it's about art as well," says Margrit. "I can thank my Swiss parents for showing me by example how they decorated—not the house, but their lives." Robert and Margrit are not only the consummate example of the gracious art of living, they are equally as anxious to share it with everyone.

"A great concern of mine is the way young people compromise their health to achieve an enjoyable lifestyle," Margrit says. "Among other things, it has a lot to do with how they view food. It's almost as if it's the enemy; they miss the point, the reason food exists in the first place—to nourish our bodies. Young girls seem to think it's all about being thin when what's really important is choosing the right foods, being able to enjoy mealtime, and being healthy so that you can truly enjoy life's many other pleasures."

For both Robert and Margrit, personal fulfillment at this stage of their lives has become increasingly spiritual. Robert, however, is still very much attuned to what's happening with the wine business. At eighty-six years of age, he still goes to his office at the flagship winery in Oakville each day when he's not on the road. "The trouble with me," says Robert, "is I'm usually thinking more about what might happen in ten years than I am about what I'm doing right now."

As for his personal philosophy, he says, "when I look at the world at large, when I look at human beings, I've found, generally speaking, that they are not willing to put the time and effort into things like people used to when I was growing up. They don't seem to put their heart and soul into the effort, nor do they seem to have the confidence in themselves." He continues, "Personally I believe that if you have faith in yourself, and you stay with it, you'll eventually have success. That's exactly what I feel has happened in my life."

Margrit is the cook in the family, although she will occasionally allow Robert into the kitchen. "After he's been to the cellar to pick out our wine for the evening, Robert may help me put the finishing touches on the meal," says Margrit. Robert and Margrit believe that good food and good wine is not only a way of life, it is the business of life. For the couple who have had quite a hand in defining "the good life," Margrit notes that "the more we learn and experience together, the more we are reminded that simple pleasures really are the best."

Spring ~ Summer

Chinese-Inspired Noodle Bowl with Chicken Broth

Halibut on Fig Leaves with Ratatouille

Moscato D'Oro Jellee with Fresh Berries

Robert Mondavi Carneros Chardonnay
La Famiglia de Robert Mondavi Pinot Grigio
or a fruity Pinot Blanc

Fall ~ Winter

Avocado Soup

Pinot Noir Duck Breast

Brown Rice Pilaf with Golden Raisins and Pine Nuts

Winter Apple Tart with Whipped Cream

Robert Mondavi Pinot Noir, Reserve
or a rich Cabernet Sauvignon

CHINESE-INSPIRED NOODLE BOWL WITH CHICKEN BROTH

SERVES 6 TO 8

2 tablespoons olive oil

1 medium onion, peeled and quartered

2 celery stalks, chopped into large pieces

2 carrots, peeled and chopped into large pieces

1 stalk lemon grass, trimmed and slightly crushed (optional)

1 green bell pepper, cored, seeded, and quartered

½ jalapeño pepper, seeded

3 cloves garlic, peeled and slightly crushed

1 whole chicken

4 tomatoes, peeled, seeded—3 quartered, 1 diced

salt and pepper to taste

1 pound dried angel hair pasta

zest of 1 lemon, thin strips

4 teaspoons chopped fresh chives

wedge of good quality Parmesan cheese

For this recipe, I was inspired by a Chinese cook. To me it is the lightest and most flavorful chicken broth.

In a non-reactive large stock pot, heat 1 tablespoon olive oil over medium heat. Add onion, celery, and carrots, and sauté for 1 to 2 minutes. Add lemon grass, bell pepper, jalapeño pepper, and garlic. Sauté until the garlic releases its aroma, 1 to 2 minutes. Add 1 quart water. Stir. Add chicken and enough additional water to cover chicken. Cover pot, bring to a boil, and boil vigorously for 3 minutes. Reduce heat and simmer for 30 to 45 minutes. Remove from heat. Let cool to room temperature. Place in refrigerator overnight.

Remove any fat that has accumulated on the surface of the broth. Remove the chicken from the broth and set aside. Strain the broth into a medium-size saucepan and warm over medium heat. Add quartered tomatoes and salt and pepper.

Bring to a boil and add angel hair pasta. Cook for length of time according to manufacturer's directions. With pasta tongs, remove pasta to a warm bowl. Drizzle remaining 1 tablespoon olive oil over pasta and toss gently. Set aside.

In the bottom of each of 4 bowls, place a few strips of lemon zest. Ladle soup into bowl and some of the pasta. Sprinkle each bowl with 1 to 2 tablespoons diced tomatoes and 1 teaspoon chives.

Pass a wedge of Parmesan cheese with a grater.

1996
NAPA VALLEY
PINOT NOIR
RESERVE
UNFILTERED
ROBERT MONDAVI WINERY
e750ml
PRODUCED AND BOTTLED BY ROBERT MONDAVI WINERY
OAKVILLE, CALIFORNIA, PRODUCE OF USA
Alc. 13.5% Vol.

HALIBUT ON FIG LEAVES WITH RATATOUILLE

Preheat oven to 400 degrees.

In small sauté pan over medium heat, sauté shallots in 1 tablespoon olive oil until translucent, 3 to 5 minutes. Add pepper and garlic and sauté until garlic releases its aroma, 1 to 2 minutes. Remove from heat. Add remaining olive oil, lemon juice, vinegar, and salt and pepper. Reserve.

Lay 4 fig leaves (or more if leaves are smaller) on a sheet pan and lightly brush with olive oil. Cut halibut into individual serving pieces, about 6 ounces each, and place on fig leaves. Brush with olive oil, and sprinkle with lemon juice, and lightly salt and pepper.

Bake for 5 to 8 minutes. Test for doneness—fish should be opaque throughout and moist (take care not to overcook, or fish will dry out).

Place fresh fig leaves on a warm serving platter and cooked halibut on top. Drizzle about 2 tablespoons of sauce over each fish portion. Sprinkle with cilantro. Serve with Ratatouille (recipe follows).

RATATOUILLE

I especially like this side dish when made with first-of-the-season, tender, young vegetables.

In a large pan over medium heat, lightly sauté the onion in olive oil until translucent, 3 to 5 minutes. Add the garlic and continue to sauté until the garlic releases its aroma, 1 to 2 minutes. Add the green pepper, eggplant, yellow squash, zucchini, and salt and pepper, and sauté to soften vegetables, 5 to 10 minutes. Stir in parsley, oregano, and hot pepper, and sauté for 1 minute longer.

Add the tomatoes and cook uncovered until the vegetables are tender-crisp, about 15 minutes. Add basil, adjust the seasoning, and serve hot or at room temperature.

SERVES 4

SAUCE:

1 shallot, peeled and minced

⅓ cup fruity, extra-virgin olive oil

1 teaspoon minced, seeded jalapeño pepper

2 garlic cloves, peeled and minced

1 tablespoon fresh lemon juice

¼ teaspoon balsamic vinegar

salt and freshly ground pepper to taste

8 large fig leaves (or more, depending on size)

1½ to 2 pounds fresh halibut

2 tablespoons olive oil

1 tablespoon lemon juice

salt and freshly ground pepper to taste

1 tablespoon chopped cilantro

SERVES 4 TO 6

1 medium red onion, peeled and diced

2 tablespoons extra-virgin olive oil

1 clove garlic, minced

1 medium green bell pepper, cored, seeded, and diced

1 medium eggplant, trimmed and diced

2 small yellow crookneck squash, trimmed and diced

2 small zucchini, trimmed and diced

salt and freshly ground pepper to taste

1 tablespoon chopped fresh Italian flat-leaf parsley

1 tablespoon fresh oregano leaves

1 small dried hot pepper, crushed

2 pounds vine-ripe tomatoes, cored, seeded, and diced

2 tablespoons chopped fresh basil

JELLEE:

1 envelope Knox gelatin, or equivalent amount of gelatin leaf

1 bottle (500cc) Moscato d'Oro, Robert Mondavi, or other dessert wine

½ teaspoon finely minced lemon zest

1 teaspoon freshly squeezed lemon juice

½ cup superfine sugar

4 cups mixed fresh berries like strawberries, raspberries, blackberries, and blueberries, rinsed

½ cup thinly sliced mint leaves

MOSCATO D'ORO JELLEE WITH FRESH BERRIES

I often make this easy and fun dessert which was inspired by my daughter, Chef Annie Roberts of Robert Mondavi Winery.

In a small saucepan over low heat, dissolve gelatin in 1 cup of Moscato d'Oro. (Do not to let mixture boil.) Add lemon zest, lemon juice, sugar, and remaining wine. Stir just until the sugar is dissolved. Remove from heat.

Rinse ring mold with cold water and dry. Fill mold with Moscato mixture and refrigerate for at least 4 hours or overnight.

Unmold jellee. Dice or slice equally into 8 portions. Place a ½ cup of fresh berries in each serving bowl and top with jellee and a sprinkle of mint. Serve.

SERVES 6 TO 8

2 carrots, peeled and finely diced

1 onion, peeled and finely diced

2 stalks celery, peeled and finely diced

1 tablespoon unsalted butter

3 cloves garlic, peeled

5 cups fresh chicken stock, or low-sodium canned chicken broth

3 sprigs parsley, with stems

2 large avocados, ripe yet firm, peeled, diced into ½-inch cubes

2 tablespoons dry sherry

AVOCADO SOUP

This soup is a favorite in the fall. It can be served as a first course or poured into mugs and served around the fireplace before sitting down to dinner.

In a medium saucepan, sauté carrots, onion, and celery in butter over medium-low heat until softened, 10 to 15 minutes. Add garlic and sauté until garlic releases its aroma, 1 to 2 minutes. Add chicken stock and parsley and bring to a simmer. Simmer to heat through, about 5 minutes. Remove from heat. Remove garlic cloves and parsley sprigs. Add avocado and sherry. Serve.

PINOT NOIR DUCK BREAST

The hearty-flavored Pinot Noir sauce makes this a wonderful cold weather dish. We're lucky in the Napa Valley to have fresh herbs year-round. If they're not available, good quality dried herbs work just as well in this recipe.

Score the duck skin in a crosshatch pattern (do not cut into the flesh). Place in a large glass dish that will hold the duck pieces in a single layer.

In a small bowl, whisk together Pinot Noir, green onions, garlic, parsley, thyme, marjoram, bay leaf, salt, and cracked pepper. Pour over duck. Cover with plastic wrap and marinate at least one hour or overnight. (If overnight, let the duck come to room temperature before cooking.)

In medium saucepan, quickly sauté shallot in olive oil over medium-high heat. Add garlic and sauté briefly, just until the garlic releases its aroma. Stir in thyme, marjoram, bay leaf, and peppercorns. Add Pinot Noir, balsamic vinegar, and tomatoes and reduce liquid by half, about 5 minutes. Add stock, reduce by half again, about 5 minutes more. Remove from heat, strain into a separate saucepan, and reserve.

Preheat the oven to 400 degrees.

Heat a nonstick sauté pan over medium-high heat. Drain the duck and pat dry. Sear the duck breasts skin side down until browned, about 5 to 10 minutes.

Place the duck breasts, skin side up, in a baking dish or on a sheet pan, and bake until medium-rare, about 10 to 15 minutes, or to desired doneness. Remove duck from oven, cover with foil, and let stand.

Heat the strained sauce over medium-low heat. When the sauce is warm, swirl in the butter a little at a time. Adjust seasonings.

Remove skin from duck breast (if desired) and slice duck ¼ inch thick on a diagonal. Arrange on a warm platter surrounded with a small amount of sauce. Serve, passing extra sauce.

SERVES 4

2 whole Long Island (or comparable) duck breasts

MARINADE:

1 cup Pinot Noir

2 green onions, thinly sliced, including ½ of the green stalk

1 fresh garlic clove, crushed

1 tablespoon chopped fresh Italian flat-leaf parsley

1 tablespoon chopped fresh thyme, or 1 teaspoon dried

1 tablespoon chopped fresh marjoram, or 1 teaspoon dried

1 bay leaf

1 tablespoon sea salt

1 tablespoon cracked black pepper

SAUCE:

1 shallot, peeled and minced

1 teaspoon olive oil

1 clove garlic, minced

2 teaspoons fresh thyme leaves, or 1 teaspoon dried

1 teaspoon fresh marjoram leaves, or ½ teaspoon dried

½ bay leaf

1 tablespoon peppercorns

1 cup Pinot Noir

2 tablespoons balsamic vinegar

one 6-ounce can diced tomatoes, drained

1 cup duck or chicken stock, or canned low-sodium chicken broth

1 tablespoon unsalted butter

salt and freshly ground pepper to taste

1 tablespoon unsalted butter

1 tablespoon canola oil

1 shallot, peeled and minced

1 cup brown rice

2¼ cups fresh chicken broth, or low-sodium canned chicken broth

½ bay leaf

½ teaspoon salt

½ teaspoon freshly ground pepper

¼ cup golden raisins, soaked in warm water until plump, drained

¼ cup pine nuts, toasted

BROWN RICE PILAF WITH GOLDEN RAISINS AND PINE NUTS

Heat butter and canola oil in a medium-size saucepan over medium-high heat. Add shallot and sauté until translucent, about 3 minutes. Stir in rice until incorporated. Add chicken broth, bay leaf, salt, and pepper. Reduce heat to low. Cover and simmer for 40 to 45 minutes or until rice is tender. Remove from heat. Gently mix in raisins and pine nuts while fluffing gently with a fork. Serve.

PASTRY:

10 tablespoons unsalted butter

1⅔ cups all-purpose flour

⅛ teaspoon salt

1 tablespoon cold water, or more as needed

FILLING:

6 large apples

1 teaspoon ground cinnamon

¼ teaspoon cardamom

¼ cup sugar

GLAZE:

¼ cup apricot jam, puréed

2 tablespoons lemon juice

½ teaspoon finely minced lemon zest

1 tablespoon brandy

1 cup heavy cream

½ teaspoon vanilla extract

1 teaspoon superfine sugar

WINTER APPLE TART WITH WHIPPED CREAM

Preheat oven to 400 degrees.

In a large bowl, mix together butter, flour, and salt with a fork or pastry cutter. Add water and continue mixing. Add more water as necessary just until the mixture sticks together. Form dough into a flattened disk. Place in freezer until cool. Cut dough in half and roll out both halves. Place in two 8-inch linzer pans. Prick dough with fork and bake until golden brown, about 15 to 20 minutes. (Check crust periodically and prick with fork if it begins to puff.) Remove from oven and set aside to cool.

Peel and chop three of the apples. Place in a small saucepan with a small amount of water and cook over medium heat until soft, about 5 minutes. Purée in a food processor. Add cinnamon, cardamom, and sugar. Spread mixture evenly over bottom of tart pans.

Peel remaining three apples and slice thinly. Arrange slices in circular design over apple mixture.

Combine apricot jam, lemon juice, lemon zest, and brandy.

Spread glaze over apple slices and bake about 15 minutes or until apples are tender. Serve warm or cooled with Whipped Cream (recipe follows).

WHIPPED CREAM

In a small bowl, whip cream until it begins to thicken, then add vanilla. Continue to whip, and gradually add sugar. Whip until stiff peaks form.

THE NOVAKS OF SPOTTSWOODE WINERY

"If there's a wine that intrigues you but you don't know much about it, take a chance."

"EVEN THOUGH I'M a skiing fanatic, I finally had to give up on the idea of heli-skiing," says Mary Novak. "But I think I've found the next best thing. A group of friends and I are on our way to try helihiking in the Bugaboos, our latest adventure!" When Mary's not exploring a faraway destination on foot, you'll find her walking her two mile loop each morning in the Napa Valley. Mary says, "I've been an outdoor person all my life. From the days when I gardened back in Brentwood, a suburb of Los Angeles that was very rural at that time, to a lot of social tennis and now even golf." All five of her children, now grown and most with families of their own, have a keen appreciation for nature and are fond of outdoor pursuits.

"To me, incorporating a lot of activity into my day really keeps me going, as does the inspiration I get from feeling the moistness of the earth as I plant and weed the vegetable and herb garden I now have at Spottswoode." The Valley affords a lot of inspiration to many in this way. And Mary's cooking is reflected by what's fresh and available as she takes a quick stroll through the garden before mealtime.

"And wine," says Mary, "is actually something I became enamored of once we moved from Southern California to the Valley." She continues, "I can still remember in the late 1960s drinking a little bit of Lancers, Mateus, and Blue Nun. Once we moved here, we started to be able to appreciate real quality in wine and began to drink better and better wine."

It was Mary's late husband that encouraged the move from San Diego County in 1972. "Once we were here, we planted a few acres of grapes to sell initially. Then, the winemaking came out of that. And here I am today!" Mary will tell you that with the lifestyle that has evolved through the years, a meal won't be the experience it could be without a bottle of wine on the table.

"Everyone should be so fortunate as I to be surrounded by such a wonderful family, great food, and delicious wine," says Mary. "And as for the wine, it's really much easier today than it ever has been to find good quality bottles not only throughout the United States, but all over the world." She continues, "One thing my travels have taught me is to continue to be curious and take a few risks. If there's a wine that intrigues you but you don't know much about it, take a chance. All that can happen is that you might learn something and you'll likely enjoy every drop!"

Spring ~ Summer

Green Salad with Fresh Corn and Pine Nuts

Linguini with Tomatoes, Mushroom Brie, and Basil

Loaf of Crusty, Hearty Bread

Fresh Peaches and Berries with Lemon

Spottswoode Sauvignon Blanc
Shafer Firebreak

Fall ~ Winter

Salad of Winter Garden Greens

Novak Family Pot Roast

Sourdough Bread

Almond Tart

Spottswoode Cabernet Sauvignon
Nalle Napa Valley Zinfandel

SERVES 6 TO 8

4 large vine-ripened tomatoes, cored, seeded, diced into ½-inch pieces, and drained

¾ pound mushroom Brie cheese, rind removed, and diced into ½-inch pieces or torn into small pieces (regular Brie or other semi-soft cheese can be substituted)

1½ cups fresh basil leaves, sliced into ribbons

2 garlic cloves, peeled and finely minced

½ cup and 1 tablespoon fruity, extra-virgin olive oil

1½ teaspoons coarsely ground sea salt

1 teaspoon freshly ground black pepper

1½ pounds fresh or dried linguini

LINGUINI WITH TOMATOES, MUSHROOM BRIE, AND BASIL

This recipe is a mainstay in my kitchen. It's so delicious the comments from my kids are, "totally awesome, great!" And best of all it's a snap to make on a hot, lazy, summer day. To round out the menu, I usually serve a salad with fresh garden greens, tossing in a handful of freshly steamed and cooled corn kernels and toasted pine nuts. The vinaigrette varies, and most often I'll use either balsamic or rice vinegar and always a good fruity, extra virgin olive oil.

In a large serving bowl, combine tomatoes, cheese, basil, garlic, ½ cup olive oil, ½ teaspoon salt, and pepper. Cover and set aside at room temperature 1 to 2 hours.

Bring a large pot of water to boil and add 1 tablespoon olive oil and remaining salt. Add the linguini and boil until al dente, 3 to 4 minutes for fresh lingiuni and 8 to 10 minutes for dried. Drain. Toss with the tomato sauce and serve.

SERVES 6 TO 8

5 large fresh peaches, sliced

½ pint fresh raspberries, rinsed and drained

½ pint fresh blueberries, rinsed and drained

1 lemon, juice

¼ teaspoon lemon zest

FRESH PEACHES AND BERRIES WITH LEMON

I like to take advantage of the bounty of fresh fruit that comes our way during the summer months. Highlighting good ingredients and keeping it simple are important and is reflected in my relaxed style of cooking and entertaining. If available, try using white-flesh peaches in this easy summer dessert.

Combine all fruit in a large serving bowl. Toss with lemon juice a few minutes before serving. Sprinkle with zest.

NOVAK FAMILY POT ROAST

The ultimate comfort food for my family is an old-fashioned pot roast. I made this recipe a couple of years ago for a family gathering, and it's been the most requested menu item ever since! Slow cooking is the key to rich, moist pot roast, so choose a wide, flat cut of beef over a high, round one—it cooks faster and better accomodates a hectic schedule. I usually serve a salad of mixed winter greens that might include, among others, mizuna, oak leaf, arugula, and radicchio tossed with a simple vinaigrette made with olive oil and red wine vinegar and a little Dijon mustard. I usually throw in some roasted pine nuts—I love the flavor they give and use them wherever I can.

Rinse and pat roast dry, season with salt and pepper, and dust with 1 tablespoon of flour. Heat oil in a heavy Dutch oven over medium-high heat. Add the roast and brown on all sides, about 15 to 20 minutes. Remove the meat to a platter. Pour off all but 2 tablespoons of fat from the pot and heat again over medium-high heat. Add onions, celery, carrots, and leeks, stirring just until they begin to lightly brown, about 4 to 5 minutes. Add garlic and cook until it releases its aroma, 1 to 2 minutes. Add 1 cup of wine and ½ cup stock. Bring to a boil and add bay leaf, thyme, and rosemary.

Return the roast to the pan and cover with a tightly-fitting lid. Reduce heat to its lowest setting and simmer very slowly, turning the roast every 30 minutes, for 1½ to 2½ hours, depending on the thickness of the roast. Add more stock, wine, or water as needed, making sure there is always some liquid in the pot. During the last 20 minutes of cooking, add potatoes.

When meat and potatoes are tender, remove to a platter and cover with foil to keep warm. Skim off any fat from the surface of the liquid. Strain. Add 1 cup wine. Place over medium-high heat and reduce by one third. Reduce heat.

Optional: To thicken the sauce, stir together and whisk in 1 tablespoon flour and 1 tablespoon butter (for each cup of liquid). Simmer, stirring constantly until thickened.

SERVES 6 TO 10

one 3- to 5-pound beef chuck roast

salt and freshly ground pepper to taste

1 tablespoon flour

2 tablespoons canola oil

2 cups chopped onions, medium diced

½ cup chopped celery, medium diced

½ cup chopped carrots, medium diced

½ cup thickly sliced leeks

4 cloves garlic, peeled and lightly smashed

2 cups red wine like Cabernet Sauvignon or Zinfandel

2 cups beef or vegetable stock, or canned low-sodium broth

1 bay leaf

2 sprigs fresh thyme, or ½ teaspoon dried

1 sprig rosemary

1¼ pound small red potatoes, washed, skin on

PASTRY:

1 cup all-purpose flour

½ cup butter

1 teaspoon vanilla extract

1 to 2 tablespoons cold water

FILLING:

¾ cup heavy cream

¾ cup sugar

2 drops almond extract

1 teaspoon Grand Marnier or Amaretto

2 cups sliced almonds

pinch salt

OPTIONAL: Serve with a dollop of crème fraîche (see page 168) or unsweetened whipped cream.

ALMOND TART

This is a recipe I adapted from a cooking class I attended at Chez Panisse in Berkeley, California, long ago. Whenever I serve this simple, yet delicious dessert for guests, it's always a hit!

Preheat oven to 425 degrees.

In a medium-size bowl, blend all pastry ingredients to form a ball using only enough water to keep ingredients together. The dough may be very soft. Shape it into a disk and refrigerate for a ½ hour. Roll dough out between 2 pieces of floured wax paper large enough to fit slightly over the edge of a tart pan, or pat the dough into a tart pan, making sure the dough's thickness is even all around. Prick lightly with a fork. Bake for 7 minutes or until lightly browned.

In a small pan over low heat, warm the cream and sugar until the sugar is dissolved. Remove from heat. Stir in the almond extract, Grand Marnier, and almonds.

Pour filling into prepared tart shell and spread evenly. Place aluminum foil around the bottom of the tart shell to catch any liquid that may bubble over during cooking. Place on sheet pan and bake 20 to 25 minutes, turning occasionally, until it browns evenly and is golden brown on top.

Remove from oven and let cool slightly. Gently loosen the tart from the pan.

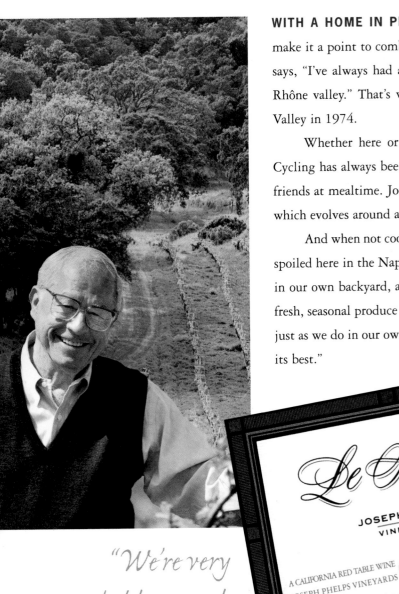

WITH A HOME IN PROVENÇE, France, as well as the Napa Valley, Joe and Lois make it a point to combine their love of food and wine with their surroundings. Joe says, "I've always had a special love for the food of Provençe and the wines of the Rhône valley." That's why Joe introduced one of his favorites, Syrah, to the Napa Valley in 1974.

Whether here or in Provençe, both he and Lois stay as active as they can. Cycling has always been a favorite sport of theirs. And they both enjoy entertaining friends at mealtime. Joe says, "There's no better camaraderie that develops than that which evolves around a good meal and a great bottle of wine."

And when not cooking at home, they both enjoy dining out as well. "We're very spoiled here in the Napa Valley," says Joe. "There are so many good restaurants right in our own backyard, all maintaining such high quality standards when it comes to fresh, seasonal produce and other ingredients. Most rely on very simple preparations, just as we do in our own home kitchen. When the food is good, it's easy to show it at its best."

"We're very spoiled here in the Napa Valley."

Le Mistral

JOSEPH PHELPS
VINEYARDS

A CALIFORNIA RED TABLE WINE
JOSEPH PHELPS VINEYARDS

PRODUCED AND BOTTLED BY
ST. HELENA, CALIFORNIA

Spring ~ Summer

Crusted Sea Bass with Tropical Salsa

Joseph Phelps, Ovation, Chardonnay
Saintsbury Brown Ranch Vineyard, Pinot Noir

Fall ~ Winter

Rib-Eye Steaks with Crushed Peppercorns

Garlic Chive "Smashed" Potatoes

Joseph Phelps, Le Mistral
Ridge Lytton Springs Zinfandel

CRUSTED SEA BASS WITH TROPICAL SALSA

SERVES 4

1½ to 2 pounds fresh sea bass, cut into 4 pieces

½ cup milk

1 cup freshly toasted bread crumbs

1 tablespoons butter

1 tablespoon olive oil

salt and pepper to taste

We enjoy fresh, lively ingredients such as those found in the salsa. And, sea bass in any preparation is a favorite. We usually serve this dish with a simple green salad tossed with a mild vinaigrette. We often have a few tortilla chips with the salsa as an appetizer as we're preparing the dish.

Dip pieces of fish first in milk, then coat with bread crumbs. Heat butter and olive oil in a nonstick sauté pan over medium-high heat. Sauté fish, browning both sides, until cooked through, about 3 minutes a side, depending on the thickness of the fish. Add salt and pepper. Serve with Tropical Salsa (recipe follows).

TROPICAL SALSA

1 medium mango, diced

1 medium papaya, diced

½ pineapple, diced

1 small jalapeño, seeded and finely chopped

2 tablespoons minced red onion

½ cup fresh cilantro leaves, chopped

1 tablespoon freshly squeezed lime juice

This can also be used as a delicious alternative to tomato-based salsa as an accompaniment to tortilla chips.

Mix all ingredients together in a medium bowl. Refrigerate until ready to serve.

RIB-EYE STEAKS WITH CRUSHED PEPPERCORNS

SERVES 4

4 large rib-eye steaks, ¾ to 1 inch thick

salt to taste

1 tablespoon olive oil

3 tablespoons coarsely crushed fresh peppercorns

We eat very simply and usually make dishes that are quick to prepare. The rib-eye steaks and potatoes are real comfort foods for us so we don't mind spending a little extra time for the "smashed" potatoes.

Preheat oven to 500 degrees.

Heat heavy cast iron skillet (preferably with ridges along the bottom) over high heat until very hot, about 5 minutes.

Meanwhile, salt steaks, rub with oil, and press peppercorns onto both sides. Place steaks in pan and sear on both sides, 2 to 3 minutes. Place skillet into oven for about 3 minutes until steaks are medium rare, or longer for desired doneness.

Remove pan from oven. Place steaks on cutting board and allow to rest 5 minutes, covered loosely with foil. Cut crosswise into ½-inch slices.

Serve with Garlic Chive "Smashed" Potatoes (recipe follows).

GARLIC CHIVE "SMASHED" POTATOES

Bring a large pot of water to boil. Add a pinch of salt and potatoes. Simmer about 20 to 25 minutes.

While potatoes are cooking, warm cream (or milk) very slowly in a small saucepan.

Drain potatoes very well and "smash" them with a fork or potato masher, leaving them slightly lumpy. Add cream, 2 tablespoons chives, and salt and pepper. Fold in the blue, garlicky chive blossoms.

SERVES 4

6 medium Yukon Gold potatoes, washed, skins on, quartered

1½ cups heavy cream, half-and-half, or milk

1 bunch chopped garlic chives* with blossoms

salt and freshly ground pepper to taste

*NOTE: If garlic chives are unavailable use 4 whole cloves of garlic: simmer in cream until garlic is soft, about 15 minutes. Remove garlic and stir cream into potatoes.

THE RODENOS OF ST. SUPERY VINEYARDS AND WINERY

"We do our best to make everything as delicious as possible."

"WE ARE BLESSED TO LIVE in the beautiful Napa Valley, where farmer's markets *always* offer organic and sometimes exotic produce," said Michaela Rodeno. "But even with the ingredients at our fingertips, the demands of modern life often make mealtime quite a challenge." Michaela says her solution is to "eat simple, wholesome, easy-to-prepare food in an atmosphere that encourages sharing at mealtimes, always with wine and with a lot of conviviality."

Being Californians, Michaela, her husband Gregory, and their teenagers Kate and John are naturally health conscious. "We eat salads and vegetables. We use little fat in cooking, although we have a family ritual where we treat ourselves to crispy bacon every Sunday morning."

"Our lifestyle has evolved. We use a fraction of the butter we used twenty years ago. But when we do, it's the real thing." Michaela says "We grill poultry, fish, meat, and vegetables (sometimes steaming them, too) either outside on a conventional grill or inside on a great cast iron skillet with ridges. Even though most is simple fare, we do our best to make everything as delicious as possible. For pizza, we use a pizza stone to make the crust crunchier. Many can identify that pizza is a given in a family with kids. You may as well make it good!"

While they do their best to eat balanced meals they also try to stay active. Michaela says, "We think about exercise a lot—that counts for something doesn't it?" At the very least, you'll usually catch Michaela in a game of doubles tennis early on Saturday mornings and usually on horseback on Sundays. Somehow she seems to find time for it all. Gregory says, "We work hard but put even more effort into making time for friends and to protect family time. And of course, we make it a point to drink lots of good wine."

"We truly see ourselves as peasants—enjoying the fruits of the land."

Spring ~ Summer

Heirloom Tomatoes with Fresh Buffalo Milk Mozzarella and Basil

Citrus and Ginger Grilled Chicken

Grilled Mustard-y Red Onions

Fresh Peach Ice Cream

St. Supery Sauvignon Blanc
Swanson Rosato

Fall ~ Winter

Prosciutto with Fall Figs

Rodeno Family Special Chicken with "Melon Seed" Pasta

Kate's Lemon Meringue Pie

St. Supery Red Meritage
Saintsbury Chardonnay
Villa Ragazzi Napa Valley Sangiovese, Rodeno Vineyard

(not yet commercially available)

SERVES 4

1 pound assorted heirloom tomatoes, sliced

½ pound fresh buffalo milk mozzarella, sliced

12 large tender fresh basil leaves, sliced into ribbons

1 tablespoon high-quality balsamic vinegar

2 tablespoons fruity, extra-virgin olive oil

salt and freshly ground pepper to taste

HEIRLOOM TOMATOES WITH
FRESH BUFFALO MILK MOZZARELLA AND BASIL

This is a Rodeno family favorite and a favorite of many in the Napa Valley, not only because it is so simple to make, but because it really shows off the flavors of the tomatoes at their peak. When we can, we shop at our local farmer's market where the selection of many varieties of tomatoes, and other fresh vegetables and herbs, is abundant.

Arrange tomatoes and mozzarella slices, alternating, on a serving platter. Drizzle first with balsamic vinegar and then with olive oil. Sprinkle with salt and freshly ground pepper. Serve.

SERVES 4

6 boneless, skinless chicken breasts

MARINADE:

½ cup freshly squeezed lemon juice

½ cup freshly squeezed orange juice

2 cloves garlic, peeled and minced

2 tablespoons freshly grated ginger

1 tablespoon soy sauce

2 teaspoons sesame oil

½ teaspoon sea salt

¼ teaspoon freshly ground pepper

CITRUS AND GINGER GRILLED CHICKEN

This dish is excellent right off the grill and even for lunch the next day.

Mix all marinade ingredients in a non-reactive bowl.

Place chicken breasts in a shallow glass pan and pour marinade over. Cover and marinate in the refrigerator for 2 to 3 hours, turning occasionally.

Preheat a grill, grill pan, or broiler. If grilling, the fire should be medium. If broiling, the rack should be close to the heat source, about 4 inches. Remove chicken from the marinade. Place on grill or under broiler. Turn 2 to 3 times during cooking, basting with a little marinade each time until it is cooked through, about 15 to 20 minutes total.

Serve with Grilled Mustard-y Red Onions (recipe follows).

SERVES 4

BASTING SAUCE:

4 ounces unsalted butter, melted

3 tablespoons Dijon mustard

2 teaspoons white wine vinegar

1 tablespoon chopped parsley (optional)

3 large red onions, peeled, and cut crosswise into ½-inch thick slices

salt and pepper to taste

GRILLED MUSTARD-Y
RED ONIONS

In a small bowl, mix together all basting sauce ingredients.

Preheat a grill to medium heat. Place onions on grill and grill for ten minutes, until tender and golden but still slightly firm, turning and basting with the sauce several times. Season to taste with salt and pepper, and serve.

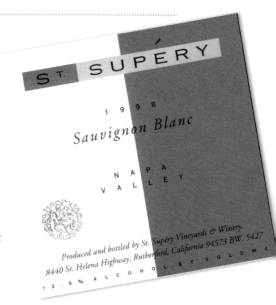

FRESH PEACH ICE CREAM

Homegrown or farmer's market peaches are best in this recipe.

Purée the peaches in a food processor or blender, adding a bit of orange juice to thin purée as needed. Blend in the remaining ingredients and pour into the freezer bowl of an ice cream maker. (Any leftover mix can be stored in the refrigerator for up to 3 days.) Freeze according to manufacturer's instructions.

Place in airtight container and place in freezer for 2 hours before serving.

MAKES TEN ½-CUP SERVINGS

8 to 10 medium, ripe and juicy peaches, peeled, pitted

2 cups heavy cream, chilled

1 cup whole milk, chilled

¾ cup superfine sugar

1 teaspoon vanilla extract

¼ cup orange juice

PROSCIUTTO WITH FALL FIGS

Place eight fig quarters on each salad plate. Drape one quarter of the prosciutto slices beside the figs. Garnish each plate with a sprig of mint and serve.

SERVES 4

8 ripe fresh figs, trimmed and quartered

½ pound Italian prosciutto, sliced paper-thin

4 sprigs tender fresh mint

RODENO FAMILY SPECIAL CHICKEN

This is our son John's absolute favorite dish. He's also our resident oenophile and is justifiably proud of his ability to taste wine and describe it. He'd like to be old enough to drink it, but until then will have to settle for tasting a little at mealtimes with the family.

In a large heavy saucepan, brown the chicken in the butter and canola oil over medium heat. Add wine and simmer until reduced by half, then add stock, lemon juice, and ¼ teaspoon lemon zest. Cover and continue to simmer until chicken is tender and cooked through, about 20 minutes.

Remove chicken and keep warm. Season remaining sauce with salt and pepper. Stir in mustard and bring broth to a boil; reduce sauce to about 1 cup, then lower heat and whisk in the cream.

Place chicken back in the finished sauce and heat through, about 3 to 5 minutes. Serve over "Melon Seed" Pasta (recipe follows) or orzo.

SERVES 4

4 boned and skinned chicken breasts

1 tablespooon unsalted butter

1 tablespoon canola oil

½ cup dry white wine

2 cups canned chicken stock, or low-sodium broth

1 lemon, juice and minced zest

salt and freshly ground pepper to taste

1 tablespoon Dijon mustard

½ cup heavy cream

"MELON SEED" PASTA

Cook pasta according to manufacturer's directions. Toss with a little butter and serve.

SERVES 4

melon seed or orzo pasta (4 servings)

butter

SERVES 8

CRUST:

1½ cups all-purpose flour

½ teaspoon salt

½ cup room temperature shortening

3 tablespoons water

FILLING:

1 cup superfine sugar

5 tablespoons cornstarch

⅛ teaspoon salt

2 cups water

3 beaten egg yolks

3 tablespoons butter

⅓ cup lemon juice

2 teaspoons finely grated lemon zest

MERINGUE:

4 egg whites

¼ teaspoon cream of tartar

1 teaspoon vanilla extract

3 tablespoons sugar

KATE'S LEMON MERINGUE PIE

Our daughter, Kate, is quite the pastry chef! She loves to bake and would do so all day long if there weren't so many activities to distract a 14-year-old. If you can find fresh eggs (we now have four chickens that give us all we need and then some) they can make a delicious difference.

CRUST: Preheat oven to 425 degrees.

In a large bowl, mix the salt into the flour, then cut in the shortening with two knives or a pastry blender. Stir in the water with a fork. Gather the mixture into a ball and roll to fit a 9-inch pie pan or, alternately, pat it evenly into the pan, creating a crimped, decorative edge. Line the pie shell with tin foil and fill it with dried beans to keep it flat. Bake for 12 to15 minutes. Cool. Refrigerate crust until ready to use.

FILLING: In the top of a double boiler, combine the sugar, cornstarch, and salt. Gradually add the water. Stir until the mixture thickens, about 8 to 10 minutes. Cover and cook for ten minutes more, stirring occasionally. Remove from heat.

Place egg yolks in a small bowl and beat lightly. Pour a little of the hot sugar mixture into the egg yolks, beating quickly. Add the egg yolk mixture to the rest of the hot sugar mixture slowly, beating constantly. Place back on double boiler and cook until thick, about 5 minutes.

Remove from heat and beat in butter, lemon juice, and lemon zest. Cool the custard by stirring gently. When room temperature, pour into the cold pie shell.

MERINGUE: Preheat oven to 325 degrees.

Beat the egg whites in a cold copper bowl until frothy. Add the cream of tartar and continue beating until the whites become stiff. Add vanilla and begin adding sugar in a slow stream while still beating. Do not over beat. Spread the meringue in decorative swoops over the pie filling, making sure the meringue touches the pie shell edges all around. Bake for 10 to 15 minutes, until the meringue is delicately golden.

ST. SUPÉRY

1995

MERITAGE

NAPA VALLEY RED WINE

PRODUCED AND BOTTLED BY ST. SUPÉRY VINEYARDS & WINERY
RUTHERFORD CALIFORNIA 94573   13.5% ALCOHOL BY VOLUME

DOUG SHAFER OF SHAFER VINEYARDS

"If I can make it fun, the kids are more willing to try new things."

"AS A SINGLE PARENT WITH three rapidly growing adolescents, mealtime is a continual challenge," says Doug Shafer. With a full-time job running a winery—and all the kids busy with lots of extracurricular activities—planning is a necessity.

"One thing I've found that makes my life simpler when it comes to dinnertime is to plan the menu a week in advance. It may sound elementary but it's saved me a lot of time and hassle. Another 'secret' I've discovered is that if I can make it fun, the kids are more willing to try new things. We'll have theme nights like 'South of the Border' night featuring a make-your-own burrito bar, or we'll have an Italian feast with appropriate music on the CD player. We make appetizers fun by turning them into tastings while making dinner. And of course, as we prepare dinner, a glass of wine for the chef is a must! As the children take an interest in wine," says Doug, "I invite them to taste a little as they want to. I've always made it a normal part of mealtime and feel it's healthy and important for them to realize that."

From his perspective, making it fun and involving all the kids serves not only to make the process easier but also encourages great discussions around the dining room table. "It gives me a chance to catch up with the children and what's going on in each of their worlds."

And what about exercise? "Well, it's important and I wish I could be more consistent as I'm sure all parents with demanding careers would agree. I do get quite a bit of activity in when the children are around. And when I'm not chasing after one of the kids playing soccer, football, one-on-one basketball, volleyball, or playing 'underwater monster' in the pool, I try to do a quick workout a few times a week at the gym or even a few laps in the pool." Walking vineyards also adds physical activity to the day. "I'm often out taking a look at the grapes, and with vineyards in the hills of Stag's Leap—that's a great workout in itself. I play an occasional game of tennis and long for more time to play golf. Family vacations are usually centered around outdoor activities as well. Here in the Napa Valley, there are so many outdoor activities to enjoy many months out of the year, and we have such an abundance of great seasonal produce readily available to us. Still, as I travel throughout the country, I see how people adapt their desire for healthy living to the environment in which they live. And good wine is usually a big part of that!"

Spring ~ Summer

Stephen's Smoothie Bar

Kevin's Grilled Flatbread and Caesar Salad Sandwiches *or*
Dad's Favorite Summer Sandwich

Libby's Best-Ever Chocolate Chip Cookies

Shafer Firebreak
Silverado Reserve Chardonnay

Fall ~ Winter

Chips and Salsa

Citrus-Marinated Red Snapper with "South of the Border" Burritos

Katherine's Flan

Shafer Merlot
Etude Pinot Blanc (Pinot Blanc grapes
grown at Shafer's Red Shoulder Ranch)

STEPHEN'S SMOOTHIE BAR

1½ cups fresh squeezed orange juice

1 cup frozen strawberries (fresh strawberries washed, trimmed, and frozen or packaged frozen)

1 medium banana, peeled and frozen

1 scoop nonfat frozen vanilla yogurt or plain nonfat yogurt

THE HOUSEHOLD FAVORITE

Place all ingredients in a blender and blend on high speed until smooth.

1½ cups nonfat raspberry sorbet

1½ cups frozen blueberries (fresh berries, washed and frozen or packaged frozen)

1 cup lemonade

A VERY-BERRY COMBINATION

Place all ingredients in blender and blend on high speed until smooth.

1½ cups freshly squeezed orange juice

¾ cup orange sections, without pith

2 cups nonfat frozen vanilla yogurt

½ teaspoon vanilla extract

THE ULTIMATE CREAMSICLE COMBO

Place all ingredients in blender and blend on high speed until smooth.

¾ cup apple juice

2 cups vine-ripe fresh frozen cantaloupe pieces

2 tablespoons finely chopped fresh mint

1 tablespoon freshly squeezed lemon juice

1 tablespoon superfine sugar

1 cup crushed ice

ADULT OPTION: Blend in 2 to 4 ounces of vodka.

MINTY MELON MADNESS

Place all ingredients in blender and blend on high speed until smooth.

Shafer

1997
Napa Valley

MERLOT

Produced & Bottled by
Shafer Vineyards, Napa, CA
Alcohol 14.0% by Volume

KEVIN'S GRILLED FLATBREAD AND CAESAR SALAD SANDWICHES

Inspired by a local St. Helena restaurant, Tomatina, piadini—or flatbread and salad sandwiches—are now a mainstay in our household. They're fun to make, and the kids enjoy getting involved helping to make the dough. They often invent new combinations of toppings for these mini pizzas. If time is short, pizza dough can usually be purchased in the freezer section of your local market or from a local pizzeria. No utensils for this recipe—just plenty of napkins!

DOUGH: In a large bowl, mix together yeast, ½ cup flour, and ½ cup warm water. Let stand until the mixture bubbles up and rises slightly, about 20 minutes. Add the remaining 2 cups flour, ½ cup warm water, 1 to 2 tablespoons olive oil, and 1 teaspoon salt. Mix thoroughly and turn the dough out onto a well-floured surface. Knead until smooth and elastic. Place dough in bowl with remaining oil and turn to coat. Cover with plastic wrap and let it rise in a warm place until doubled, about 1 hour. (Or let dough rise in refrigerator overnight, bringing to room temperature before using.)

SAUCE: Place basil in a food processor or blender. Chop with a few pulses. Add garlic, pine nuts, walnuts, balsamic vinegar, lemon juice, and Parmesan. Purée as you drizzle olive oil into the feed tube. Process until smooth. Makes about ¾ cup. (Can be made ahead and refrigerated or frozen.)

DRESSING: In a small bowl, whisk together lemon zest, juice, garlic, soy sauce, and vinegar. Add the olive oil slowly, whisking constantly to incorporate. Add pepper and Parmesan cheese.

Preheat grill to medium heat. Remove dough from the bowl and punch down. Let rest 5 minutes. On a floured work surface, divide the dough into 16 pieces. With a rolling pin, roll each piece of dough into a very thin 7- to 8-inch circle, about 1/16 inch thick. Let rest for 10 minutes.

Place dough pieces on grill and grill them in batches until golden around the edges, turning once. Spread with pesto or your choice of toppings once turned. Flatbreads should be soft enough to fold in half, about 5 to 7 minutes.

Place the lettuce in a large bowl and toss with the dressing. Place salad on top of grilled dough and fold in half. Serve immediately.

SERVES 6 TO 8

DOUGH:

2½ teaspoons dry yeast

2½ to 3 cups all-purpose flour

1 cup warm water

1 teaspoon salt

¼ cup extra-virgin olive oil

SAUCE: (you can substitute pre-made pesto sauce found in the refrigerated section of many markets)

2 cups fresh basil leaves, rinsed and spun dry

3 cloves garlic, peeled

¼ cup pine nuts, lightly toasted

¼ cup walnuts, lightly toasted

1 tablespoon balsamic vinegar

1 tablespoon lemon juice

¼ cup freshly grated Parmesan cheese

¼ cup olive oil

DRESSING:

1 teaspoon finely grated lemon zest

¼ cup freshly squeezed lemon juice

2 cloves garlic, peeled and finely minced

1 tablespoon low-sodium soy sauce

1 teaspoon white wine vinegar

½ cup fruity olive oil

½ teaspoon freshly grated pepper

2 tablespoons freshly grated Parmesan

½ large head romaine lettuce, washed and spun dry

OPTION: Since we always have an overabundance of figs from our trees in the summertime, we've discovered a great way to use them as a flatbread topping: Carmelize sliced onions, add a touch of balsamic vinaigrette, toss in some sliced figs, and place mixture atop flatbread. Sprinkle a little goat cheese over the top, and garnish with thinly sliced mint.

1 vine-ripe tomato, sliced

1 red onion, peeled and thickly sliced

garden fresh lettuce leaves, washed and patted dry

2 tablespoons blue cheese dressing

2 slices sourdough bread, toasted

DAD'S FAVORITE SUMMER SANDWICH

Place tomatoes, red onion, and lettuce leaves on one slice of bread. Drizzle with a little blue cheese dressing and top with other bread slice. Enjoy!

MAKES 60 SMALL COOKIES

1 cup unsalted, sweet butter

2/3 cup golden brown sugar

1 1/3 cup granulated sugar

3 large eggs

2 teaspoons vanilla

3 cups flour

1 teaspoon baking soda

1 teaspoon salt

12 to 24 ounces semi-sweet chocolate chips

1 cup chopped, lightly toasted pecans

1 cup chopped, lightly toasted walnuts

LIBBY'S BEST-EVER CHOCOLATE CHIP COOKIES

A staple with the kids and a definite must every now and then for the adults. Doug's sister Libby shares her secret for what are often the neighborhood's most requested chocolate chip cookies. The real secret to wonderful cookie consistency is to mix the dry ingredients into the wet ingredients, squishing with your fingers—it's great therapy, too!

Preheat oven to 325 degrees.

In a large mixing bowl, cream butter and sugars until light. Beat in eggs, one at a time, and then vanilla until smooth. In a separate bowl, mix together flour, baking soda, and salt. Add to wet ingredient mixture.

Stir in chocolate chips and nuts. Drop onto baking sheets using a small ice cream scoop or dropping 1 tablespoonful at a time. Bake until golden brown, about 12 to 17 minutes. Remove from oven and let cookies cool slightly before removing from baking sheet.

CITRUS MARINATED RED SNAPPER WITH "SOUTH OF THE BORDER" BURRITOS

CITRUS MARINATED RED SNAPPER

Whisk the marinade ingredients together in a small bowl. Place snapper in a glass, flat-bottom dish and pour marinade over. Cover with plastic wrap and refrigerate from 1 hour to overnight.

TO GRILL: Preheat grill to medium heat. Place soaked thyme sprigs on coals, and place snapper in a hinged wire fish basket (if available). Grill, basting often with marinade, about 2½ minutes per side for ½ inch thickness. Remove to warm platter and cover to keep warm.

TO SAUTÉ: Heat olive oil in a non-stick sauté pan over medium-high heat. Drain snapper and place in pan. Sauté until fish is cooked through, turning once, about 3 to 5 minutes.

"SOUTH OF THE BORDER" BURRITOS

This is a crowd-pleaser for even the pickiest eaters since everyone chooses their own filling.

BLACK BEANS: In a small saucepan, sauté onion in olive oil over medium-high heat. When the onion begins to soften, about 3 minutes, add minced garlic and cook until it releases its aroma, about 1 minute. Stir in vinegar and beans. Heat through. Cover and set aside.

Preheat oven to 350 degrees. Wrap tortillas in foil and place in oven about 15 minutes.

Place warm tortillas in a basket with a clean, dry linen towel and cover loosely.

To serve, place all optional filling ingredients as desired, except rice, in small, individual bowls, cover with plastic wrap and refrigerate. Make rice approximately 1 hour before you're ready to serve. Arrange filling ingredients, sour cream, salsas, and lime wedges buffet-style. Hand out plates, and let everyone make their own burrito.

MARINADE:

1 orange, juice and 1 teaspoon zest

1 lemon, juice and 1 teaspoon zest

2 tablespoons olive oil

1 tablespoon minced red onion

2 tablespoons coarsely chopped cilantro

1 tablespoon fresh thyme leaves

2 garlic cloves, peeled and smashed

1 teaspoon dried, ground coriander

thyme sprigs, soaked (if grilling)

1 tablespoon olive oil (if sautéing)

1½ pounds red snapper, boned and skinned

1 small yellow onion, peeled and diced small

1 tablespoon olive oil

1 clove fresh minced garlic

1 tablespoon red wine vinegar

one 15-ounce can whole black beans, drained

1 package 8-inch flour tortillas

OPTIONAL FILLINGS:

1 cup avocado, diced and sprinkled with lime or lemon juice

1 cup diced cucumbers, peeled and seeded

1 cup broccoli florets, steamed and cooled

1 cup shredded green cabbage

1 cup diced Roma tomatoes, seeded

2 cups mixed shredded Monterey Jack and cheddar cheese

2 cups cooked brown rice, warm

1 cup sour cream

Mango Salsa (recipe follows)

Tomato Salsa (recipe follows)

Lime wedges

MAKES 1 CUP

3 ripe mangos

1 jalapeño pepper, cored, seeded, and finely diced

2 limes, juice

1 clove garlic, minced

1 teaspoon chili oil

¼ cup chopped cilantro leaves

MANGO SALSA

Mix together all ingredients in a medium-size non-reactive bowl. Cover tightly and refrigerate 1 hour to overnight. Serve.

MAKES 1 CUP

4 medium tomatoes or 6 Roma tomatoes, seeded and diced

1 small sweet yellow onion, peeled and diced

2 jalapeño peppers, stemmed, seeded, and minced

1 medium serrano chili, stemmed, seeded, and minced

1 clove garlic, peeled and minced

¼ cup chopped fresh cilantro leaves

¼ cup fresh squeezed lime juice

1 tablespoon lemon juice

1 teaspoon coarsely ground sea salt

½ teaspoon freshly ground pepper

TOMATO SALSA

Mix together all ingredients in a medium-size non-reactive bowl. Cover tightly and refrigerate 1 hour to overnight. Serve.

KATHERINE'S FLAN

This is a favorite with all the kids. It's an easy-to-make comfort food—rich, yet light and satisfying.

Preheat oven to 325 degrees.

Mix ¾ cup sugar and water in a small saucepan over medium heat until a clear syrup forms. (It is important that the syrup clarify before it comes to a boil.) Increase heat to high and bring to a rolling boil. Cover pan and boil for 2 minutes. Uncover and cook, stirring occasionally until the syrup turns a dark caramel color. Pour quickly into a 2-quart souffle dish. Tilt the dish to spread the caramel over the bottom of the dish and halfway up the sides.

Heat milk in a medium saucepan with vanilla bean.

In a separate bowl, whisk eggs, remaining sugar, and salt. Scrape the vanilla seeds out of the vanilla bean pod and add to egg mixture. Discard pod. Gradually whisk the milk into the egg mixture and stir until the sugar is dissolved. Pour into dish and bake in a water bath until the center is firmly set, about 1 to 1½ hours. Remove from oven and refrigerate for at least 4 hours or up to 2 days.

To unmold, loosen the edges by dipping the dish in hot water for a short time. Invert onto a large plate, making sure it's deep enough to catch all the syrupy caramel.

SERVES 6 TO 8

1½ cups sugar
¼ cup water
3 cups lowfat milk
5 large eggs
⅛ teaspoon salt
1 vanilla bean

"Don't limit yourself. Have fun exploring."

"SEASONAL INGREDIENTS ARE the way to go," says Tracey Skupny, "no matter your level of expertise in the kitchen." The Skupnys belong to a local produce service that brings an organic vegetable box once a week practically all year long. "That forces us to explore ingredients we might ordinarily pass over in a market and makes cooking more of an adventure," she says.

John says, "I'm usually the cook in the kitchen with Tracey as my very able sous chef. We always open a bottle of wine as we're preparing dinner and at the same time we have a chance to catch up on the day's events." Tracey adds, "We may have a glass or two out of a bottle, put the cork back in, and save it again for the next day since we usually enjoy trying a different wine with dinner. Many might feel an obligation to finish a bottle once it's opened, but we can attest that one or two days later the wine may be even better!"

"Both John and I really began exploring food and wine in college, which was an outgrowth of a French food and culture class I was taking at the time. While dating we became more and more familiar with food of the regions and the wines as we ventured into unknown areas for both. John honed his cooking skills, and we both learned a tremendous amount about wine."

"We were married soon thereafter," says John, "and began our own great wine and food adventure. So it was either France or the Napa Valley." Their pocketbooks dictated the more obvious choice, the Napa Valley. "We're fortunate to both have continued to learn so much more about wine since the early days and now are fortunate to have a wine of our own."

Their two quickly growing, adolescent boys, Jersey and Reed, help prepare dinner. Tracey says, "We really feel it's important that they participate. It's an activity we can all easily do together."

The Skupnys will often prepare more than one day's meal at a time to make it easier for the following day. "To make it through a busy work week you have to adopt some handy hints, and this is ours," says Tracey. "We may be grilling fish for tonight's dinner, but we'll also throw some simply marinated chicken on the grill next to it to have the following day."

"As for wine," John said, "Don't limit yourself. Have fun exploring."

Spring ~ Summer

Grilled Rocky Chicken Breast with Mushrooms, Peppers, and Carmelized Onions

Rosemary Roasted Yams and Sweet Potatoes

Lang & Reed Cabernet Franc

Fall ~ Winter

Chilean Sea Bass with Ginger and Garlic

Jasmine Rice

Stir-Fry Winter Greens

Experiment with Sauvignon Blanc from different regions:

Cain Musque, Selene Sauvignon Blanc or
Spottswoode or Sancerre Sauvignon Blanc

SERVES 4

2 Rocky chickens* full breast fillets with skin

2 teaspoons Beau Monde seasoning**

2 teaspoons chopped fresh tarragon,
or 1 teaspoon dried

2 cloves garlic, finely minced

salt and pepper to taste

2 small sweet, yellow onions, peeled and
sliced into thin rings

1 tablespoon butter

1 tablespoon olive oil

1 cup fresh shiitake mushrooms, sliced

2 red bell peppers, cored, seeded, and thinly sliced

*NOTE: Free range, organic chickens.

**NOTE: Celery-salt-like seasoning mixture found in most
grocery stores.

GRILLED ROCKY CHICKEN BREAST WITH MUSHROOMS, PEPPERS, AND CARMELIZED ONIONS

Rinse chicken fillets and dry. Leaving skin on, trim excess fat and lightly pound to flatten. Season both sides with Beau Monde and tarragon. Rub skin with garlic and sprinkle with salt and pepper. Set aside.

In a large skillet over medium heat, sauté onion with butter until onion is translucent, 3 to 5 minutes. Add olive oil, mushrooms, and peppers. Reduce heat and continue cooking on low heat until all vegetables are soft and onions carmelized, about 20 to 30 minutes. Remove from heat and set aside.

Preheat grill to medium heat.

Place chicken on grill, skin side down. Grill for 5 minutes. Turn and grill 3 to 5 minutes, depending on the thickness. If more time is needed, move chicken away from direct heat, cover grill, and cook for 3 to 5 more minutes.

Place on a serving platter along with Rosemary Roasted Yams and Sweet Potatoes (recipe follows), slice, and smother with onion mixture.

ROSEMARY ROASTED YAMS AND SWEET POTATOES

Preheat oven to 450 degrees.

Place yams, sweet potatoes, carrots, garlic, and rosemary in large mixing bowl. Toss with olive oil and salt and pepper.

Spread into a large baking pan with shallow sides. Bake for 20 minutes. Stir thoroughly and bake for another 20 minutes. Continue roasting until vegetables are completely tender. Keep warm until service.

SERVES 4

2 yams, peeled and cubed

2 sweet potatoes, peeled and cubed

6 to 8 carrots, peeled and cubed

10 cloves garlic, peeled

1 tablespoon olive oil

1 tablespoon chopped fresh rosemary, or 1 teaspoon dried

4 or 5 sprigs fresh rosemary

salt and pepper to taste

CHILEAN SEA BASS WITH GINGER AND GARLIC

This is a quick, easy, and delicious dinner for our family of four. The portions of sea bass should be purchased according to appetite, remembering that it is a rich, flavorful fish. Serve this dish with jasmine rice. Start the rice first, so it can cook while you prepare the fish.

Preheat oven to 400 degrees.

Rinse fish and pat dry with paper towel. Cut into 4 pieces.

In a small bowl, mix the ginger and garlic together and spread equal portions on each piece of fish, both sides. Gently roll fish in bread crumbs until completely coated.

Place the fish on an oiled rack with a drip pan underneath. Bake for 5 minutes. Remove, and turn the oven to broil. Return fish and broil until the top is crispy, about 3 minutes.

SERVES 4

2 large filleted (1½ pounds) Chilean sea bass

1 tablespoon crushed fresh ginger

1 tablespoon crushed fresh garlic

½ cup non-seasoned bread crumbs

NOTE: Chilean Sea Bass is delicate and cooks quickly. Cooking time can be longer if the fish is very thick.

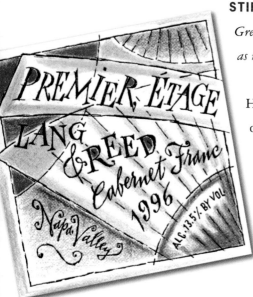

STIR-FRY WINTER GREENS

Greens wilt in size dramatically, so we generally cook as much as our wok will hold.

Rinse greens and pat thoroughly dry. Heat a wok over medium heat, and add sesame oil. When oil is hot, add greens. Stir frequently. (Greens cook quickly and are done when they are wilted and heated through.) Sprinkle with sesame seeds and soy sauce. Stir once more and serve.

SERVES 4

6 to 8 cups mixed winter greens like radicchio, kale, chard, and napa cabbage

2 to 3 tablespoons sesame oil

1 teaspoon sesame seeds

2 tablespoons soy sauce

THE STAGLINS OF STAGLIN FAMILY VINEYARD

"We're fortunate to be able to see our dream finally become a reality."

FOR GAREN AND SHARI STAGLIN, exercise is the top priority. "Even when traveling, when you have those 'body-clock blues,' you have to remain committed to exercise. When you're fit, everything else is so much easier."

Along with exercise, they see wine playing a big part in their overall health and well being. "Even before all the good health news was so widely publicized we made wine a part of our routine with dinner," Garen says. "I'm from an Italian family, and just like the obligatory bowl of pasta, wine was on the table each evening. It's a tradition we're proud to pass on to our children."

Shari says, "Having come from South Dakota, you can imagine I didn't have much experience with wine early in life. It was Garen who introduced me to it as we would travel up to the Napa Valley from the San Francisco area on day dates when he was attending Stanford's business school."

"There weren't nearly the amount of wineries there are today. Not even close," says Garen. "As we picnicked, munching on the best olives, salami, berries, and cheese—and of course always drinking a delicious wine—we would dream of someday owning a vineyard of our own."

"We definitely always had the dream," says Shari, "but not the means early on. And now we're fortunate to be able to see that dream finally become a reality. In regard to diet, our motto is to keep it simple. Garen loves pasta, which must have something to do with those Italian roots! And I adore meat and potatoes. My midwest upbringing is showing! Often we'll have one or the other and sometimes both—like in a good hearty soup." Garen added, "We always try to have some type of vegetable which is easy to do with the long growing season we have here. Our organic vegetable garden provides us the inspiration and motivation we need to vary our selections and try out new seasonal recipes."

They feel their children have certainly benefitted from growing up in the Valley, particularly when it comes to their outlook on wine. "Our children, Brandon and Shannon, were always allowed to taste wine growing up," says Shari. "Most of Shannon's friends actually prefer wine to beer because they grew up with it. Since wine was here and available to try, they didn't abuse it." And for all the Staglins, it's made life that much more pleasurable.

Spring ~ Summer

Green Salad

Stir-Fry Pasta Primavera

Fresh Berries with Tropical Coulis

Staglin Family Sangiovese
Pride Mountain Viognier

Fall ~ Winter

Shari's Hearty Fall Vegetable Soup

Crusty Country Bread

Mustard Marinated Veal Chops with Fall Mushrooms

Smoked Gouda, Pears, and Apple Slices

Staglin Family Cabernet Sauvignon
Pinot Noir

STIR-FRY PASTA PRIMAVERA

Cook pasta with 1 tablespoon olive oil in large pot of salted boiling water until al dente. Drain. Toss with 1 teaspoon olive oil and return to pot to keep warm.

Meanwhile, heat 1 tablespoon olive oil in large wok or skillet over medium heat. Add onions and sauté for 2 minutes, or until translucent. Add garlic and sauté for 1 to 2 minutes. Add asparagus, zucchini, and carrots, and stir-fry 2 minutes. Add mushrooms and peppers, and stir-fry an additional 1 to 2 minutes. Add chicken stock, wine, milk, red pepper flakes, and salt and pepper. Turn heat to high and cook another 2 to 3 minutes. Add peas, basil, and chicken (optional). Reduce heat and simmer for 1 to 2 minutes.

Place cooked, hot pasta into a large serving bowl. Using slotted spoon, remove all vegetables and meat and toss with pasta.

Reduce remaining liquid by half over high heat and pour over pasta.

Toss in one cup of grated Parmesan cheese and serve in individual pasta bowls, with remaining cheese sprinkled on top.

FRESH BERRIES WITH TROPICAL COULIS

In food processor, purée banana and pineapple. Add coconut extract.

Divide berries among four bowls. Pour banana mixture over. Serve.

STAGLIN FAMILY
VINEYARD
CABERNET SAUVIGNON
RUTHERFORD, NAPA VALLEY
1996

SHARI'S HEARTY FALL VEGETABLE SOUP

Heat olive oil in a large, deep saucepan over medium heat. Add onion, celery, and carrots, and sauté until onion is tender, 3 to 5 minutes. Add garlic and continue to sauté until it releases its aroma, 1 to 2 minutes. Add rosemary, thyme, oregano, garbanzo beans, kidney beans, chicken stock, salt and pepper, tomatoes, butternut squash, and potatoes. Bring to a gentle boil. Cover and reduce heat, and simmer until all vegetables are tender, about 20 to 30 minutes. Stir in chard. Add pasta and continue to simmer until tender, about 5 minutes.

Pass the Parmesan, and serve with a hearty country bread.

SERVES 6 TO 8

½ tablespoon extra-virgin olive oil

½ cup diced yellow onion

½ cup diced celery

¼ cup diced carrots

1 clove garlic, minced

½ tablespoon chopped fresh rosemary

1 tablespoon chopped fresh thyme

1 tablespoon chopped fresh oregano

1 cup canned garbanzo beans

1 cup canned kidney beans

3 cups chicken stock, or low-sodium canned chicken broth

salt and freshly ground pepper to taste

1 cup canned chopped Roma tomatoes

½ cup diced butternut squash

1 small potato, peeled and diced

1 cup chopped chard, kale, or spinach

¼ cup small macaroni, uncooked

2 tablespoons freshly grated Parmesan cheese

MUSTARD MARINATED VEAL CHOPS WITH FALL MUSHROOMS

Inspired by Ben Davis, former chef of the Cypress Club in San Francisco, this dish has always been a cold-weather favorite of ours.

Mix all marinade ingredients except salt, and spread over both sides of chops. Cover and refrigerate at least 8 hours. One half hour before cooking chops, sprinkle with salt and let stand at room temperature.

Melt half of the butter in a large heavy-bottomed, non-stick pan over medium-high heat. Add mushrooms and cook for 1 to 2 minutes or until mushrooms start to brown. Remove mushrooms and set aside.

Add remaining butter to pan. Add onions and sauté 2 to 3 minutes. Add white wine and continue to cook until wine is evaporated. Add stock and simmer over low heat until onions are soft. You may need to add more stock or water to keep onions simmering.

Return mushrooms to pan, add cream, and bring slowly back to a simmer. Season with salt, white pepper, and lemon juice. Keep warm until serving.

Preheat grill to medium heat.

Grill veal chops 4 to 6 minutes each side to medium rare, or desired doneness. Or broil chops 4 to 6 minutes on each side, 3 inches from heat source. Let meat rest 2 to 3 minutes before serving. Serve with the mushroom mixture.

SERVES 4

MARINADE:

1 cup whole grain mustard

4 tablespoons freshly squeezed lemon juice

2 tablespoons chopped fresh tarragon

2 tablespoons olive oil

2 teaspoons freshly ground black pepper

salt to taste

four 8- to 10-ounce veal loin chops

1 tablespoon unsalted butter

8 ounces fresh fall mushrooms like porcini or shiitake, or 4 ounces dried, reconstituted

16 green onions, washed, tops trimmed, cut into 2-inch pieces

½ cup white wine

2 cups veal, chicken, or beef stock

½ cup heavy cream

salt, white pepper, and lemon juice to taste

THE TRUCHARDS OF TRUCHARD VINEYARDS

"We so enjoy the people and the business."

ACCORDING TO JO ANN TRUCHARD, being a vintner in the Napa Valley takes on a lifestyle all its own. "When you own a winery, and are involved in its day-to-day management—my husband Tony manages our 250 acres of vineyards and I do the accounting—you're always working. You're doing tours whenever it's most convenient for your potential customers. That may mean weekdays but more often than not, weekends are fair game, too."

"I always get a kick out of telling people how Tony likes to relax after he's put in a hard day in the vineyards. Believe it or not he 'relaxes' by coming home to work in the vegetable garden!" That's actually good fortune for Jo Ann since she very much enjoys cooking the fruits of his labor.

"I always use fresh ingredients when I can," she says. "Seasonal vegetables and herbs are a must. We make every effort to eat healthy. And for us, another criteria is that whatever I'm cooking has to be fast. And, of course, we heartily believe wine has the incomparable ability to truly round out a meal."

Jo Ann and Tony are originally from Texas. Jo Ann says, "At first I always thought we'd move back, but the Valley tends to grow on you!" Tony grew up on a farm in Texas. Tilling the soil is something with which he is very familiar, so farming vineyards is a natural extension. As a doctor of internal medicine in Reno, he and Jo Ann longed to get back to the small twenty-acre piece of land they bought years before in the Napa Valley while Tony was still in the Army. In the meantime, they had six children and commuted to their vineyard property on weekends for many years until finally moving there full-time in 1987.

Jo Ann says, "We so enjoy the people and the business." And now it's a family affair. "For the first time, our two sons will be trying their hand at producing a Chardonnay from their own vineyard this year!"

Spring ~ Summer

Southern Catfish

Garlic Mashed Potatoes

Truchard Garden Sauté

Spicy Cornbread Muffins

French Vanilla Ice Cream with Poached Pears and Pear Liqueur

Truchard Chardonnay
St. Supery Sauvignon Blanc

Fall ~ Winter

Turkey Cutlets in Mushroom Wine Sauce

Easy Basmati Rice

Swiss Chard with Fresh Garlic

French Bread

Stilton Cheese with Walnuts and Pears

Truchard Pinot Noir
Frog's Leap Chardonnay

½ cup cornmeal

2 teaspoons chopped fresh thyme leaves

1 teaspoon finely minced garlic

four 4- to 6-ounce catfish fillets

1 teaspoon lemon pepper seasoning

½ teaspoon salt

1 egg, lightly beaten

1 tablespoon water

2 tablespoons olive oil

SOUTHERN CATFISH

Preheat oven to 400 degrees.

On a large plate, toss together the cornmeal and thyme. Set aside. Rub garlic on each filet, sprinkle with lemon pepper seasoning and salt. In a small bowl, whisk together egg and water. Dip each filet in egg mixture and then into cornmeal mixture.

Pour 1 tablespoon olive oil into a heavy, nonstick sauté pan, coating the pan evenly. Heat over high heat and add catfish fillets, browning both sides. You may need to add additional olive oil when turning.

Transfer to baking sheet and place in oven. Bake until fish is firm and flaky, about 15 minutes.

SERVES 4

2 pounds Yukon Gold or all-purpose potatoes, peeled and cubed

2 cloves garlic, peeled

½ teaspoon salt

½ cup whole or skim milk, heated

1 tablespoon butter

salt and coarsely ground black pepper to taste

GARLIC MASHED POTATOES

Place the potatoes in a large saucepan, cover with cold water, and add garlic cloves and salt. Bring to a boil. Reduce heat slightly and cook until tender, about 20 minutes.

Drain the potatoes, reserving the garlic. Return the potatoes to the saucepan, cover, and set aside. In a small food processor, purée the garlic together with the warm milk.

Transfer the potatoes to the bowl of an electric mixer with paddle attachment, and add the butter, garlic and milk mixture, and ground pepper. Beat until desired smoothness (or mash by hand). Add salt and pepper to taste. Serve.

TRUCHARD GARDEN SAUTÉ

In a medium, non-stick sauté pan, sauté vegetables in olive oil over medium-high heat just until they begin to soften, about 5 minutes. Add onion and jalapeño pepper and continue to sauté until the onion becomes translucent, another 1 to 2 minutes. Remove from heat. Spoon into heated serving bowl. Add the lime juice, salt, pepper, and cilantro. Sprinkle with cheese. Serve.

SERVES 4

4 cups sliced or diced, mixed summer garden vegetables like tomatoes, peppers, yellow crookneck squash, and zucchini

1 tablespoon olive oil

½ cup diced sweet yellow onion

½ jalapeño pepper, cored, seeded, and diced

1 to 2 teaspoons freshly squeezed lime juice

salt and freshly ground pepper to taste

¼ cup coarsely chopped fresh cilantro

¼ to ½ cup shredded dry Jack cheese, or other hard, aged cheese

SPICY CORNBREAD MUFFINS

Preheat oven to 400 degrees.

Mix the first six ingredients in a medium-size mixing bowl. Add fresh corn and toss. In a separate bowl, mix together sour cream, milk, eggs, and jalapeño. Add to the dry ingredients and mix just until combined.

Pour the batter into a preheated, greased, cast-iron muffin tin. Place in oven, reduce heat to 375 degrees. Bake until golden and the center is cooked through, about 12 to 15 minutes.

12 MUFFINS

1 cup yellow cornmeal

1 cup all-purpose flour

1 teaspoon baking powder

½ teaspoon salt

½ teaspoon baking soda

1 teaspoon sugar

¾ cup fresh corn kernels

¾ cup nonfat sour cream or plain nonfat yogurt

¼ cup milk

2 eggs, lightly beaten

1 jalapeño pepper, cored, seeded, and minced

½ cup sugar

¼ teaspoon salt

2 egg yolks, lightly beaten

2 cups hot 2-percent milk

1 vanilla bean, split lengthwise

2 cups heavy cream, or half-and-half

FRENCH VANILLA ICE CREAM WITH POACHED PEARS AND PEAR LIQUEUR

Creamy and smooth, this vanilla ice cream is best right from the ice cream freezer. Or, if you don't have the time to make it yourself, there are many high-quality varieties available in most markets.

In a medium saucepan, whisk together the sugar, salt, and egg yolks and warm over medium heat. Slowly whisk in the hot milk. Add the vanilla bean and stir over medium-low heat until slightly thickened. Remove from heat. Scrape the seeds from the vanilla bean into the milk mixture and discard the hull. Chill for ½ hour in the refrigerator.

Whisk in heavy cream, pour into ice cream freezer, and freeze according to manufacturer's instructions.

2 cups dry white wine

1 cups water

¾ cup sugar

4 ripe pears, peeled, halved, and cored

4 tablespoons pear liqueur

POACHED PEARS AND PEAR LIQUEUR

Place the wine, water, and sugar in a medium-size saucepan. Bring to a low boil over medium heat. Gently place the pears in the liquid and reduce heat to a simmer. If necessary, add more water until the pears are completely submerged. Simmer pears until tender, about 15 to 20 minutes. Remove with slotted spoon and set aside to cool. Continue to reduce the liquid until it reaches a syrupy consistency. Remove from heat.

Place 1 pear half in serving bowl. Add 1 scoop of ice cream and drizzle with pear liqueur and some of the reserved syrup. Serve.

SERVES 4

4 turkey cutlets, flattened

salt and freshly ground pepper to taste

1 cup sliced fresh button mushrooms

2 tablespoons olive oil

2 teaspoons butter

½ cup white wine

1 cup sour cream, or nonfat sour cream

TURKEY CUTLETS IN MUSHROOM WINE SAUCE

Sprinkle cutlets with salt and pepper. In a medium-size sauté pan over medium heat, sauté mushrooms in 1 tablespoon olive oil and butter until all of liquid has evaporated. Remove from pan and set aside.

Add remaining olive oil to the same pan and brown cutlets over medium-high heat. Reduce the heat to medium, add white wine, and reduce by half. Stir in sour cream and mushrooms and continue to simmer until the turkey is cooked through, about 15 to 20 minutes. Add more white wine to thin the sauce as needed.

EASY BASMATI RICE

This recipe produces perfectly cooked, fluffy rice every time!

Grease a medium-size casserole dish. Add all ingredients and stir. Cover with plastic wrap, leaving a small gap to allow steam to escape.

Microwave on ½ power until desired doneness, about 18 minutes.

SERVES 4

1½ cups water

¾ cup rice

¾ teaspoon salt

1 tablespoon butter

1 tablespoon coarsely chopped fresh parsley leaves

SWISS CHARD WITH FRESH GARLIC

Trim chard stems and coarsely chop. Cut chard leaves into bite-size pieces and set aside. In a medium sauté pan over medium heat, sauté stems in olive oil until tender, add the leaves and sauté until wilted. Stir in red pepper flakes and garlic. Sauté until the garlic releases aroma, 1 to 2 minutes more. Remove from heat. Serve.

SERVES 4

1 bunch fresh Swiss chard, washed

1 tablespoon olive oil

1 teaspoon red pepper flakes

1 teaspoon minced fresh garlic

DELIA VIADER OF VIADER VINEYARDS

"That's what the Napa Valley is all about—bringing the best traditions of the old world over to the new."

"WHEN I FIRST CAME TO finish my business studies at Berkeley, my father and I would travel up to the Napa Valley to look at land there. He saw that an opportunity existed so many years ago," said Delia Viader. "The piece of property he bought on a hillside was totally undeveloped then. His rationale was that he liked the view!" Now those same hillsides produce luscious Cabernet Sauvignon.

"Wine was always an important part of my experience growing up since it was always a part of our mealtime during my teenage years in Europe," says Delia. And it still is. "Even though some days are very long, when you love what you do it doesn't seem much like work. And that's the ideal!"

Many years and four children later, Delia enjoys every aspect of the business. "And to get my exercise, I walk the hillside vineyards often. During harvest I'm out there even more checking 'sugars' so we'll know just when to pick the grapes."

"Mealtime," says Delia, "is an important part of the day for my family. We've always made it a point to sit down to breakfast and dinner together. It's a time to talk and catch up on the day's events. Three of my children are college age now, with individual food likes and dislikes. So I usually build simple meals to make sure everyone has something they'll eat. My five-year-old is the easiest because he will eat anything his teenage brothers do."

The food philosophy Delia learned in Europe was to look first to what's fresh and seasonally available around you. "In Europe," she says, "we bought fresh produce every day. Where that might not be as practical with our lifestyle today, I still make it a point to go to the local farmer's market weekly. There's such a tremendous variety of fresh produce and locally produced products available—and I sometimes feel quite nostalgic since it really reminds me so much of the European markets." But that's really what Napa Valley is all about—bringing the best traditions of the old world over to the new.

Spring ~ Summer

Brie Quiche

Ginger Orange Butterflied Leg of Lamb

Chocolate and Raspberry Brownies

Viader 1997 (Blend of Cabernet Sauvignon and Cabernet Franc)
Spottswoode Sauvignon Blanc

Fall ~ Winter

Sherried Cream of Mushroom Soup

Roasted Pork Tenderloin with Mustard Sauce

White Chocolate Mousse with Raspberry Sauce

Viader 1989 (Blend of Cabernet Sauvignon and Cabernet Franc)
Truchard Syrah

SERVES 12

PASTRY:

1¼ cups all-purpose flour

½ teaspoon salt

2 teaspoons fresh thyme leaves

4 tablespoons unsalted butter, cold,
cut into small pieces

3 tablespoons vegetable shortening, cold

2 to 3 tablespoons ice water

1 egg white, lightly beaten

FILLING:

4 egg yolks, lightly beaten

½ cup half-and-half, or whole milk

1 pound Brie cheese, rind trimmed, softened

⅛ teaspoon salt

4 egg whites

½ cup sour cream (optional)

caviar (optional)

BRIE QUICHE

Even though this recipe is rich and a bit decadent, it's one of my very favorite appetizers and always meets with rave reviews!

Combine flour and salt in a medium-size mixing bowl. Add thyme and toss. Add butter and shortening and mix with a pastry blender or two knives until mixture resembles coarse crumbs. Add ice water 1 tablespoon at a time, blending flour mixture until it forms a ball. Place on cool marble slab or wooden board sprinkled with a little flour and shape into a disk. Wrap in plastic and refrigerate at least 30 minutes.

Roll dough into an 11-inch disk and place in a 9-inch pie plate. Chill 30 minutes. Preheat oven to 375 degrees.

Prick the bottom and sides of the shell with a fork and line with foil. Bake for 10 minutes. Remove foil, prick any bubbles that have formed during baking. Brush the crust with egg white and bake until it begins to brown, about 5 to 7 minutes. Remove crust from oven. Set aside.

In a large bowl, beat the egg yolks and half-and-half together. Mash softened brie and add to the mixture. Mix thoroughly. In a separate bowl, beat egg whites until stiff peaks form. Gently fold one third of the egg whites into the brie mixture. Then, continue folding in the egg whites one third at a time.

Reduce oven heat to 350 degrees.

Pour mixture into shell. Bake until set, about 30 minutes. Cut into twelve or more small wedges and serve with sour cream and caviar, if desired.

GINGER ORANGE BUTTERFLIED LEG OF LAMB

Place lamb in a shallow roasting pan, fat side down. Combine remaining ingredients in a medium saucepan and simmer at medium heat, uncovered for 20 minutes. Cool to lukewarm and pour over lamb. Marinate at room temperature for 1 hour. Return meat to refrigerator and continue to marinate 6 to 8 hours or overnight, turning frequently.

TO GRILL: Preheat grill at medium heat. Place lamb on grill for 30 to 45 minutes. Turn several times basting with the marinade. Take care not to pierce the lamb when turning. Continue to grill to desired doneness. Remove lamb from grill and let stand for 10 minutes before slicing to allow juices to reabsorb.

TO BROIL: Preheat broiler to 500 degrees. Place lamb fat side down under broiler 4 inches from the heat. Broil 10 minutes per side, basting with marinade as you turn it. Reduce oven heat to 425 degrees and continue baking for 15 minutes. Remove from heat and let stand before carving.

SERVES 8 TO 10

one 4- to 5-pound leg of lamb, butterflied and trimmed of fat

1 cup dry red wine

¾ cup beef stock, or low-sodium beef broth

3 tablespoons orange marmalade

2 tablespoons red wine vinegar

2 tablespoons minced fresh onion

2 tablespoons chopped fresh marjoram

1 tablespoon chopped fresh rosemary

1 large bay leaf

1 teaspoon sea salt

1 teaspoon freshly grated ginger

1 clove garlic, peeled and crushed

CHOCOLATE AND RASPBERRY BROWNIES

A favorite with the children!

Preheat oven to 350 degrees.

Melt chocolate and butter in a double boiler. When smooth, add 2 cups of sugar and vanilla. Beat in 4 eggs. Add flour, baking powder, and salt. Pour one half of the batter in a greased and floured 9 x 13-inch baking pan.

In a small bowl, combine cream cheese, ⅓ cup sugar, and 1 egg. Mix well and spread over batter in pan. Cover with raspberry jam.

Spoon remainder of batter over raspberry jam.

Bake for 35 to 40 minutes. Cool and cut into squares.

4 ounces unsweetened chocolate

½ cup butter

2 cups and ⅓ cup sugar

1 teaspoon vanilla extract

5 large eggs

1 cup all-purpose flour

¼ teaspoon baking powder

¼ teaspoon salt

8 ounces cream cheese, softened

¾ cup raspberry jam

4 tablespoons unsalted butter

2 leeks, washed, white part only, diced

1 small yellow onion, peeled and diced

2 ribs celery, peeled and diced

1½ pounds fresh button mushrooms, sliced

½ cup fresh shiitake mushrooms (or 1 ounce dried, reconstituted)

3 tablespoons flour

3½ cups milk

½ cup dry sherry

2 cups rich chicken stock, or low-sodium chicken broth

salt and freshly ground pepper to taste

½ cup crème fraîche

2 tablespoons chopped chives

OPTIONAL: In a blender purée the soup in small batches. Return it to the soup pot to warm through over low heat.

½ cup heavy cream

½ cup sour cream

SERVES 4

2- to 2½-pound pork tenderloin

¼ cup soy sauce

¼ cup bourbon

2 tablespoons brown sugar

SAUCE:

⅓ cup sour cream

⅓ cup mayonnaise

1 tablespoon Dijon mustard

1 tablespoon chopped onion

1½ teaspoons vinegar

¼ teaspoon salt

SHERRIED CREAM OF MUSHROOM SOUP

Melt the butter in a large soup pot over medium-low heat. Add the leeks, onion, celery, and mushrooms and cook until softened and the mushroom liquid has almost evaporated, about 5 minutes.

Reduce heat to low, stir in flour, and cook an additional 5 minutes, stirring periodically. Slowly whisk in the milk, sherry, chicken stock, and salt and pepper. Simmer uncovered until the soup has thickened, about 15 to 20 minutes.

Allow it to cool just slightly.

Serve garnished with a dollop of crème fraîche (recipe follows) and a sprinkle of chives.

HOMEMADE CRÈME FRAÎCHE

Whisk the creams together in a small bowl. Cover with plastic wrap and let stand at room temperature for 12 hours. Stir and then refrigerate for another 24 hours before use.

ROASTED PORK TENDERLOIN WITH MUSTARD SAUCE

Combine soy sauce, bourbon, and brown sugar in large glass dish. Marinate pork in mixture for at least 2 hours.

Preheat oven to 325 degrees.

Place pork on a roasting pan and into oven. Roast pork until it reaches desired doneness, at least until it registers 150 to 160 degrees on a meat thermometer, about 1 hour and 20 minutes. Baste often while roasting. Remove from oven. Let stand, covered with aluminum foil 5 to 10 minutes before slicing.

In a small bowl, whisk together all ingredients for sauce. Pass with the pork.

WHITE CHOCOLATE MOUSSE WITH RASPBERRY SAUCE

Melt 4 ounces chocolate in double boiler. Whisk in milk and sugar until smooth. Cool to room temperature. In a small bowl, beat egg white with lemon juice and salt until it forms stiff peaks. Fold egg white into chocolate. Fold in whipped cream. Spoon into individual molds. Refrigerate overnight.

Place raspberries (or 10 ounces frozen raspberries) and liquid in saucepan over medium heat. Add cornstarch, bring to a slow boil, and stir as the sauce thickens. Add sugar and simmer for 5 minutes stirring frequently. Press mixture through strainer into bowl. Whisk in lemon juice and brandy.

Unmold white chocolate mousse onto chilled dessert plates. Surround with raspberry sauce. Shave remaining 1 ounce of white chocolate and sprinkle over mousse. Serve.

YIELDS ABOUT 1 CUP

MOUSSE:

5 ounces white chocolate

2 tablespoons warm milk

1 egg white

½ teaspoon fresh lemon juice

pinch salt

½ cup whipping cream

SAUCE:

2 pints fresh raspberries, rinsed and drained, or one 10-ounce package frozen raspberries

¼ teaspoon cornstarch

2 tablespoons sugar

1 teaspoon fresh lemon juice

2 teaspoons brandy

DICK WARD AND LINDA REIFF OF SAINTSBURY WINERY

"Wine goes with food and always enhances the experience."

"WE MAKE IT A POINT to sit down to dinner together each night," says Dick Ward. "Even if we're both working late, we'll still make a simple dinner and use the mealtime to unwind and relax from the day's events."

For Dick's wife, Linda, who is head of the Napa Valley Vintner's Association, "It's something we always look forward to at the end of our day. And fortunately for me, Dick is such a skilled cook. I've learned a lot by watching and helping! One of us will usually stop by the market on the way home from work, choose what's fresh, and then Dick will almost magically bring together a healthy and delicious dinner."

Dinner is also the perfect opportunity to update the Wards' "tasting library." Linda says, "It's so much fun to taste, talk, and learn about wines while enjoying the meal. After all, in the true European tradition, wine goes with food and always enhances the experience."

Gardening is also a passion they share. With both a garden at the Saintsbury winery and at their home, there's always a project that needs a little work. Dick says, "We really enjoy working in the garden together. It's a time we can share, and it also gives us such a sense of gratification once we see that special flower bloom or we pick the first ripe, juicy tomato of the season."

Dick and Linda stay active with other outdoor activities and seasonal sports. Dick says, "When we're on the road, we'll usually take running shoes. It's a great way to explore a new city between meetings!"

Spring ~ Summer

Bread Salad with Tomatoes and Fresh Mozzarella

Grilled Swordfish with Tarragon and Lime

Saintsbury Vincent Van Gris

Swanson Rosato

Fall ~ Winter

Fennel, Pear, and Parmesan Salad

Garlic Horseradish Mashed Potatoes

Garlic and Rosemary Grilled Pheasant

Saintsbury Pinot Noir

Joseph Phelps Le Mistral

BREAD SALAD WITH TOMATOES AND FRESH MOZZARELLA

SERVES 4

¼ cup extra-virgin olive oil

1 tablespoon balsamic vinegar

2 teaspoons freshly ground sea salt

3 to 4 thick slices rustic Italian bread

3 large vine-ripe beefsteak tomatoes or equivalent of good Roma tomatoes cut into ¾-inch cubes

1½ balls (size of a small fist) fresh mozzarella

6 sprigs fresh basil, coarsely chopped

1 teaspoon freshly ground black pepper

OPTIONAL: ½ small red onion, thinly sliced; 1 cucumber, seeded, peeled, and diced; 1 tablespoon coarse grain mustard; 1 clove garlic, crushed

The bread salad is a wonderful summer specialty with juicy garden fresh tomatoes, basil, fresh mozzarella, and rustic bread tossed with lots of fruity olive oil and sweet, balsamic vinegar.

In a small bowl, mix half of the olive oil and a third of the balsamic vinegar together. Add a pinch of salt. Drizzling the vinaigrette over the bread cubes creates little flavor pockets and prevents the bread from soaking up too much of the tomato juice.

In a large bowl, toss the tomatoes, mozzarella, and basil with the remaining olive oil, balsamic vinegar, salt, and pepper. Add bread and optional ingredients as desired. Lightly toss. Adjust salt and pepper to taste.

GRILLED SWORDFISH WITH TARRAGON AND LIME

SERVES 4

¼ cup fruity olive oil

1 lime, juiced

1 teaspoon lime zest

2 tablespoons coarsely chopped fresh tarragon

1 teaspoon freshly ground sea salt

1 teaspoon freshly ground black pepper

4 medium swordfish steaks (totaling about 1½ pounds), skinned

A simple yet delicious preparation where the lime juice melds with the tarragon to give the swordfish a lively and savory flavor.

In a small bowl, whisk together olive oil and lime juice. Add zest, tarragon, salt, and pepper. Place swordfish in a shallow pan and coat swordfish with marinade. Let marinate for several hours.

Preheat grill over high heat and grill swordfish 3 minutes per side.

FENNEL, PEAR, AND PARMESAN SALAD

SERVES 4

2 Bosc pears or other seasonal variety, cored and sliced diagonally

1 teaspoon lemon juice

2 medium-size fennel bulbs, stalk, base, and thick outer layers removed

2 tablespoons olive oil

1 teaspoon Balsamic vinegar

½ teaspoon freshly ground sea salt

freshly ground pepper to taste

4 ounces fresh Parmesano Reggiano cheese, sliced medium-thin

Fresh sliced fennel is tossed with Bosc pear slices and slices of Parmesano Reggiano and dressed lightly with olive oil flavored with a dash of Balsamic and lemon juice.

Toss pears with lemon juice to prevent browning. Thinly slice fennel bulbs on the diagonal. Combine fennel and pears and drizzle olive oil and balsamic vinegar over the mixture. Add salt and pepper to taste. Add cheese and gently toss. Serve.

GARLIC HORSERADISH MASHED POTATOES

Red potatoes are simmered with lots of unpeeled garlic cloves and then mashed with butter, olive oil, sour cream, and horseradish.

Boil unpeeled potatoes and unpeeled garlic cloves in large pot of water for 15 minutes, or until tender. Drain. Remove garlic skins that have come off during boiling and squeeze off any skins that remain on the cloves. Mash potatoes and garlic cloves together with hand masher or electric mixer with paddle attachment. Add butter, olive oil, sour cream, horseradish, salt, and pepper. Continue to mash/mix until desired texture. Serve.

SERVES 4

10 medium-size red potatoes

6 cloves garlic, unpeeled

2 tablespoons butter

2 tablespoons olive oil

¼ cup sour cream, or nonfat sour cream

1 tablespoon horseradish

2 teaspoons salt

1 teaspoon pepper

GARLIC AND ROSEMARY GRILLED PHEASANT

In a medium bowl, mix olive oil, garlic, rosemary, salt, and pepper. Coat pheasant with mixture.

Preheat grill to medium-high heat. Grill 4 minutes per side. (Take care not to overcook, or pheasant will become dry and tough.)

SERVES 4

½ cup olive oil

8 cloves garlic, crushed

1 tablespoon chopped rosemary

4 teaspoons freshly ground salt

2 teaspoons freshly ground pepper

2 pheasants, halved

Carneros

PINOT NOIR

1997

SAINTSBURY

PRODUCED AND BOTTLED BY SAINTSBURY
NAPA, CALIFORNIA, USA   ALCOHOL 13.5% BY VOLUME

JULIE WILLIAMS AND JOHN WILLIAMS OF FROG'S LEAP WINERY

"It's important to help them learn where the best produce and herbs come from—our own garden, of course."

"SPRING IS A TIME OF AWAKENING in the garden," says Julie Williams. "A foray into the flower borders provides a rewarding wake-up to the senses as well." Julie plants many heirloom varieties of flowers and vegetables. She says, "I never thought of daffodils and tulips as particularly aromatic until I began planting heirloom bulbs. There's a world of difference between those and the hybrid bulbs more familiar to most."

"At Frog's Leap, we plant Johnny Jump-Ups and pansies under the bigger, more showy blooms to give us both a lush carpet of color and a source of delicate edible flowers." When planting, she thinks not only of color scheme but of the biodynamic environment the plants create as well. "I'll also plant calendula in an area close to the pansies since earliest blooms of these hearty, long-blooming plants not only offer a complement of color, they're also a great source of nectar for beneficial insects. And the pansies will add a dash of peppery spice when used as a garnish on any dish."

Among the flowers sit raised beds for vegetables. "We'll always put in an early and tightly sown mixed planting of carrots, radishes, and lettuces," says Julie.

The three children will sometimes get into the act, too. Julie says, "The children very much enjoy the outdoors, and I've always felt it was important to help them learn where the best produce and herbs come from—our own garden, of course, but then there are equally good sources locally as well."

"Harvest is a special time of year for me," says John Williams. "We've worked all year long nurturing and coddling those grapes. And then in the fall, they reward us with the rich and concentrated juice that will soon turn into delicious wine."

When harvest arrives in the Napa Valley, no one has much time for anything other than making sure the grapes get picked at the right time and begin their fermentation. My basis for a healthy diet at that time of year is a warm hearty soup that might be made with last-of-the-season tomatoes or even a chili that will give me the energy I need to work late into the night. Often when I'm in the fields all day long, covered with sticky grape juice, and all purple, I rely on a thermos of simple soup to keep me going. At that point, there's just nothing more satisfying." In the Napa Valley, hard work—physical labor that's good exercise—a healthy attitude, and an appreciation for fresh produce and wine are the ingredients for the good life.

Spring ~ Summer

Salad of Spring Greens and Edible Flowers

Light and Easy Prawn Barbeque

Herbed Rice Salad

Frog's Leap "Leapfrogmilch" (Riesling and Chenin Blanc blend)
Turnbull Cellars Zinfandel

Fall ~ Winter

Roasted Tomato Soup

Rustic Country Bread

Frog's Leap Merlot

or

Cashew Chili

Cheesy Cornbread

Napa Pumpkin Pie

Frog's Leap Zinfandel

4 cups mixed young and tender spring salad greens like baby lettuce, arugula, watercress, beet greens, baby chard, radish, and carrot shoots, washed and spun dry

1 cup mini-baby vegetables, like carrots, first-of-the-season peas, and radishes, washed and spun dry

DRESSING:

6 tablespoons olive oil

2 tablespoons hazelnut oil

2 tablespoons raspberry (or other fruit) vinegar

1 teaspoon Dijon mustard

1 teaspoon fresh lemon zest

1 tablespoon lemon juice

1 clove garlic, minced

2 tablespoons grated aged goat cheese

1 cup mixed edible flowers like pansy, viola, and calendula petals

OPTIONAL: chopped fresh basil, dill, tarragon, or thyme

SALAD OF SPRING GREENS AND EDIBLE FLOWERS

You may want to add a squeeze of lemon to make the dressing more piquant, creating a balance of tastes, without making it too assertive for the wine. If you are inclined to add herbs, my personal favorites to try with Sauvignon Blanc are basil, dill, and thyme. And with Chardonnay, try tarragon.

Place greens and vegetables in a large salad bowl.

In a small jar with a tightly fitting lid, combine all dressing ingredients. Shake well. Adjust the seasonings to taste.

Toss the salad with just enough dressing to coat the leaves. Sprinkle with a handful of pansy, viola, or calendula petals. Serve.

SERVES 4

MARINADE:

1 cup olive oil

6 tablespoons fresh lemon juice

4 cloves garlic, minced

1 teaspoon sea salt

½ teaspoon freshly ground black pepper

2 teaspoons red pepper flakes

½ cup chopped fresh basil leaves

½ cup chopped fresh cilantro leaves

½ cup chopped fresh flat-leaf parsley leaves

2 teaspoons finely minced lemon grass (or pulverized with mortar and pestle)

2 teaspoons finely minced lemon zest

48 medium-size fresh prawns, or thawed frozen prawns, about 3 pounds, rinsed and patted dry

LIGHT AND EASY PRAWN BARBECUE

This is a favorite summer recipe and especially nice to grill—keeping all the summer heat outdoors. It also works well for entertaining. Festively cover your table with a few layers of newspaper. Set out large, bright cotton or paper napkins, and a couple of bowls per person to hold both prawns and shells. Slice up a generous amount of crusty, whole grain bread. Set out several different dishes of fresh goat cheeses, prepared red pepper, or sun-dried tomato spreads as well as any other finger foods such as fresh baby carrots, spring onions, and green olives. Guests will enjoy a dining adventure that is both sensuous and delicious. The real secret to this dish is to keep the wine flowing and the napkins handy!

Mix together all marinade ingredients. Set aside.

Place prawns with shells on in a large glass baking dish. Toss the prawns with the marinade. Cover tightly and refrigerate for up to 6 hours. (Or lift shells off, keeping them connected at the tail. Clean both sides of the shrimp and replace shell—with the shell on, the shrimp will stay moister during grilling.)

Preheat the grill to medium heat.

Grill prawns until pink, turning once, about 3 to 5 minutes per side. Serve immediately and pass the bottle of Sauvignon Blanc... and open a bottle of Zinfandel, too!

HERBED RICE SALAD

In a small bowl, whisk together all dressing ingredients. Toss with rice in a large serving bowl. Refrigerate until ready to serve.

DRESSING:

1 tablespoon chopped mint, basil, cilantro, flat-leaf parsley

⅓ cup olive oil

2 tablespoons freshly squeezed lemon juice

1 teaspoon fresh minced garlic

salt and freshly ground pepper to taste

3 cups cooked basmati rice, cooled to lukewarm

CASHEW CHILI

Inspired by a good friend from Ithaca, New York, Julie Jordan, this is a dish with just the right amount of spice for a cool fall day. Bursting with cashews and raisins, it's especially good when topped with grated sharp cheddar and accompanied by hearty cornbread.

In a heavy-gauge soup pot over medium heat, sauté onions in olive oil until translucent, about 3 minutes. Add peppers, celery, and carrots, and sauté until peppers become soft, about 3 to 5 minutes. Add garlic and stir until the garlic releases its aroma, 1 to 2 minutes. Stir in basil, oregano, chili powder, cumin, and pepper flakes. Add tomatoes, red wine, salt, black pepper, bay leaf, cashews, and molasses. Bring mixture to a boil. Reduce heat and simmer for 20 minutes, stirring often.

Add raisins, adjust seasonings, and continue cooking 10 to 15 minutes more.

Remove from heat when desired consistency is reached. Add red wine vinegar and serve. Pass the grated cheddar.

SERVES 6 TO 8

2 small, medium-sweet yellow onions, peeled and diced

2 tablespoons olive oil

2 green bell peppers, cored, seeded, and diced

2 stalks celery, peeled and diced

2 carrots, peeled and diced

3 cloves fresh garlic, peeled and finely minced

1 tablespoon chopped fresh basil, or 1 teaspoon dried

1 tablespoon fresh oregano leaves, or 2 teaspoons dried

2 cups canned kidney beans (if using dried beans, soak overnight)

1 cup canned garbanzo beans (if using dried beans, soak overnight)

3 tablespoon chili powder

1 tablespoon ground cumin

2 teaspoons red pepper flakes, or to taste

4 cups canned diced tomatoes, substitute fresh diced tomatoes if in season

½ cup red wine

sea salt and freshly ground black pepper to taste

1 bay leaf

1 cup raw cashews, coarsely chopped and lightly toasted

1 tablespoon molasses

½ cup raisins

¼ cup red wine vinegar

1 to 2 cups grated sharp cheddar cheese

FROG'S LEAP

1997 MERLOT NAPA VALLEY

ALC. 13% BY VOL.

PRODUCED & BOTTLED BY FROG'S LEAP, RUTHERFORD, CA

SERVES 4

1 medium sweet yellow onion, peeled and coarsely chopped

2 tablespoons olive oil

1 clove garlic, peeled and minced

1 teaspoon grated orange zest

1 teaspoon thyme

1 teaspoon fennel seeds, crushed

3 to 4 pounds vine-ripened tomatoes, roasted*

1 cup fresh chicken stock, or low-sodium canned chicken broth

½ cup red wine

salt and freshly ground pepper to taste

1 tablespoon lemon juice

1 teaspoon balsamic vinegar

2 tablespoons chopped fresh basil

dash of Tabasco sauce or hot chili oil

*ROASTING THE TOMATOES: Halve the tomatoes and brush both sides with olive oil. Place skin side up in a roasting pan and broil the tomatoes on both sides until slightly charred. Set aside to let cool. Or heat a cast iron skillet over medium-high heat until very hot. Add whole tomatoes and cook, turning often until the skins are lightly blackened and blistered, about 5 to 10 minutes. Set aside to let cool.

ROASTED TOMATO SOUP

I enjoy making this rustic-style roasted tomato soup with richly flavored, last-of-the-season tomatoes. It's delightful either warm or cold, but I prefer it warm since the evenings during harvest-time in the Napa Valley can be quite chilly. Roasting the tomatoes brings out their sweetness and also adds a subtle smoky flavor.

In a medium soup/stock pot over medium-high heat, sauté the onions in 1 tablespoon olive oil until soft, about 3 minutes. Add the garlic and stir until it releases its aroma, 1 to 2 minutes. Add orange zest, thyme, and fennel seeds. Add the tomatoes, stirring to break them up. Stir in chicken stock and red wine and simmer for 30 minutes, stirring occasionally. Remove from heat.

In small batches, with a blender or food processor, purée soup. Strain if desired, to remove tomato skins. Adjust with salt and pepper to taste. Stir in lemon juice, vinegar and fresh basil. Serve.

SERVES 6 TO 8

¾ cup coarse, stone-ground white cornmeal

1¼ cups all-purpose flour

1½ teaspoons baking powder

¼ teaspoon baking soda

½ teaspoon salt

1 tablespoon sugar

½ cup coarsely grated sharp cheddar cheese

½ cup nonfat, plain yogurt

½ cup milk

2 eggs, beaten lightly

2½ tablespoons canola oil

CHEESY CORNBREAD

Preheat oven to 400 degrees.

Grease an 8-inch round cast-iron skillet or baking pan. (If using skillet, preheat before adding batter.)

In a medium bowl, mix together first six ingredients. Toss with cheese. In another medium-size mixing bowl, whisk together yogurt, milk, eggs, and oil. Stir in dry ingredients until incorporated.

Pour batter into pan and bake until golden brown and cooked through, about 20 to 25 minutes.

NAPA PUMPKIN PIE

Preheat oven to 425 degrees.

Place eggs in a medium-size bowl and beat in pumpkin. Stir in vanilla, sugar, brown sugar, salt, cinnamon, ginger, cloves, half-and-half, and whole milk. Pour into pastry shell and bake for 15 minutes. Reduce heat to 350 degrees and bake until the filling is firm, about 40 to 50 minutes more.

3 eggs, slightly beaten

1¾ cups cooked pumpkin (15-ounce can)

1½ teaspoons vanilla extract

½ cup sugar

¼ cup brown sugar

½ teaspoon salt

1½ teaspoons cinnamon

½ teaspoon ground ginger

¼ teaspoon ground cloves

1½ cups half-and-half, or evaporated milk

1 unbaked 9-inch, deep dish pie shell

"Hard work, a healthy attitude, and an appreciation for fresh produce and wine are the ingredients for the good life."

THE LANGUAGE OF WINE—
MAKING SENSE OF WINESPEAK

WALKING DOWN THE AISLE of your local wine shop, you're barraged with information. There are brochures, side displays, wine scores, and ratings—some even hung around the necks of bottles, like Olympic gold medals. You'll find wines described as having a "big nose," "great legs," or being floral, fruity, jammy, or spicy. One bottle boasts of "a wonderful sense of harmony and finesse with pure fruit in a lively, balanced package." Another is "bright and crisp with a feisty mineral quality that finishes with good length." You find yourself lost in a sea of description. What do these words really mean?

If you're like most, wine terminology is somewhat of a mystery, but having some fluency in the language can be useful.

Andrea Immer, beverage director for Starwood Hotels and Resorts and formerly wine director at Windows on the World in New York City gave me a good example: "A friend of mine phoned the other day excited about a wine. She said it was a white, but she couldn't remember the name or the label. When I asked her to describe it, she said it was 'so delicious and, well, um, well, uh, white.' And that's pretty much where the conversation ended because she couldn't help me and I didn't have much more to go on."

Unless we have some way to describe the tastes and flavors of wine, it's difficult to relate much of the experience to anyone else. And it's really difficult to duplicate the experience the next time you're looking for a wine with similar characteristics.

"We pull a cork to encourage a sensual experience, and our words should reflect that."

LEARNING A COMMON LANGUAGE

Wine tasting is about *appreciation*. Imagine describing the taste of a banana to someone who has never tasted one. You peel the banana and take a bite. At first you think it tastes like, well, a banana. But think about it, as if it were new. The words pour forth: pleasantly mild, sweet, with a thick, almost creamy texture that is distinctly tropical. That sounds like a wine description, doesn't it? Now you're getting the hang of it.

WINE TASTING MADE EASY

"Our language provides a wealth of opportunities to be clear and concise," says Joseph Spellman, Master Sommelier formerly at Charlie Trotter's in Chicago. "We should describe a wine in terms of fruit, earth, wood, place, food, instead of jargon about pH, ML, varietal oddities, and phenolics. "We pull a cork to encourage a sensual experience, and our words should reflect that."

"Wine is a very special beverage—some even call it a food," says Immer. "It can take on many different styles depending on so many variables. To understand the possibilities, think of milk and cheese." Milk from different producers still tastes pretty much the same. When milk is processed, it changes dramatically... into a luscious cheese. Think for a moment how many varieties of cheese there are. "With wine, it's similar," says Immer. "Once you ferment grape juice, a world of stylistic possibilities opens before you."

THE BASICS

First, evaluate what you see, the wine's *appearance*. Second, swirl the wine in the glass to release the aromas, and with your nose well in the glass, breathe in the *"bouquet."* Third, *taste* the wine by taking a sip and letting it roll over all your tastebuds. The wine should be balanced, taste "fruity," with no peculiar or objectionable sensations. Finally, swallow. Only after you've swallowed do you get the true impression of the wine—the finish, how long—and how pleasantly, or not—the flavor lingers on the palate. The aromas you experience after swallowing can be remarkable.

"If we simply pay attention each time we taste a wine, we build a library of memorable experiences," says Immer. And it's paying attention each and every time you taste a wine, from the least expensive to the most expensive, that will add the volumes to your library.

Balance

Balance means that the individual components of a wine intertwine on the palate so that no single characteristic overwhelms the senses. Balance is the most important characteristic of a good wine.

APPEARANCE

Evaluating Color

A white wine should have a light straw to medium gold color. A darker yellow color, unless it's a dessert wine, may indicate a wine is past its prime. A young red wine should have a vibrant ruby color. As it ages, the pigments (color) begin to fall out in the form of sediment and the vibrant red will become more of a brick color. With both white and red wine, you'll want to evaluate the wine's clarity. The wine should be bright, clear, and inviting.

Evaluating the Legs

Great legs are always a good thing! In the case of wine, legs give a hint as to how powerful a wine will be. Technically, glycerin is a by-product of alcohol production, responsible for the "legs," which is the term for how wine streams back down the glass after it's swirled. The richer and fuller the wine, the more distinct the "legs."

SWIRL AND SMELL

Swirling the wine in a glass allows the wine to come in contact with the air, releasing its aromas. "If wine has a big 'nose' it simply means it has a lot of powerful aromas," says Andrea Immer. The term *aroma* is associated with a young wine. A *bouquet* usually develops over time as all the elements meld together in the bottle.

So what do you look for when smelling a wine? For starters, Immer says, "The presence of fruit, herbs, and spices."

Wine Aromatherapy 101

A good friend, Jeff Prather, formerly a wine educator with Beaulieu Vineyard and now a wine merchant with *wine.com*, offered to develop my own appreciation for "aroma" and "bouquet."

There are few tastes, but thousands of aromas. "To learn how to distinguish some of those aromas in wine—to sensitize yourself—use foods and spices to which you're more accustomed," says Prather. "That way you'll be able to relate the aroma to something more familiar right away." What really happens when you smell a wine is the aroma reminds you of a sense memory… of a smell you've experienced before. "The fact that wine reminds you of rose petals, honey, beeswax, or pepper doesn't mean the wine has the exact aroma of those things," says Prather. "It just triggers something in your brain that brings those things to mind and gives us a common language with which to talk about wine's individual characteristics. It allows us to share our impressions. The idea is to give aroma and flavor metaphors a more tangible, memorable meaning."

Prather poured 2 ounces of inexpensive, generic white wine into four glasses. He crushed a green apple slice in the first, a pear slice in the second, a vanilla bean in the third, and added a few drops of imitation butter flavor in the fourth. I swirled and sniffed each glass, commiting the scents to memory.

He then poured a glass of 1997 Cakebread Chardonnay Reserve to test my nose. I swirled and smelled. Remarkable. They were all there—apple, pear, vanilla, and butter. It was easier than I thought! And there's a science behind it. The compounds that give green apples their flavor are also in Chardonnay. The buttery-aroma comes from part of the fermentation process. And the vanilla fragrance comes from aging wine in oak, which contains vanillin.

This quality of balanced complexity is why some wines command a higher price than others. It comes from the standard of the grapes and the time and care that is taken in the wine's aging and fermentation. So while a $5 bottle of wine may be a great everyday wine, the $40 bottle will offer higher rewards to your nose and palate.

Wine Aromatherapy—Lesson Two

Cabernet Sauvignon evokes more herbal flavors if it comes from a cooler climate or, as Prather noted, it can have "almost bell pepper characteristics." Some people really enjoy these flavors and others prefer the dark berry flavors or warmer climate Cabernets."

Prather poured 2 ounces of inexpensive red wine and crushed a few slices of bell pepper into it, then had me smell it.

Next he poured a glass of 1995 Smith & Hook Cabernet Sauvignon from Monterey. I swirled and smelled. Incredible. The bell pepper smell was unmistakable.

Then Prather poured 2 ounces of the red wine in a glass and crushed vine-ripened blackberries and currants into it. I swirled and smelled. Prather says, "What you'll usually experience is a rich, concentrated flavor somewhat reminiscent of blackberry jam."

Prather poured another 2 ounces of red wine into a wine glass and ground black pepper into it. First I swirled and smelled the wine mixture. Oh, yes—I definitely smelled black pepper, as I held back a sneeze.

He then poured a glass of Guigal Côte Rotie. A Syrah that comes from the northern Rhône Valley in France and promises a nasal-clearing black pepper aroma. I swirl and smell. Amazing again. It's absolutely there! The wine almost "needs a place of its own on my kitchen spice rack," Prather says.

The tart cherry pie or red berry aroma can also be a distinct wine aroma characteristic, especially in one style of Pinot Noir.

Prather poured another 2 ounces of the generic red wine into a glass and crushed sweet-tart red pie cherries into it.

He then poured a glass of Saintsbury Pinot Noir. I put down the glass of cherries and picked up the glass of Pinot Noir. Then, swirled and sniffed… the tart cherry aroma was definitely there!

DETERMINING WINE FLAWS OR OFF AROMAS

Today, with the latest technology used in winemaking and more attention being given to wine storage, it's less likely that you'll find a flawed wine.

An "off" wine can usually be detected by smelling it. But allow the wine to be exposed to the air for a while and then try smelling it again. A minor flaw in the wine might dissipate after it's been poured. But the smell of a truly flawed bottle of wine will remain constant. A flawed wine may have a stale or musty smell that can develop during bottle aging.

A flawed wine may have a stale or musty smell that can develop during bottle aging.

There are a variety of things that can cause off aromas in wine. While you'll likely encounter few, those you may come across are most likely to be "corked" wine and oxidized wine.

"Corked"

"Think of a damp, drizzly morning. You've just gone out to the front porch to get the newspaper which is now also damp because the papergirl forgot to wrap it in plastic. Think of how it smells—dank and musty," says Andrea Immer. "That's just how a wine smells if it's 'corked.'" A random poll of local winemakers elicited these additional descriptions: your grandmother's attic, a damp basement, a mildewed book, and even sweaty gym clothes left in the locker overnight—which would certainly be an extreme case! Nevertheless, you get the idea. "Remember," Immer says, "you'll know for sure if it doesn't go away even after the wine has been in the glass awhile."

How does it happen? "Remember, cork is really the bark of a tree," Immer says. "All kinds of mold spores and microorganisms reside in that bark before it's harvested. To remove them, and to lighten the cork, a chlorine rinse is most often used." Corks are then dried and stored, usually in a humidity-controlled environment, until they're needed. "On occasion, if the processed corks are exposed to moisture, mold spores begin to grow." If such a cork is then placed in a bottle of wine, the wine will take on the off aromas produced by the presence of the mold.

Oxidized

A principal characteristic of a wine that's been aged too long is oxidization. "An oxidized wine smells a little like a madiera or sherry," Immer says. While this aroma is desirable for those fortified wines, it isn't for table wine. A table wine that's aged too long will lose its freshness and fruitiness.

TUTORING THE TASTEBUDS

Taste and flavor are sometimes used interchangeably, when in actuality "taste" is something we sense on our tongue and flavor is something more. Bill Briwa, currently a chef instructor at the Culinary Insitute of America, Greystone, in St. Helena, Napa Valley, helped me learn the differences. Briwa set out three fruit-flavored jelly-

A table wine that's aged too long will lose its freshness and fruitiness.

beans. He says, "Close your eyes and choose one. Now, hold your nose, put the jelly-bean in your mouth and chew. What do you taste?" Try it for yourself. I bet you'll taste a nondescript sweet and chewy substance. Now, let go of your nose. What do you taste now?" Wow. A burst of fruit flavor. It works with wine, too.

"People often confuse sweetness and fruitiness when talking about wine, but sweetness is a taste on the tongue and fruitiness is perceived when your nose gets involved," says Andrea Immer. If the grape fermentation has been stopped before all the sugar is converted to alcohol, then what's left is called residual sugar. It's when the wine has more than 1 percent sugar left over that we really begin to taste the sweetness.

"In actuality, I think many Americans prefer wines with a touch of sweetness. People talk 'dry' but consume mostly 'sweet,'" says Immer. "I know that's why some California wineries leave a trace of sugar in their Chardonnays." It's rarely, if ever, advertised because consumers have been conditioned, wrongly, to believe that the more sophisticated wine is a "dry" wine.

To reinforce your perception of sweetness, mix a ½ teaspoon of sugar into a small glass with about 4 ounces of water. First, smell it. Nothing. Then, taste it. You may get a tingle on the tip of your tongue where the sweetness tastebuds are concentrated. You can't smell sweetness, right? So, if you think a wine is sweet by the smell, remember that it will certainly be "fruity" but the taste will tell you whether it has residual sugar or not. A wine can be bone dry yet very fruity.

Immer says, "Taste the difference in a dry wine and a sweet wine, one with residual sugar, and you'll now notice the difference immediately." Her examples included:

- Dry Riesling, Hugel 1997... fermented dry; fruity but not sweet.
- Late Harvest Riesling, Durney 1994, from Carmel Valley... its sweetness is readily evident.

Acidity

"Acidity kicks up the flavor of wine," says Immer. "It's the engine for flavor; it turbo charges it." It is crisp, tangy, and tart and gives wine "elegance." Some say it's a wine's backbone, the element that gives it structure and protects it from microbes as it ages.

And acidity causes you to salivate. When you salivate, foods taste better; acid helps to release the flavor elements of the food. "I can never have too much acid in wine. I just love it," says Immer. "Acid keeps the tastebuds awake." If wine doesn't have enough acidity to balance the other components, the taste seems "flat." Although some varieties characteristically have more acidity than others, you can guess that a wine might have more acidity if it comes from a cooler climate. And conversely, if you want a wine with more "fruit forward" flavors, and less acidity, look for one that comes from a warmer climate.

Tartaric acid is the main acid in wine, and its presence in grapes is higher than in most other fruits. It's accompanied by the green apple taste of malic acid and the citrus taste of citric acid.

As a reminder for your tastebuds, you can mix a ½ teaspoon of citric acid (a white powder sold in most supermarkets) or 2 tablespoons of lemon juice into 4 ounces of water. Sip it and you immediately begin to salivate and inevitably pucker up. That's sour!

In wine, "acidity" describes this mouth-puckering feeling. The word *sour* is reserved for wine that tastes vinegary, which is a negative. When acidity is a positive attribute, it is "crisp," "lively," or "tart." So the next time you're drinking a Sauvignon Blanc from the Loire in France, maybe a Sancerre, you can show off your wine vocabulary because it's one of the tartest wines around.

The Loire Valley in France has a cooler climate and Kenwood, in California's Sonoma Valley, has a much warmer climate. Sancerre, Jolivet, from the Loire makes you salivate with its vibrant acidity. The flavor lingers and sometimes your tongue will tingle. A 1997 Sauvignon Blanc from the Kenwood Vineyards will come from much riper grapes and a warmer climate. The acidity will not be as pronounced, and it might be described as smoother, more buttery, rather than tingly.

Bitterness

Bitterness is the third taste that can be perceived in wine. It's the tannin in wine—yes, the same substance that holds wine's antioxidants—that adds the element of bitterness and can also create a tactile sensation of astringency, perceived as a drying effect in the mouth. Alcohol leaches the tannin from the grape skins during fermentation. Immer says, "There is little or no perceptible tannin in white wine since the skins of red wine are in contact with the juice all through fermentation, and not so with white wine." The seeds and stems can also add tannin, and the oak barrels, in which wine is aged, can add even more.

Tannin contributes to the body and texture of wine and, along with acid and alcohol, is needed to preserve the wine as it ages. As a red wine ages, the tannins combine with pigments in the wine to form larger solids that precipitate out of the wine as sediment. "That's how the taste of an aged red mellows," says Andrea Immer. That's why you need to carefully decant an older red wine, so the sediment stays in the bottle and doesn't make it into your glass.

To remind your senses of both bitterness and astringency, brew a cup of tea. Leave the tea bag in as you let it cool. Tea tannins can be much more bitter than grape-skin tannins, but can readily demonstrate the effect of tannin on your palate. Of course you know what tea tastes like, but this time pay close attention to what happens as you sip it. Sip the tea slowly. I'll bet your expression changes immediately as your nose crinkles up in response to its bitterness. Following closely behind is the power of astringency as you suddenly feel as though you've eaten a piece of chalk. The drying effect of the tannin makes it seem as though your tongue will forever be stuck to the roof of your mouth.

"The tannins bind with the proteins on your tongue, which causes the astringent effect, the drying sensation," Immer explains.

"Taste the difference in a tannic red wine as compared to one with low tannin." encourages Immer. For example:

- Napa Ridge Pinot Noir, 1997—Very little tannin, easy to drink, relatively no perceptible bitterness.
- Cabernet Sauvignon, Mayacamas Vineyards, 1995—The tannin is very evident. The wine has a decidedly drying effect… almost makes your tongue stick to the roof of your mouth.

Great wines are like great literature—they last and reside in your memory.

FLAVOR

Flavor involves taste, smell, your sense of touch, and also, Immer says, "your expectations."

A good example of "flavor" is the perceptible "fruit" characteristic. A wine is said to have good "fruit," when the flavor aromas caress the nose and the palate.

Oak vs. Fruit

"Aging wine in oak barrels, in wine terms, adds 'complexity,'" says Immer. Oak aging is like adding a spice to a recipe. It also adds color, often evident as a golden hue, and texture, causing the wine to feel oilier, fatter, and creamier on the palate. It also inevitably adds cost since barrel aging adds a step to the winemaking process (often a lengthy one), and oak barrels are quite costly. Oak barrels, sometimes costing upwards of $700 each, can often be used only once or twice.

"Tasting the next two wines, you'll be able to discern the difference between the flavor of fruit and an added dimension when the same varietal is aged in oak," Immer says.

- Pouilly Fuisse, Bouchard—A Chardonnay from Burgundy (cooler climate)—lighter bodied wine, refreshing.
- Chardonnay, Beringer, Napa 1997—A Chardonnay from California's Napa Valley (warmer climate)—wine with more body, richer, creamier.

"You'll immediately notice a difference in color and intensity of the fruit. The characteristics from a cooler climate are higher acid, lighter color, and less pronounced fruit flavors. In a warmer climate you get less acidity, deeper color, and more intense fruit flavors." Oak aging in the California Chardonnay is responsible for the increased texture and the pronounced vanilla, oaky, buttery aroma and taste."

ALCOHOL

"Alcohol contributes to the body of wine, " says Andrea Immer. "It gives wine a richness and 'thickness.'" The viscosity of a low-alcohol wine could be compared to skim milk. As you move up the scale with more and more alcohol, you go through whole milk all the way to heavy cream. And when the alcohol is high, greater than 14 percent, it can wreak havoc with a wine's balance, "sometimes tasting 'hot' by creating a burning sensation at the back of your throat," says Immer.

FINISH

We conclude appropriately with wine's "finish"—tastes that linger after you've swallowed the wine. A highly regarded attribute, the higher the wine's quality, the longer the finish. Great wines are like great literature—they last and reside in your memory.

BREAKING ALL THE RULES—FOOD AND WINE PAIRING

YOU'RE SEATED WITH A GROUP OF FRIENDS at a restaurant. The waiter offers the wine list. With a smile and nod you reluctantly accept it. You try to get rid of it by passing it to the next person. The list is passed from one person to the next like a hot potato. It finally lands in your hands again and everyone at the table agrees that you have the most wine knowledge. You panic as you look over the list. Everyone's having something completely different to eat. Which wine should you choose? How can you possibly decide? Will you be shunned forever by your fellow diners and, even worse, the restaurant sommelier if you make the 'wrong' choice? Quick, what were those "rules" again?

Most of us have heard the "rules" at one time or another: red wine with red meat and white wine with chicken or fish, but which red and which white? And what if you prefer white, but love beef; or prefer chicken, but lean toward gangbuster Syrahs? According to the rules, salad can never be paired successfully with any wine. Does that mean you're out of luck if your idea of lunch or dinner is a big garden salad?

REVISITING THE "OLD RULES"

The "old rules" appear simple but obviously they still don't make things any easier. "It was someone's marketing scheme run amok," says Tim Hanni, the first American to pass the arduous tests run by England's Institute of Master of Wine. "Thirty years ago, Americans just weren't drinking very much wine so someone thought up a scheme of making some simple rules so it would be less intimidating for people to make wine choices," says Hanni. "Trouble is, the rules don't have any sound basis on which to fall back. They also leave no room to talk about the big difference in taste a sauce or other ingredients can add to a dish." Now that Americans are enjoying wine more often, "they're willing to try varietals, and the old rules are too limiting."

So, how can we drink what we like and eat what we enjoy?

CELEBRATING OUR DIFFERENCES

We all have unique taste preferences. What seems sour to some might seem delicious to someone else. What seems hot and spicy to one might seem mild to another. Some of us naturally prefer stronger tastes and some milder. These preferences determine the wine we enjoy and how we respond to wine and food combinations. Perhaps the most important concept to remember is that there is no strict right and wrong in food pairing or wine appreciation.

Hanni, formerly with Beringer Wine Estates, owns his own company, Wine Logic, Inc., and is a professional chef. He says, "Our industry is arrogant when it comes to explanations of wine and food pairings. I think the attitude is frankly just a defense to cover up what many just don't know." How many times have you heard food and wine pairing descriptions like this: "The big, oaky, butterscotch flavors in the Chardonnay complement the smoky flavor of the grilled halibut, and the wine's slightly herbal character accentuates the tarragon in the cream sauce ever so slightly, creating a match made in Heaven." While this might be a sensory reality for some, it just adds to confusion for others.

Granted, some professionals have their own elaborate pairing philosophies. While this might help them grasp subtler, deeper textures and shades, it is far too elaborate and unhelpful to the average or self-educated wine drinker. Most of us just want to be able to drink good wine and enjoy our meal, without the oversimplification of the red/meat–white/poultry and fish paradigm, or the advanced oenological calculus of the most advanced and sophisticated professionals.

DRINK WHAT YOU ENJOY WITH CONFIDENCE

The good news is that the wine industry is itself taking the lead to help make wine more approachable and scupper its myths. Jancis Robinson, internationally renowned wine writer and wine educator, says, "It's perfectly possible to drink anything while eating anything. There may truly be one perfect food match for each and every wine but for most of us life is just too short to work out what it is." What a refreshing and radical departure from the usual complicated wine and food pairing philosophies.

Tim Hanni led a group of three of us—Sarah Scott, executive chef at Robert Mondavi winery; Mark DeVere, a Master of Wine and wine educator at Robert Mondavi; and me—through his unique and much simplified version of wine and food pairing. We came together out of our shared professional curiosity about food and wine pairing.

Sarah Scott frequently presents food and wine demonstrations and wanted a way to give her audiences "the tools they needed" to do their own food and wine pairing without recourse to a vintner's slide rule.

Mark DeVere noted that as a presenter of wines during winemaker dinners, "The guests expected me to have all the answers because I had the Master of Wine designation. Before I understood the cause-and-effect reaction from the balance of taste components in food, I couldn't explain why one dish might affect the taste of a particular wine and another wouldn't."

Hanni's office is in the loft of a charming old winery at the south end of the Napa Valley. On a classically sunny wine country afternoon we made our way up the creaking wooden staircase.

It was here we learned the two fundamental principles of Tim Hanni's Wine Logic.

You can drink any wine with any food as long as the food is in "balance."

1. SWEET OR "SAVORY" FOODS MAKE ANY WINE TASTE "STRONGER." "Sweet or savory foods make a wine taste drier, more sour (*acidic* is the wine term), and more tannic, sometimes even bitter." Sweet foods are anything that includes some form of sugar: fruit, fruit juice, honey, or even hoisin sauce. Examples of savory foods are ripe tomatoes, scallops, mushrooms, beef, stocks, and sauces.

2. WINES WILL TASTE "MILDER" WITH SOUR (MORE ACIDIC) OR SALTY FOODS. "A wine can seem less tart/acidic and therefore fruitier or even less tannic or bitter," adds Hanni, when it is paired with sour tastes that come from lemons, limes, vinegars, capers, mustards, and verjus (the unfermented juice from underripe grapes often used in French cooking). A salty taste can come from things like olives that were cured in a brine, soy sauce, anchovy paste, or Thai fish sauce.

HOW BASIC INGREDIENTS INFLUENCE WINE TASTE

sweet —>stronger

savory —>stronger

salt —>milder

acid (sour) —>milder

As we age, our taste buds mature and some people obviously develop more of a tolerance than others for certain tastes in food. When we talk about wine, the same is true. "Some like a stronger, more bitter taste;—a high-alcohol, tannic Cabernet Sauvignon;—and some really only enjoy wine with a milder, sweeter taste, an off-dry Riesling or White Zinfandel (both have a bit of residual sugar)," says Hanni. "The key is to slow down enough to be able to recognize the tastes and discover just what our individual preferences are."

Scott, who traded in her chef coat to become a taster for the day, told us about an exercise she participated in to relearn the art of tasting. "I was given a handful of raisins, and told to put one in my mouth. First, I felt the raisin's texture. Then I bit down to taste it. The idea was to get all the senses engaged." After swallowing, the raisin's taste quickly disappeared, but Scott had a desire to try another. "It was a fascinating experience and one that showed me that, even as a chef, I rarely pay as close attention as I could to what I'm tasting. I'm guilty, as I'm sure many of us are, of eating for the sake of sustenance and not necessarily to really enjoy the experience of tasting."

TUNE INTO THE ELEMENTS OF BALANCE

Hanni firmly believes you can drink any wine with any food as long as the food is in "balance." When food is in "balance" it won't overly accentuate any one characteristic in the wine. This is a new concept for some but, as Hanni says, "it's the absolute key. Once you have become accustomed to what each of the individual taste components can do to create balance, then you can easily adjust for your taste preferences." He emphasizes, "You have to experiment to learn what tastes you prefer and to under-

Balace is part of the food culture in France, and can be adapted to your own kitchen with a pinch of salt or a wedge of lemon.

stand each element's effect on the whole. Keep in mind, some combinations work because it's a combination a diner is emotionally connected to and not because it's the only right way to go."

SEE FOR YOURSELF

There's nothing like firsthand experience. All you need is a glass of wine, any wine, a Red Delicious apple, a wedge of lemon or lime, honey, and some salt.

First, taste the wine. What do you taste? Remember taste is what you sense on your tongue, before you notice the wine's flavor. Is it sweet, sour (acidic), astringent, bitter?

Now taste the apple. Chew it; concentrate on what you're tasting. It's probably more sweet than sour. Swallow.

Taste the wine again. What happened? Does it taste different? Most likely it does, and possibly some characteristic is "stronger." If it's a Cabernet Sauvignon with a lot of tannin (astringency) you might taste more astringency (that drying sensation in your mouth) and the wine can seem bitter.

Squeeze some lemon or lime juice on the apple and add a light sprinkling of salt. Now taste the apple again. You'll taste the acidity right away. What you're doing is beginning to condition your tastebuds for the coming sip of wine.

Taste the wine again. Is the wine milder, stronger, or does it stay the same? Does it seem as balanced, as it did originally? Likely, the wine seems milder, closer to its taste before you tasted the apple.

One last confirmation: take another slice of apple and drizzle some honey on it. Taste it. Then taste the wine. Likely, it tastes more tannic or bitter.

It's really pretty simple, once you become accustomed to thinking in terms of balance—and of balancing your meal's tastes to suit the wine you enjoy. The adjustment will very likely become second nature.

OLD WORLD TRADITIONS REVISITED

Balance isn't a new concept. "Think of how a beefsteak is served in Tuscany," says Hanni. "It comes with a generous squeeze of lemon, a sprinkling of salt, and a glass of Chianti—wine made from mostly Sangiovese grapes that characteristically are higher in acid." By tasting the lemon juice with the steak, your palate has already somewhat adapted to the acidity, so acidity in the wine should be less pronounced— it will taste "milder" and seem more in balance with the other elements. "In Burgundy," Hanni added, "your hearty red wine will often be accompanied by rabbit in a sauce with mustard or vinegar, both high in acid."

Sarah Scott noted that on a trip to Bordeaux, "Everywhere I ordered fresh oysters, a mignonette sauce of vinegar and shallots came alongside. A wine pairing was difficult unless I ate the mignonette sauce with the oysters. When I cooked there, my French assistant always finished everything off with a squeeze of lemon, or splash of vinegar, and a dash of salt." Balance is part of the food culture in France, and can be adapted to your own kitchen with a pinch of salt or a wedge of lemon.

PREVIOUSLY DAUNTING COMBINATIONS

But, what about the "rule" that you can't serve wine with salad? Again, it's all really a matter of achieving balance. With salads, the trick is balancing the acidic content. In salads with very high acid—as is characteristic of most vinaigrettes—most wine will taste flat or out of balance. A solution might be to use a sweeter vinegar, such as balsamic, or even to add a little honey, or raisins. If one of the wine's leading characteristics is acid, as is the case with a cool climate Sauvignon Blanc, the adjustment needed will be minimal since the acid levels are similar.

The savory characteristic of asparagus and artichokes, traditionally known as "enemies" of wine, can often be balanced with a zesty vinaigrette. I usually just squeeze a wedge of lemon over the top of a steamed artichoke, or steamed, fresh asparagus, and it allows me to enjoy almost any wine selection.

The bottom line? You *can* enjoy the food you like with the wine you like, if you remember the principle of balance, which is simply this: If your food causes your wine to taste stronger—more bitter, more acidic, less fruity—in a way that's not pleasing to your palate—season your food with sour and salty ingredients; if your wine tastes too mild—sweeter, fruitier, less acidic, less tannic than you enjoy—season your food with sweet or savory tastes. One example is the classic combination of salty prosciutto and sweet melon. The salty prosciutto makes wine taste "milder" or even bland. Add sweet melon and you restore balance. When you taste the wine, it's again a pleasant taste. Conversely, the melon on its own will sway the balance in the other direction and the wine will taste "stronger." It's clearly the combination that does the trick.

SCIENCE TO THE RESCUE

There is, of course, science behind the taste test. "It's called 'adaptation,'" says Hanni. "There are two types: sensory and cross-adaptation." Sensory adaptation is when you squeeze the lemon juice over the beefsteak to balance it with a high-acid Chianti. Says Hanni, "Your senses have already begun to adapt to the acid levels so the wine's acidity won't dominate its other tastes in combination with the food. It's the same thing when you walk out to your mailbox on a brisk, cold day without your jacket. When you return to the house you feel the need to adjust your thermostat because it seems warmer than it was a few minutes ago. What's happened is that your body has adapted to the cold."

A "cross-adaptation" is one where a taste seems unnaturally exaggerated. You've just brushed your teeth but forgot to drink the rest of the grapefruit juice you poured minutes earlier. When you take a sip it's almost unbearably sour. The acidity becomes over-exaggerated.

There are seasonings that can wreak havoc with wine because they adversely sensitize your mouth. In scientific terms it's called "chemesthesis." A reaction from raw garlic, spicy seasonings, hot chilies, white pepper, and others will inevitably make a wine taste more bitter. And sometimes the sensation lingers. Says Hanni, "The good news is that food with salty and sour tastes are inclined to ease the effect."

On those occasions when the wine itself is, for example, a big, heavily oaked, high-alcohol Zinfandel, it may be impossible to taste anything else. Nothing can compete or compensate.

THE REAL TEST

To get out of the laboratory and around the dining table, we decided to test the theory on "real" food. "Real" food to those of us with Southern roots, like Hanni's, Scott's, and mine, means good ol', down home Southern cookin'. So we had a platter of fried chicken, baked ham, barbecued ribs, coleslaw, garden fresh tomatoes, juicy, sweet cantaloupe, and rich, gooey brownies fresh from the oven. If it worked with

The balance theory makes sense—taste sense.

those foods, it was bound to work in many other situations, even with English cooking (a little humor, since our partner Mark DeVere is an Englishman).

With a plate of lemons, a salt shaker, and a bit of honey nearby, we tried the balance theory for ourselves. We tasted the wine before the food, and then again after.

Our wine choices: a hearty, rich Borolo (highly acidic and tannic); a luscious, oaky Chardonnay (dry with a touch of tannin—added by the oak aging); a sweet thick dessert wine (almost as syrupy sweet as the honey); and a crisp, elegant champagne (characteristically high in acid). We proceeded by swirling, smelling, sipping, "slurping," and then swallowing the wine.

First, the champagne (OK, we didn't swirl and slurp the champagne, just smelled and sipped). We each took a bite of chicken and then another sip of champagne. At first the champagne seemed too stark a contrast to the savory Southern fried chicken. The acid was exaggerated. So we squeezed a little lemon and sprinkled a little salt on the chicken. Now the combination worked. The balance had been reestablished.

We tried the other dishes and wine combinations, always tasting the wine first, then the food, then the wine again. Small adjustments restored balance, creating delicious combinations. The ham was very salty, so we had a little cantaloupe alongside to compensate. The BBQ ribs were both sweet and acidic, but their sweet and savory characteristic seemed overpowering. So we added a splash of red wine vinegar. The coleslaw was acidic and sweet, with the mayonnaise moving it a bit over the edge. But with a squeeze of lemon, it complemented the wine. And the tomatoes, those vine-ripe luscious tomatoes, were both very sweet and slightly acidic. For balance, they actually needed a little more acid, so we added a touch of red wine vinegar and a dash of salt.

Finally, at dessert, we all wanted to test the chocolate–and–red wine combination. "What you'll find," said Hanni, "is that if your wine isn't sweeter than your dessert, the dessert can make the wine taste stronger, objectionable to some but a taste others crave." He was right. The brownie emphasized the Cabernet Sauvignon's tannins—good for some, not so good for others. But the sweet dessert wine was a 100 percent success, unaltered by the dessert.

Together, we found the balance theory makes sense—taste sense, that is. Hanni reminded us, "It's important to remember everyone's taste is different. One person might like the strong taste of a wine created by the combination and someone else might not. At least now we have a way to help everyone achieve the taste they enjoy."

So, the next time the wine list goes flying around the table, grab it with confidence and ask for the wine everyone would most like to drink, regardless of the food they've ordered. And if your fellow diners press you into a discussion of what goes best with their choice of entrée, take it with a grain of salt, or a drizzle of honey, and pass the lemons!

WINE TRENDS FOR THE NEW MILLENNIUM

NOT EVEN SO TRADITIONAL AN INDUSTRY as the wine industry can afford to stay still. Change has helped preserve and expand on vintners' good traditions. So what does the future hold for wine? The good news is—even more improvement. In particular, you'll see increased emphasis on the dining experience. The public will begin to understand that meals—as times of great joy and sharing—are enhanced by wine. "Wine snobbery" will fade—with a hearty push from the wine industry itself.

LET THE EXPLORATION BEGIN

You'll likely see more expensive "cult" wines from the wine industry equivalent of microbrewers. Meanwhile, from the bigger labels, we'll continue to see improving quality wine and lower prices—a trend that will be accelerated by wine's growing popularity. And new wine-drinkers, as they become more experienced, will begin to search out varietals beyond Chardonnay, Cabernet Sauvignon, and Merlot, expanding the universe of popular varietals.

UNDERSTANDING HOW "WINEGROWING" INFLUENCES FLAVOR

Consumers will become increasingly aware of the relationship between location and the ultimate expression and style of grape varieties. The region in which a grape is grown (*Appellation*) and farming practices can greatly influence a wine's flavor and other characteristics. New wine drinkers will not only learn to identify these characteristics, but articulate them as well. And their descriptions of taste, will lead them to new wines. If dry and crisp are the adjectives they prefer, they'll learn more, for example, about Alsatian Rieslings, Pinot Gris, Italian Pinot Grigios, among others. And as the popularity of alternate wine varietals increases, prices will fall.

What does the future hold for wine? Even more improvement.

WINE IN CYBERSPACE

Increasing availability through the Internet is an area well worth mentioning. In this age of convenience, many are likely to turn to the Internet, to sites such as *wine.com* or *wineshopper.com* for speedy advice and speedy delivery. Imagine the wine arriving on your doorstep the day after you order. We still have hurdles to get over in regard to wine shipping regulations into several U.S. states that don't currently allow direct shipment. But inevitably the demand will be such that the consumer will have a tremendous influence. (Visit *winesense.com* for information on moderate wine consumption and a balanced, healthy lifestyle.)

MORE GOOD HEALTH NEWS

Studies on the positive affects of moderate wine consumption will continue to be published and publicized as the evidence becomes increasingly more conclusive that benefits—outside of the already well-documented cardiovascular benefits—are far reaching.

WINE TASTINGS TO DINE FOR

More restaurants will make wine more accessible by offering carefully selected samplings—usually of two or three similar wines/varietals with different characteristics—as recommended choices to accompany a meal. Also, the number of wines available by-the-glass, or even by-the-half-glass, will increase, as will the availability of half-bottles.

STRATEGIC PARTNERSHIPS

Watch for more strategic partnering between wine companies in different countries. They'll share their winemaking knowledge, vineyard development techniques, and marketing expertise.

VARIETALS TO WATCH FOR

WHITE WINE

Chardonnay

Big, rich, oaky, high-alcohol Chardonnay will remain popular, but you'll also find the same wine drinker searching out the best value from Chablis, where styles are lighter and crisper and less oaky.

Pinot Grigio

Here's a wine that's easy to like whether you're looking for an aperitif, something to sip on a warm afternoon, or a light white for a first course. European varieties are more tart than those from California that, while equally light and refreshing, emphasize a fruity flavor.

Sauvignon Blanc

Another white that's easy to like. I know many White Zinfandel lovers who have recently discovered California Sauvignon Blanc and have made it their wine of choice with a meal. Sauvignon Blancs from France and New Zealand can be pleasingly tart with citrus, kiwi, and lime flavors or even a slightly herbal accent, while those from California have more ripe melon, peach, and fig flavors while retaining crisp acidity.

RED WINE

Syrah and Syrah Blends

Perhaps best known from the Rhône region in France, the Syrah grape is now being more widely planted in the Napa Valley and beyond. It's also known as Shiraz in Australia. These wines can be plummy, peppery, rich, and spicy. They're often full of ripe berry flavors and lively acidity. Styles will range from the elegant to a "big dog" red.

You'll also see U.S. producers making traditional Rhône blends with Syrah, grenache, mourvedre, and carignane.

Zinfandel

A tradition in California, Zinfandel even has its own promotional society! Those who enjoy blockbuster, high-alcohol, chewy, jammy wines are among its biggest fans. While there are more styles that lean toward elegance, the direction of the trend seems to be the more "rustic" and powerful.

Sangiovese

Sangiovese, known in Italy as the Chianti grape, has an acidity level higher than many red wines and can be a refreshing change from some of the heavier, tannic red wines. It's often light, fresh, and reminiscent of raspberries or other red berry fruit. It can be pleasantly spicy and always an easy favorite at mealtime—known among other attributes for its ability to bring out the best in a meal when a classic tomato sauce is served. Look for Sangiovese blends to become more readily available.

Pinot Noir

A red that's easy to like, and deserves to be more popular. It's known for its soft, inviting tannins and rich fruit. In California—and the Northwest where it's also grown—you're likely to experience cherry-berry fruit flavors, with rich texture. Pinot Noirs from Europe, while equally as inviting, can have a more earthy character which some wine-drinkers prefer.

BACK TO THE FUTURE... AND THEN SOME

So the future of wine in America is one of booming growth and popularity, bringing treasured and joyous traditions from the steadfast, fruitful "old" world to the fast-paced, exciting new. It is a marriage of past and present that should make for a wonderful, healthy future.

NOTES

1 Blackwelder, W.C., et al., Alcohol and Mortality: The Honolulu Heart Study, *American Journal of Medicine*, 1980; 68(2);164–169.

2 Fuchs, C.S., et al., Alcohol consumption and mortality among women, *New England Journal of Medicine*, 1995; 332(19): 1245–1250.

3 Yuan, J. (USC researcher), et al., Follow-up study of moderate alcohol intake and mortality among middle-aged men in Shanghai, China, *British Medical Journal*, 1997; 314:18–23.

4 Doll, R., and Peto, R., Mortality in relation to consumption of alcohol: 13 years' observations on male British doctors, *British Medical Journal*, 1994; 39:911–918.

5 Klatsky, A., et al., Alcohol and Mortality: A Ten-Year Kaiser Permanente Experience, *Annals of Internal Medicine*, 1981; 117. LaPorte, R.E., et al., Alcohol, Coronary Heart Disease, and Total Mortality, *Recent Developments in Alcohol*, 1985; 3:157–163.

6 Dennis Schaeffer, as reported in *Guest West Magazine*.

7 Coate, D., Moderate Drinking and Coronary Heart Disease Mortality; Evidence from NHANES I and NHANES I Follow-Up, *American Journal of Public Health*, 1993; 83 (6):888–890.

8 Holbrook, T., and Barrett-Connor, E., A prospective study of alcohol consumption and bone mineral density, *British Medical Journal*, 1993; 306:1506–1509.

9 Nelson, H., et al., Smoking, alcohol, and neuromuscular and physical function of older women, *Journal of the American Medical Association*, 1994; 272(223):1825–1831.

10 Malloy, Dr. Mary Ann, Psychological benefits to wine consumption…, *Lancet*, September 1998.

11 Lipton, R., The effect of moderate alcohol use on the relationship between stress and depression, *American Journal of Public Health*, 1994; 84(12):1913–1917.

12 National Institute on Alcohol Abuse and Alcoholism, Moderate Drinking, *Alcohol Alert*, 1992; 16(315).

13 Ibid.

14 Columbia University, findings published in January 6, 1999, issue of the *Journal of the American Medical Association*, as reported by Reuters, January 5, 1999.

15 Physicians' Health Study, ongoing Harvard study including 22,000 doctors, as reported by American Academy of Neurology (Reuters, April 22, 1999).

16 Camargo, C.A., Jr., et al., Prospective study of moderate alcohol consumption and risk of peripheral arterial disease in U.S. male physicians, *Circulation*, 1997; 95(3):577–580.

17 Jepson, R.G., et al., Alcohol intake as a risk factor for peripheral arterial disease in the general population in the Edinburgh Artery Study, *European Journal of Epidemiology*, 1995; 11:9–14

18 Gillman, W.M., et al., Relationship of alcohol intake with blood pressure, *Hypertension*, 1995; 25:1106–1110. Klatsky, A., et al., Alcohol Consumption and Blood Pressure: Kaiser Permanente Multiphasic Health Examination Data, *New England Journal of Medicine*, 1987; 296(21):1194–2001. Stamler, J., Blood Pressure and High Blood Pressure: Aspects of Risk, *Hypertension*, 1991; 18(3 Suppl.).

19 American Heart Association (AHA), Mary Ann Malloy, M.D., spokesperson for AHA and a cardiologist at Loyola University Stritch School of Medicine in Maywood, Illinois (*Food and Wine*, February 1998).

20 Gammon, Marlie, et al., *(American) Journal of the National Cancer Institute*, 1997

21 Shaffer, Alyssa Lustigman, "Healthy Living."

22 Prescott, Dr. Eva, Copenhagen University Hospital, Denmark, *American Journal of Epidemiology*, 1999; 149:463–470.

23 Michaud, Dominique S., Harvard School of Public Health, National Institute of Health, and American Cancer Society, *New England Journal of Medicine*, May 6, 1999.

24 Curhan, G., et al., Prospective study of beverage use and the risk of kidney stones, *American Journal of Epidemiology*, 1996; 143(5):487–494.

25 Tripler Army Medical Center, Honolulu, 1995. Peterson, Walter, M.D., University of Texas Southwestern Medical Center in Dallas.

26 Brenner, Hermann, M.D., German Institute for Human Nutrition in Pastdam-Rehbrucke, Germany.

27 Gronbaek, M., et al., Mortality associated with moderate intakes of wine, beer, and spirits, *British Medical Journal*, 1995; 310:1165–1169.

28 Carmelli, D., Christian, C., et al., World War II-veteran male twins who are discordant for alcohol consumption: 24-year mortality, *American Journal of Public Health*, 1995; 85(1):99–101.

29 Rimm, E.B., et al., Prospective study of cigarette smoking, alcohol use, and risk of diabetes in men, *British Medical Journal*, 1995; 310:555–559.

30 Voit, L., et al., Smoking, obesity, alcohol consumption, and the risk of rheumatoid arthritis, *Epidemiology*, 1994; 5:525–532.

31 Cohen, S., et al., Smoking, alcohol consumption, and susceptibility to the common cold, *American Journal of Public Health*, 1993; 83(9):1277–1283.

PHOTOGRAPHY CREDITS

INDEX

acidity, 187–88

acids, 188

adaption, 199

Age-Related Macular Degeneration (AMD), 16

aging, wine, 2, 3, 9–10

alcohol: abuse of, 6; benefit to women of, 16; digestive system and, 6; as diuretic, 15; fermentation and, 188–89; French consumption of, 3; health benefits of, 5; heart disease and, 4, 8; longevity and, 8–9; physical performance and, 10; production of, 183; psychological benefits of, 10–11; weight regulation and, 9; in wine, 190–91. *See also* wine

Alexander Vineyards Gewürtztraminer, 91

almonds, 68, 75; macaroons with, 114; tart with, 130

Alsatian Riesling, 203

Alzheimer's disease, 3

Amaretto, 130

AMD. *See* Age-Related Macular Degeneration

American Health Society, 14

American Heart Association's Nutrition Committee, 8

American Journal of Epidemiology, 15

Andrus, Nancy and Gary, 26

angula, 62

antioxidants: cancer and, 13; in fruits, 7; in grape skin, 8; quercetin, 13; in red wine, 4, 7, 13; resveratrol, 13; in vegetables, 7; in wine, 7–8

Appelation, 203

apples: juice of, 144; in salad, 101; in tarts, 124; torte with, 75

Archery Summit Pinot Noir, 27, 91

arthritis, 3, 15

artichokes: Moroccan, 93; in salad, 58; spring, 58; wine and, 198

arugula, 42, 176

Asiago, 60, 94

asparagus, 58, 198

aspirin, 5

astringency, 188

atherosclerosis, 3, 4, 5, 13

Australia, 205

avocados, 72, 92, 122

bacon, 59

Baked Alaska "Snowballs", 102

balance: food in, 196–97; health and, 2; tradition and, x; wine and, 191, 196–97

bamboo shoots, 100

bananas, in smoothies, 144

Bancroft Vineyard Cabernet Sauvignon, 27

Bandol, 113

barbecuing, 39

Barret, Bo, 36

Barret, Heidi Peterson, 36, 96

basil, 55, 128

bass. *See* sea bass

beans: black, 147; fava, 84; garbanzo, 177; green, 29, 84; kidney, 79, 177; vanilla, 162

Beau Monde seasoning, 152

beef: chuck meat, 129; filet mignon, 32; in lasagna, 55; New York strip, 115; pot roast, 129; red wine and, 32; rib-eye steaks, 134; sautéed steaks of, 32; sirloin, 32; strip, 32; testing for doneness of, 32

beets: baby, 42; chioggia, 42, 106; gold, 42; red, 42; roasted, 42; in salad, 31, 106

Beringer Wine Estates, 194

berries: blackberries, 49, 109, 122; blueberries, 49, 128; cranberries, 71; fresh, 122; raspberries, 49, 122, 128; in smoothies, 144; strawberries, 30, 44, 49, 122; with tropical coulis, 156

bismuth salicylate, 15

Bistro Jeanty, 88

bitter, 96

black beans, 147

blackberries, 49, 109, 122

Blanc de Blancs: Domaine Chandon, 83; Schramsberg, 71

Blanc de Noirs: Domaine Chandon, 83; Schramsberg, 71, 74

blood alcohol, 6

blood clotting, 5, 7

blueberries, 49, 128, 144

Blue Nun, 126

Bon Appétit, 96

bone density, 10

Borolo, 200

E. coli, 15
eating: moderation in, x; rules for, 21–22
edible flowers, 176
Edmunds St. John Syrah, 105
eggplant, 50, 114
Ellison, R. Curtis, 3–4, 6, 16
endive, Belgian, 106
England, 193
estrogen, 4, 9–10
Etude Pinot Blanc, 57, 143
Europe, 164
Europeans, wine consumption of, 4
exercise, 22, 40, 142, 154

Fall-Winter menus, 27, 41, 47, 53, 57, 65,
    77, 83, 91, 99, 105, 113, 119, 127, 133,
    137, 143, 151, 155, 159, 165, 171, 175
Far Niente Dolce, 117
fats, 21
fennel, 172
fermentation, 182, 184, 187
feta cheese, 92, 101, 106
Fife, Dennis, 104
Fife Vineyards, 104
Fife Vineyards L'Attitude 39, 105
Fife Vineyards Max Curee, 105
Fife Vineyards "Redhead Vineyard" Petite
    Syrah, 105
Fife Vineyards "Redhead Vineyard" Zinfandel,
    105
figs, 86, 139, 145
filet mignon, 32
fish: catfish, 160; grilled, 58; red snapper,
    147; sea bass, 74, 78, 134, 153; swordfish,
    172; testing for doneness of, 121
flan, 149
flatbread, grilled, 145
flavonoids, 8, 13
flowers, edible, 176
foie gras, 3
food: in balance, 196–97; pairing of wine and,
    xi, 193–201; "real", 199; saturated-fat, 3;
    sea salt and, 96–97; wine and, x, xi, 118,
    170
food poisoning, 3, 15
France: alcohol consumption in, 3; food
    culture in, 198; incidence of heart disease
    in, 3; Loire Valley in, 188; Mediterranean
    diet in, 1; Rhone Valley in, 185, 205;
    Sauvignon Blanc of, 205; unfermented
    juice of unripe grapes used in, 87

Freemark Abbey Merlot, 53
Freemark Abbey Riesling, 52, 53, 54
Freemark Abbey Winery, 52
The French Paradox, 3, 5
Frog's Leap Chardonnay, 159
Frog's Leap "Leapfrogmilch", 175
Frog's Leap Merlot, 175
Frog's Leap Winery, 174
Frog's Leap Zinfandel, 175
fruits, antioxidants in, 7
Fume Blanc. *See* Sauvignon Blanc
Fussell, Barry, 96

garlic: broccoli sautéed with, 33; elephant, 28;
    raw, 28; roasted, 28; sautéed, 28; swiss
    chard with fresh, 163
German sparkling wine, 90
Gewürztraminer: Alexander Vineyards, 91;
    Lazy Creek, 65
glycerin, 183
Goldberg, David, 6
Grace Family Vineyard, 36
Grand Marnier, 130
grapefruit, in champagne, 73
grape juice, 182
grapes: Chianti, 206; fermentation of, 187;
    harvesting, 174; juice of red, 8; Pinot
    Blanc, 143; in salad, 72; Sangiovese,
    197–98; standard of, 184; style of varieties
    of, 203; Syrah, 205; tartaric acid in, 188;
    unfermented juice of unripe, 87
grape skin, antioxidants in, 8
gratin, potato, 87
gravy, smoked turkey, 39
greens: baby, 50; baby lettuce, 48; baby spring
    salad, 43; beet, 176; chard, 153; kale, 153;
    mixed torn lettuce, 48; napa cabbage, 153;
    radicchio, 153; with Spicy Lamb Stew,
    110; spring, 176; wilting of, 153; winter,
    153. *See also* salad
grenache, 205
Guigal Côte Rotie, 185

H. pylori, 15
halibut, 58; on fig leaves with ratatouille, 121;
    in lemon ginger marinade, 48; steaks of,
    48
Hanni, Tim, wine-food pairing and, 193–201
Harrison Zebra Zinfandel, 99
Harvard School of Public Health, 14

Patz & Hall Hyde Vineyard Pinot Noir, 57

peaches: baked summer, 114; fresh, 128; in ice cream, 139; white, 92

pears: baked, 94; Bartlett, 117; Bosc, 94, 111; caramel, 117; liqueur with, 162; poached, 111, 162; in salad, 72, 172

Pearsell, Paul, 20

peas, 59, 84

pecans, 42, 75

peppercorns, 49, 134

peppers, 161; with grilled chicken, 152; jalapeno, 121, 134, 148; red, 43, 117; roasted, 43; roasted, stuffed, 117; serrano chili, 148

Pepto-Bismol, 15

peripheral artery disease (PAD), 3, 12

pesto sauce, 145

pheasant, grilled, 173

Phelps, Joe and Lois, 132

Phoenicia, 96

Physicians' Health Study, 12

pie: lemon meringue, 140; Napa Pumpkin, 179

pilaf, rice, 124

pineapples, 156; in salsa, 134

pine nuts, 74, 124

Pine Ridge Chenin Blanc, 47

Pine Ridge Merlot, 27

Pine Ridge Napa Valley Chardonnay, 27

Pine Ridge Winery, 26

Pinot Blanc: Etude, 57, 143; fruity, 119

Pinot Grigio, xi, 205; Italian, 203; La Famiglia de Robert Mondavi, 119

Pinot Gris, 203

Pinot Noir, 83, 86, 155, 185, 206; Archery Summit, 27, 91; morel mushrooms and, 85; Patz & Hall Hyde Vineyard, 57; Robert Mondavi, 119; Saintsbury, 77, 133, 171; sauce with, 123; Truchard, 159

platelets, 5, 11

polenta: with Asiago, 94; cheesecake with, 44; traditional preparation of, 94

pork: grilled, 101; honey-roasted, 32; loin, 32, 101; roasted tenderloin of, 168

potatoes: garlic horseradish mashed, 173; garlic mashed, 160; Gold, 66; gratin with, 87; pancakes with zucchini and, 33; pan fried, 49; red, 49, 173; "smashed", 134, 135; in soup, 66; sweet, 153; Yukon Gold, 135, 160

pot roast, 129

Pouilly Fuisse, Bouchard, 190

Prather, Jeff, 184

prawns, barbecued, 176

Pride Mountain Viognier, 155

primavera, pasta, 156

produce, freshness of, ix–x

prosciutto, 59, 139, 198

protein, 21

Provençe, 132

pumpkin pie, 179

purée, vegetable, 101

quality of life, 2

quercitin, 13

quiche, Brie, 166

rabbit stew, 93

radicchio, 153

radishes, 176

raisins, 68, 124, 177

raita, cucumber, 114

raspberries, 122, 128; brownies with chocolate and, 167; cabernet sauce with, 49; in champagne, 73; sauce with, 169; in smoothies, 144; vinegar with, 72

Ratatouille, 121

red grape juice, 8, 13

red snapper, 147

red wine: antioxidants in, 4, 7, 13; appearance of, 183; beef and, 32; in cashew chili, 177; health benefits of, 4, 8; heart disease and, 2–3; with leg of lamb, 116; leg of lamb and, 116; pears poached in, 111; polenta cheesecake with strawberries in, 44; in raspberry cabernet sauce, 49; with rigatoni and sausage, 45; in Roquefort Butter, 115; tannin in, 189. See also white wine; wine

Reiff, Linda, 170

Renaud, Serge, 3, 5

resveratrol, 13

rheumatoid arthritis, 3, 15

Rhône Valley, 132, 185, 205

rice: Arborio, 29, 59, 115; basmati, 78, 80, 163, 177; brown, 124; wild, 66, 67

ricotta, 114

Ridge Zinfandel, 41, 133

Riesling: Alsatian, 203; Freemark Abbey, 52, 53; Freemark Abbey Riesling, 54; Frog's Leap "Leapfrogmilch", 175; Hugel Dry, 33; Late Harvest, 33; white peaches with, 92

sorbet, 54

sorrel, 92

soup: avocado, 122; avocado and lime, 92; butternut squash, 38; roasted tomato, 178; sherried cream of mushroom, 168; sweet corn and potato, 66; vegetable, 157

sour, 96, 188

sparkling wine, 74; German, 90; mussels in, 86; Schramsberg Blanc de Noirs, 71; Schramsberg Napa Valley, 73

Spellman, Joseph, 182

spinach, 42

Spottswoode Sauvignon Blanc, 77, 127, 151, 165

Spottswoode Winery, 126

Spring-Summer menus, 27, 37, 41, 47, 53, 57, 65, 77, 83, 91, 99, 105, 113, 119, 127, 133, 137, 143, 151, 155, 159, 165, 171, 175

squash: butternut, 38; in garden pasta toss, 54; in lasagna, 55; in soup, 38; summer, 84; yellow, 54, 55; yellow crookneck, 161

St. Helena, 17, 56, 112

St. Supery Red Meritage, 137

St. Supery Sauvignon Blanc, 137, 159

St. Supery Vineyards and Winery, 136

Staglin Family Cabernet Sauvignon, 155

Staglin Family Sangiovanese, 155

Staglin, Garen and Shari, 154

Starwood Hotels and Resorts, 181

State University of New York, 20

steak. *See* beef

Sterling Vineyards, 82

stew, rabbit and olive, 93

stock, chicken, 59

stomach cancer, 13

stomach ulcers, 3, 15–16

Stone, Arthur, 20

Stony Brook School of Medicine, 20

strawberries, 122; olive oil cake with, 30; "Pazzo", 60; with raspberry cabernet sauce, 49; in red wine, 44; in smoothies, 144; spiced, 100

stress, 3, 10, 11

stroke, 3, 4, 11–12

Summer menus. *See* Spring-Summer menus

Swanson Rosato, 113, 137, 171

sweet, 96

sweet potatoes, 153

swordfish, grilled, 172

Syrah, 113, 132, 185, 205; Edmunds St. John, 105; Fife Vineyards "Redhead Vineyard" Petite, 105; with leg of lamb, 116; Truchard, 165

tandoori paste, 106

tannin, 188–89, 197

tapenade, black olive, 83, 86, 113, 116

tartaric acid, 188

tarts: almond, 130; winter apple, 124

taste, elements of, 96

tastes and flavors: acidity, 187; bitterness, 188–89

terrines, bittersweet chocolate, 69

testosterone, 9

Thun, Michael, 14

Tomatina, 63, 145

tomatoes, 161; beefsteak, 172; bread salad with, 172; crostini with, 84; heirloom, 78, 138; with lemon vinaigrette, 78; with linguini, 128; in Mediterranean salad, 38; roasting, 178; Roma, 62, 84, 148, 172; soup with, 178; sun-dried, 62; vine-ripened, 178; vine-ripened red, 106

tomato sauce, 61, 62

torte: apple, 75; chocolate mousse, 33

tortellini, on bamboo skewers, 28

tortilla chips, 134

tradition, x

Tra Vigne Ristorante, 18, 56

Trefethen Merlot, 47

triglycerides, 7

Tripler Army Medical Center, 15

Truchard Chardonnay, 159

Truchard Pinot Noir, 159

Truchard Syrah, 165

Truchard, Tony and Jo Ann, 158

Truchard Vineyards, 158

turkey: chili with, 79; cutlets, 162; smoked, 39

Turnbull Cellars Zinfandel, 175

turnips, 31

Tuscany, 197

ulcers, 3, 15–16

United States, cardiovascular disease in, 4

United States Department of Agriculture (USDA), 4–5

University of California at Davis, 14

University of Edinburgh, 12

University of Toronto, 6

USDA. *See* United States Department of Agriculture

varietals: popular, 203; red wine, 205–6; white wine, 205

veal, 157
vegetables: antioxidants in, 7; garden, 161; purée of, 101
vermouth, King Eider, 80
Viader, Delia, 164
Viader 1989, 165
Viader 1997, 165
Viader Vineyards, 164
Villa Ragazzi Napa Valley Sangiovese, 137
vinaigrette: champagne, 83, 86; feta and orange-apricot, 106; honey mustard, 77, 79; lemon, 57, 60, 77, 78; orange-apricot, 105, 106
vinegar: raspberry, 72; rice wine, 71
Vineyard 29, 36
Viognier, xi; crisp, 83
Vitamin E, 7
vodka, 144
Voss Sauvignon Blanc, 65

walnuts, 75, 88, 101
Ward, Dick, 170
watercress, 101, 176
watermelon, 92
water smoker, 39
weight: alcohol and regulation of, 9; losing, 2; maintenance of, 2; regulation of, 3; wine and regulation of, 9
whipped cream, 34, 124, 130
white wine: antioxidants in, 8; appearance of, 183; Chardonnay, 205; in chicken, 139; griddled salmon and, 29; with halibut, 48; with honey-roasted pork, 32; in lemon risotto, 29; in olive oil cake, 30; in pan fried potatoes, 49; in risotto, 115; tannin in, 189; in turkey cutlets, 162; with veal, 157. *See also* red wine; wine
White Zinfandel, 205
Williams, John and Julie, 174
Windows on the World, 181
wine: aging and, 2, 3, 9–10, 184, 190; alcohol in, 190–91; Alzheimer's disease and, 3; as anti-inflammatory, 5, 11; antioxidants in, 7–8; appearance of, 182, 183; appreciation for, 182; aromas in, 184–85; atherosclerosis and, 3, 13; balance and, 196–97; balance in, 183; balance of, 191; benefits of, x, 2–3; blindness and, 3, 16; bouquet of, 182, 183–85; cancer and, 3; choosing, x–xi, 193–94; clarity of, 183; common cold and, 3; complexity of, 184, 190; "corked", 186; depression and, 11; dessert, 122; dry, 187; "enemies" of, 198;

experimentation in, xi; fermentation of, 184; finish of, 191; flavor and making of, 203–4; flawed, 185–86; as a food, xi; food and, x, xi, 118, 170; food poisoning and, 3, 15; future of, 206; healthy lifestyle and, xi, 16; heart disease and, 4–6, 7; high blood pressure and, 3; hypertension and, 12–13; incorporated into diet, 2; influence of food ingredients on, 196; Internet and, 204; intoxicating effect of, 6; kidney stones and, 3, 15; legs of, 183; lifestyle and, 40; longevity and, 2, 8–9; long-term benefits of, 2; making of, xi; meals and, x, 2, 6, 23, 26, 36, 90; off aromas in, 185–86; "old rules" in, 193–94; oxidized, 186; pairing of food and, xi, 193–201; pattern of consumption of, 3–4; peripheral artery disease and, 3, 12; physiological effects of, 7–8; pre-dinner, 26; psychological benefits of, 3, 10–11; science and, 199; short-term effects of, 4; sparkling, 71, 73, 74; stroke and, 3, 11–12; sweet, 187; swirling, 183; table, 186; tastes and flavors of, 181, 186–91; tasting of, 182–83; terminology for, 181; ulcers and, 3, 15–16; USDA and, 4–5; varietals of, xi, 205–6; weight and, 2, 3, 9; white varietals of, xi; young, 183. *See also* alcohol
wine.com, 184, 204
The Wine Institute, 6
Wine Logic, 195–96
Wine Logic, Inc., 194
"wine sense", xi
winesense.com, 204
wineshopper.com, 204
Wine Spectator, 96
Winter menus. *See* Fall-Winter menus
winter root, 101
women: alcohol's benefits to, 16; estrogen level in, 9–10; physical performance in, 10; wine's mortality benefits and, 8; wrinkles in, 9–10
wrinkles, 9–10

yams, roasted, 153

Zinfandel, 37, 199, 206; Fife Vineyards "Redhead Vineyard", 105; Frog's Leap, 175; Harrison Zebra, 99; Nalle Napa Valley, 127; in pot roast, 129; Ridge, 41, 133; in turkey chili, 79; Turnbull Cellars, 175
Zone diet, 2
zucchini, 161; in garden pasta toss, 54; grated, 33; in lasagna, 55; pancakes with potatoes and, 33

RECIPE INDEX